THE YAMASHITA PRECEDENT:
War Crimes and Command Responsibility

THE YAMASHITA PRECEDENT
War Crimes and Command Responsibility

By Richard L. Lael

SR Scholarly Resources Inc.
Wilmington, Delaware

Scholarly Resources Inc.
104 Greenhill Avenue
Wilmington, Delaware 19805

Library of Congress Cataloging in Publication Data

Lael, Richard L., 1946–
  The Yamashita precedent.

  Bibliography:
  1. Yamashita, Tomoyuki, 1885–1946. 2. War crimes—
Philippines. 3. War crimes—United States. 4. Com-
mand of troops. 5. War crime trials—United States.
I. Title.
JX5441.M3L33 1982   341.6'9'02852   82–17024
ISBN 0-8420-2202-3

Dedicated to
Kemp and Elsie Lael

CONTENTS

PREFACE

Some years ago I became fascinated with the trial of General Tomoyuki Yamashita and that concept of command responsibility so closely associated with his name. A preliminary reading of the trial transcript, of A. Frank Reel's delightful reminiscences of the proceedings, and of the majority and dissenting opinions of the U.S. Supreme Court, together with other available published accounts, convinced me that Reel and Associate Justices Frank Murphy and Wiley B. Rutledge were correct: that Yamashita's trial had been a travesty of American justice, that the concept of command responsibility, as then defined, had been illegal, and that General Douglas MacArthur bore the heaviest responsibility for the questionable prosecution and execution of Yamashita in 1945 and 1946.

This current study, however, based on my subsequent research in the records and papers of governmental agencies, army commands, presidents, cabinet members, and Supreme Court justices, together with my examination of postwar statements and interrogations of captured Japanese soldiers, reveals the weaknesses in those earlier, oversimplified conclusions. The chapters that follow reveal neither black-hearted villains nor perfect saints, just human beings who, given their unfamiliarity with war-crimes proceedings, sometimes made questionable decisions.

———

Many librarians, archivists, and friends have made this study possible. I would like to express my deep appreciation to them all. The personnel at the National Archives, the Library of Congress Manuscript Division, the Washington National Records Center, the Center for Military History, the MacArthur Memorial and Archives, the Michigan Historical Collections, the Franklin D. Roosevelt Library, the Harry S Truman Library, and the Reeves Library provided invaluable assistance. John Taylor at the National Archives and Fred Pernell at the Washington National Records Center deserve special mention since their advice, assistance, and labors on my behalf far exceeded the normal call of duty.

I also would like to acknowledge the generous assistance of Judy Barnes, Ellen Marquardt, Kent Palmer, Linda Killen, Mary Standifer, Sam Wells, and Cathy Zade. Furthermore, I am indebted to Westminster College for its continued financial support of this research project.

Richard L. Lael

INTRODUCTION

General Douglas MacArthur, vividly remembering his harrowing flight from the Philippines, solemnly pledged in the dark days of 1942 that he would return. Fulfilling that promise in 1944, his forces invaded Leyte in October and Luzon, the most important island in the archipelago, in January 1945. His ensuing struggle with General Tomoyuki Yamashita's 14th Area Army, however, proved to be a long, bloody one. Indeed, by the time Tokyo accepted the terms of unconditional surrender imposed on it by the Allied governments, the number of American and Japanese soldiers who had lost their lives in the Philippines since MacArthur's invasion exceeded two hundred sixty-five thousand. But it was the slaying of over thirty-five thousand apparently innocent Filipino civilians by Japanese soldiers during those same ten months that most shocked American and Japanese leaders.

As reports surfaced, detailing the rape, murder, and torture of tens of thousands of civilians in Manila and in Batangas Province, General MacArthur, angered that Yamashita had so clearly failed to exercise adequate control over his subordinates, ordered his trial as a war criminal. In formulating the policies and procedures by which Yamashita would be tried, MacArthur naturally borrowed freely from the policies and procedures already formulated in Washington and in London to govern the European war-crimes trials.

Despite its procedural similarities with later trials at Nuremberg and Tokyo, however, the Yamashita proceeding proved unique. As far as the prosecution and defense could determine, it was the first war-crimes trial that charged a commanding officer with a failure to exercise adequately his command responsibility when no conclusive evidence directly linked him to the violations. Furthermore, it was the first trial of any Japanese official under MacArthur's new streamlined legal methods. Not surprisingly, therefore, the proceeding eventually sparked a legal controversy that not even the U.S. Supreme Court could permanently still.

Rather than silencing the debate, the Court's opinion in early 1946 only fueled the controversy surrounding the novel charge and the legal proceedings by which it had been upheld. Twenty-five years after that ruling, legal experts and pseudoexperts in the United States were still engaged in a vigorous discussion of that concept of command responsibility enunciated by the MacArthur commission in Manila. By the early 1970s, however, those experts were seeking to determine whether U.S. officials, including General William Westmoreland and President Lyndon B. Johnson, should be tried for violations of the law of war committed by their subordinates in Vietnam.

A decade later the controversy has yet to be fully resolved despite those earlier discussions and despite an international conference that addressed the subject in a protocol signed in 1977. After more than thirty years, nations have not one but three different legal definitions of command responsibility from which to choose. But in order for them or for individuals to assess intelligently those definitions, one needs to recall the events of 1944 and 1945. One needs to understand the battle conditions in the Philippines which led to the charges against the 14th Area Army commander. Furthermore, one needs to discover the general nature of war-crimes policy formulation in Europe and in the Far East, to reexamine Yamashita's trial before the MacArthur tribunal, to grasp the arguments of a divided U.S. Supreme Court, and to evaluate the conflicting legal decisions rendered between 1946 and 1977. Only by reexamining the past can one sensibly determine the current legal validity of that concept of command responsibility which led to Yamashita's execution in February 1946 and prompted the subsequent lengthy debate.

CHAPTER ONE
WAR IN THE PHILIPPINES, 1944–45

Evaluating both the progress of the Japanese invasion launched against the Philippines at Lingayen Gulf on 22 December 1941 and the state of his own command, Major General Jonathan Wainwright, leader of the last beleagured and beseiged remnants of General Douglas MacArthur's Philippine command, solemnly informed President Franklin D. Roosevelt on 6 May that he could no longer hold Corregidor. "With broken heart and head bowed in sadness but not in shame," he declared:

> I report to Your Excellency that today I must arrange terms for the surrender of the fortified islands of Manila Bay. . . . There is a limit of human endurance and that limit has long since been past [sic]. Without prospect of relief I feel it is my duty to my country and to my gallant troops to end this useless effusion of blood and human sacrifice.[1]

Within seventy-two hours of that depressing news, the last vestige of American control of the Philippines slipped away as formal resistance to the Japanese throughout the islands ceased.

While the defeat of American forces on these islands had taken only five months, the treacherous and bloody road leading the United States back to the archipelago would take two and one-half years. Starting at Papua and Guadalcanal, General MacArthur, as commander of the Southwest Pacific Area, would direct the crucial phase of that counter-attack. A natural choice to lead the American offensive because of his distinguished military career and his familiarity with the southwest Pacific, MacArthur felt personally compelled to regain control of the Philippines in particular. Had he not been ordered by the president to transfer command to Wainwright and to proceed with his family to Australia, he, not his subordinate, would have been defeated by Lieutenant General Masaharu Homma in 1942. According to his foremost biographer, the memory of his lost command and of his own forced flight

---

[1]Wainwright to Roosevelt, Jonathan Wainwright, *General Wainwright's Story* (Garden City, NY: Doubleday & Co., 1946), p. 122. Also see John Jacob Beck's *MacArthur and Wainwright* (Albuquerque: University of New Mexico Press, 1974), p. 219; and John Toland's *The Rising Sun* (New York: Random House, 1971), p. 357.

in the face of Homma's forces made the return to the Philippines MacArthur's "obsession." The general's famous phrase, "I came through and I shall return," had been no idle comment. It had been a solemn pledge.[2]

Not until June 1944, after successfully driving the Japanese from the islands lying south of the archipelago, was MacArthur able to concentrate on plans for "his return." Considering various military scenarios, MacArthur decided during the summer that a preliminary attack against Mindanao in October would be the best opening stratagem.[3] Once his forces secured the strategic airfields on that large island lying in the southern Philippines, he reasoned that he could launch a major offensive against Leyte in mid-November. After Leyte fell he would then finally be ready to return to Luzon, the site of his own escape and of Wainwright's surrender in 1942.

Meeting with President Roosevelt and top naval commanders at Pearl Harbor in late July, MacArthur urged the adoption of his Mindanao-Leyte-Luzon proposal. Admirals Ernest J. King and Chester W. Nimitz, however, favored a more direct strike at Japan, which would mean, they conceded, bypassing either all or part of the Philippines. Although Roosevelt and his military advisers reached no final decision at that conference, they would formally adopt MacArthur's plan within a month.

By early September the Joint Chiefs of Staff notified MacArthur that, while they left the preliminary tactical details, including an operation against Mindanao, to his discretion, they expected the major operation against Leyte to be launched on 20 December. Within a week the Joint Chiefs, studying reports from Admiral William F. Halsey's Third Fleet that revealed the weakened condition of Japanese defenses in the Philippines, altered that timetable. Following consultations with MacArthur and Nimitz, they dropped the Mindanao operation and advanced the invasion of Leyte by two months. Since the attack on Leyte would now occur on 20 October, the Joint Chiefs scheduled an attack on Luzon for 20 December, the date originally designated for the Leyte invasion.

While the American command debated invasion tactics and timing in the summer and early fall of 1944, Lieutenant General Shigenori

---

[2]D. Clayton James, *The Years of MacArthur* (Boston: Houghton Mifflin Co., 1975), 2:154. Also see Wainwright, *Story*, pp. 4–5. For a more detailed examination of the defeat of American forces on the islands in 1942, see Louis Morton, *U.S. Army in World War II: The Fall of the Philippines* (Washington: Government Printing Office, 1953).

[3]Robert R. Smith's *U.S. Army in World War II: The Approach to the Philippines* (Washington: Government Printing Office, 1953) examines American operations leading to MacArthur's return. M. Hamlin Cannon's *U.S. Army in World War II: Leyte, The Return to the Philippines* (1954; reprint ed., Washington: Government Printing Office, 1978), studies the tactics relating to an invasion of the islands.

Kuroda and Field Marshal Count Hisaichi Terauchi were planning methods to thwart just such an American invasion of the archipelago. Terauchi, as commander of Southern Army, controlled land operations in Malaya, Sumatra, Java, Borneo, Burma, Thailand, and IndoChina as well as in the Philippines. Kuroda, his immediate subordinate in the former American territory and the man most concerned with an attack on Mindanao, Leyte, or Luzon, commanded the 14th Army (later reorganized and renamed the 14th Area Army).

Both men realized the strategic importance of the Philippines in the defense of the Japanese homeland. As Terauchi had explained to his army commanders on 5 May 1944, those islands would be "the final decisive battle area" where Japanese forces would halt the Americans' 1944 Pacific offensive.[4] Preoccupied with battles in Burma, the southern Pacific, and New Guinea, Terauchi, however, miscalculated the time needed to transform Kuroda's command from garrison to combat status and misjudged the date of the anticipated American strike.

In July the Imperial General Headquarters in Tokyo, concerned over Southern Army's delay in strengthening the Philippines, prompted Terauchi to action. Finally focusing on Philippine defense, the field marshal discovered that Kuroda, acting on his own initiative, already had developed a defensive strategy for the 14th Army. Striking when the enemy would be most disorganized and most susceptible, Kuroda expected to defeat decisively the American invasion on the beaches of Luzon. But should battle conditions become precarious, rather than risk the annihilation of his command, he planned to order his army to retire to the nearest mountains and engage in "delaying warfare."[5]

Following the ominous loss of Saipan on 7 July, Kuroda, also on his own initiative, had clarified the operational responsibilities of his forces so that his defensive scheme could be implemented more easily. The 35th Army, he ordered, would defend the central and southern Philippines, while the remainder of the 14th Army would defend Luzon.[6] Kuroda also hoped to use in his defensive arrangement four newly formed divisions and mixed brigades recently transferred into his command by Southern Army. He discovered, however, that since "some of the newly organized units had not even received the prescribed basic training," the new soldiers were ill adapted to battle conditions in the Philippines.[7] Furthermore, his efforts

[4] "History of the Southern Army, 1941–1945," Japanese Monograph Series No. 24, p. 109, Center for Military History, Washington, DC (hereafter cited as JMS).

[5] "Philippine Operations Record, Phase III," JMS 4, p. 6.

[6] JMS 24, pp. 113–14.

[7] 10th Information and Historical Service Headquarters, Eighth Army, "Staff Study of Japanese Operations on Luzon," sect. 1, p. 3 (hereafter cited as 10th I & H). This study is based on accounts prepared by Colonel Ryoichiro Aoshima, chief of staff of the Line of Communications, 14th Area Army, and is located at the Center for Military History.

to reorganize and train his land units were hampered by a Southern Army directive insisting that military preparation of air and naval facilities, considered by Terauchi as essential if he was to parry an American thrust, was more important. Southern Army's decision to upgrade its air and naval power also deprived the 14th Army of vital supplies needed for an adequate defense. Unable to secure scarce shipping space, allocated by Southern Army on a priority basis, the 14th Area Army by late August and early September had only 50 percent of its prescribed munitions and supplies.[8]

Southern Army complicated Kuroda's life further when Count Terauchi opposed the 14th Area Army's withdrawal from the Luzon beaches if threatened with destruction by the enemy.[9] Terauchi and his staff, as well as Imperial General Headquarters in Tokyo, envisioned a "decisive" battle on those same beaches, with victory and not retreat or delay as the result.[10] As to the proposed scene of the major military campaign against the Americans, Southern Army differed with Kuroda and also with the Imperial General Headquarters. Whereas Kuroda and the army staff at Tokyo favored a holding action against the Americans in other sectors of the Philippines while fighting the decisive campaign on Luzon, Terauchi, vigorously supported by the navy, favored fighting decisive battles "whenever and wherever the enemy attacked." Once the Japanese lost air and naval bases to the Americans in other parts of the Philippines, Terauchi reasoned, a Luzon defensive battle would inevitably fail no matter how hotly contested. To achieve victory, the Japanese had to overwhelm the Americans before they could establish bases from which to launch air and naval strikes against Japanese land forces on the islands.

Needing to discuss strategy and tactics for the defense of the Philippines and hoping to convince air and army personnel within his command that his plan was the most suitable, Terauchi convened a commanders' conference in early August. When representatives of the air, naval, and army services arrived at Southern Army Headquarters in Manila, they immediately engaged in tabletop maneuvers simulating Japanese responses to an American invasion. For Terauchi and the navy the results of those games confirmed their earlier arguments that the strategy best suited to holding the Philippines and defeating the enemy was a decisive battle located at the initial point of the American thrust. Those same results, however, convinced Kuroda and his staff that the

---

[8]JMS 4, pp. 2–3; JMS 24, p. 117; 10th I & H, "Staff Study of Japanese Operations on Luzon," sec. 1, p. 3.

[9]For the view of Count Terauchi and Southern Army, see JMS 4, p. 12; and JMS 24, p. 117.

[10]For the view of Imperial General Headquarters, see JMS 24, pp. 113, 117. Also see Imperial General Headquarters Army Orders, vol. 3, pt. 1, p. 46, Center for Military History.

decision to fight the major action on Luzon was still more desirable.[11] Kuroda was a lieutenant general; Terauchi, a field marshal. Unless Imperial General Headquarters intervened in the final decision making, Terauchi's view would obviously prevail. Although disagreeing with Southern Army's decision to fight the decisive battle wherever the Americans invaded, the Tokyo generals refused to usurp Terauchi's powers to control his command as he saw fit. By mid-August, therefore, the field marshal began dispatching Japanese forces not only to Luzon but also to those other islands in the archipelago where a major American attack could be expected.

Had Lieutenant General Kuroda been more forceful during the August conference and had he been held in higher esteem by Terauchi and the War Ministry in Tokyo, his plan may have received more careful consideration. But Terauchi's staff, if not the field marshal himself, considered Kuroda a lightweight by the summer of 1944. Major Kyuya Sato, aide-de-camp to the field marshal, revealed at the end of the war that one of the factors that influenced Terauchi to move Southern Army Headquarters to Manila in May 1944 was his lack of confidence in Kuroda's ability to organize the Philippine defense.[12]

After observing the 14th Area Army commander for several months and perhaps influenced by their disagreement over defensive strategy, Terauchi recommended that the War Ministry relieve Kuroda and select experienced combat officers to replace both the 14th Area Army commander and his staff.[13] Responding to Terauchi's request and to additional reports already received in Tokyo, the War Ministry dispatched Lieutenant Colonel Seiichi Yoshie, a member of its powerful Personnel Bureau, to Manila on 4 September. Upon arriving at the Philippine capital, he was to determine whether the "unfavorable stories in regard to Lt. General Kuroda" were true. The unflattering stories that had reached the War Ministry asserted that the general was "devoting more time to his golf, reading and personal matters than to the execution of his official duties." Further, they reported that discipline within his command was "becoming very lax" since Kuroda was losing the respect and confidence of his officers and men.[14]

---

[11]"Philippine Area Naval Operations, Part IV," JMS 114, pp. 1–2. For a discussion of the navy's position, see "Outline of the Third Phase Operations, Feb 43–Aug 45," JMS 117, pp. 21–22. Also see Interrogation of Vice Admiral Takeo Kurita, commander in chief, Second Fleet, RG 243, Records of the U.S. Strategic Bombing Survey, National Archives, Washington, DC (hereafter cited as RG 243 Interrogations).

[12]Interrogation of Major Kyuya Sato, aide-de-camp to Terauchi, Interrogations of Japanese Officials on World War II, vol. 2, p. 177, Center for Military History (hereafter cited as CMH Interrogations).

[13]JMS 24, p. 114.

[14]Statement of LTC Seiichi Yoshie, aide to the chief of the Personnel Bureau of the War Ministry, Statements of Japanese Officials on World War II, vol. 5, Center for Military History (hereafter cited as Statements).

After a whirlwind of interviews on 6 September, the day he arrived in Manila, Yoshie discovered that some officers of Kuroda's staff believed that their commander's responsibilities "were beyond his powers."[15] Evaluating that and other data with what appeared to be unseemly haste, he concluded that Kuroda ought to be relieved as soon as possible. Writing to the chief of the Personnel Bureau that night, he recommended that General Tomoyuki Yamashita replace Lieutenant General Kuroda. Yoshie's findings, confirming Field Marshal Terauchi's earlier evaluation, induced the War Ministry to remove the 14th Area Army commander on 26 September and to name as his successor General Yamashita, commander of the First Area Army in Manchuria.

Born in 1885, Yamashita had risen to the rank of lieutenant general by 1937, after serving thirty-one years in the Japanese Army.[16] By November 1941 Japanese military leaders, realizing that war against Great Britain and the United States was increasingly likely, had designated Yamashita commander of the 25th Japanese Army and had ordered him to prepare and execute operational plans for the invasion of the Malay peninsula. Hours before the first bombs crashed into the anchored ships of the U.S. Pacific Fleet at Pearl Harbor, Yamashita's 25th Army had landed in Malaya. Employing a tactic later made famous by MacArthur, Yamashita had moved southward toward the British bastion of Singapore, bypassing strong pockets of Allied resistance. Maneuvering his troops through jungle considered almost impenetrable by the British, Yamashita had been able to lay siege to Singapore by land, while the main British fortifications and guns faced the sea—the direction from which the British had expected a major attack. Taking maximum advantage of his surprise tactics, Yamashita had demanded the surrender of the Allied garrisons in Malaya. British Lieutenant General Sir Arthur Percival, faced with an enemy army of unknown strength at his rear, a city full of civilians, and a diminishing stockpile of food and water, surrendered his entire complement of 130,000 troops to General Yamashita on 15 February 1942, only seventy-three days after Yamashita had begun his invasion. Not until after the surrender did Percival learn that the Japanese forces opposing him had numbered less than 60,000 and that their supply situation had been critical, with artillery ammunition for the Japanese siege guns extremely low. By boldness and daring Yamashita had won a tremendous victory for

---

[15]CMH Interrogations, Colonel Shujiro Kobayashi, senior operations staff officer, 14th Area Army, 1:427.

[16]See Yamashita's 201 File, box 1217, RG 331, Records of the Allied Operational & Occupation Headquarters, World War II: Supreme Commander for the Allied Powers (Washington National Records Center, Suitland, MD) for a detailed chronology of his military career. Also see Aubrey Kenworthy, *The Tiger of Malaya* (New York: Exposition Press, 1953); John Deane Potter, *The Life and Death of a Japanese General* (New York: New American Library, 1962); Arthur Swinson, *Four Samurai* (London: Hutchinson & Co., 1968); and A. J. Barker, *Yamashita* (Ballantine Books, 1973).

Japan with the loss of only 3,000 Japanese dead and 6,824 wounded. That victory also had gained him an international reputation and the nickname "Tiger of Malaya."[17]

For Premier Hideki Tojo, Yamashita had received too much prominence by his victory over Percival. Fearing that his political position might be undermined if Yamashita, an old rival of an opposing military clique, gained too much recognition because of his triumph, Tojo, in July 1942, had ordered the "Tiger" to the Japanese puppet state of Manchukuo. While that new command would assume great significance if Japan went to war with the Soviet Union, Tojo intended it to isolate Yamashita from further prestigious victories that could increase his political influence in Japan. Not until after the Tojo government fell on 18 July 1944 did Yamashita's near exile in Manchukuo end. Within sixty-nine days of Tojo's political demise, Yamashita had received his orders to proceed to the Philippines.

Three days before Yamashita formally received his appointment as commanding officer of the 14th Area Army, the Imperial General Headquarters notified Terauchi to prepare for a decisive battle in the Philippines, a battle that War Ministry intelligence believed would occur in late October.[18] Some of the staff officers of Southern Army, notably in the Operations Section, heartily applauded days later the choice of Yamashita but felt "that the appointment had been made too late," especially in light of the new intelligence on the American invasion plan.[19] Yamashita, they thought, simply did not have enough time to whip the Philippine forces into shape. They realized that, when Terauchi had recommended Kuroda's relief and requested the appointment of an active commander capable of converting a garrison army into a combat force, the field marshal had estimated that three months would be the minimum time needed to prepare the Japanese forces in the Philippines for the inevitable American invasion.[20]

The task facing Yamashita was awesome. He needed to select a competent staff and integrate it into the Philippine command; to familiarize himself with his general officers in order to use them effectively in combat; to continue the supervision, integration, and training of the new

---

[17]For accounts of the Singapore operation, see Sir Arthur Percival, *The War in Malaya* (London: Eyre & Spottiswoode, 1949); Major General S. Woodburn Kirby, *The War Against Japan: The Loss of Singapore* (London: Her Majesty's Stationery Office, 1957); James Leasor, *Singapore: The Battle that Changed the World* (Garden City, NY: Doubleday & Company, 1968); Ivan Simson, *Singapore: Too Little, Too Late* (London: Leo Cooper, 1970); and Colonel Masanobu Tsuji, *Singapore: The Japanese Version*, trans. Margaret E. Lake (New York: St. Martin's Press, 1960).

[18]Imperial Gen. HQ Army Orders, No. 1135, 22 September 1944, 3:pt. 2, p. 48.

[19]JMS 24, p. 117.

[20]Ibid., p. 114.

units that had arrived in July, August, and September from China and
Manchuria; and to cope with the three additional divisions and two
brigades that arrived from Korea, China, Manchuria, and Japan during
October and November.[21] He needed to learn the terrain of the Philippines
and the disposition of his forces; to study and evaluate current strategies of
defense and formulate a new concept if he believed the old ones unwork-
able; and to coordinate his command with Southern Army, the 4th Air
Army, the Southwest Naval Forces, and the 3d Shipping Command. He
also needed to deal with the deteriorating economic conditions in the
Philippines as well as with the deteriorating relations between Japanese
troops and Filipinos.[22] And he had, if the estimate of Imperial General
Headquarters was correct, fewer than thirty days to accomplish these
tasks before the Americans launched their invasion.

Shortly after Yamashita assumed control of the 14th Area Army
on 9 October, Lieutenant General Kuroda departed without either formally
discussing tactics that might have proved useful on the islands or leaving
Yamashita any major formal written reports concerning the status, extent,
and operations of his troops. Nor did Yamashita obtain the assistance of
Kuroda's chief of staff, who had become ill and had been evacuated to
Japan before he could brief Yamashita on the status of his new command.[23]

Yamashita's problems in mid-October were complicated further
by the absence of a complete staff. His own chief of staff, Major General
Akira Muto, transferring his command in Sumatra in a more orderly
fashion than had Kuroda, did not arrive in the Philippines until 20 October, the day the American invasion of Leyte began. Of the remaining
fifteen staff members, only three had served under Kuroda in the Philippines. The rest just recently had arrived from Manchuria and other
locations. Most of the 14th Area Army staff, therefore, had arrived at
approximately the same time as Yamashita and were as unfamiliar with
affairs on the islands as were their commander and his chief of staff.[24]

The loss of Kuroda's experienced staff at such a critical moment
cost Yamashita precious time while he and his own officers tried to
familiarize themselves with the Philippine situation. Yamashita, however,

---

[21]JMS 4, pp. 44–45; 10th I & H, "Staff Study of Japanese Operations on Luzon,"
sect. 1, p. 10; "Memoirs of Akira Muto," chief of staff, 14th Area Army, p. 12, Translation
of Japanese Documents, General HQ, Far Eastern Command Military Intelligence Section,
Historical Division, Center for Military History (hereafter cited as CMH Translations).
[22]Intelligence Report 95046, 11 September 1944, RG 226, Records of the Office
of Strategic Services, National Archives.
[23]Interrogation of Yamashita by Charles A. Willoughby, 20 September 1945, box
79, p. 4, RG 5, Records of General Headquarters, Supreme Commander for the Allied
Powers, 1945–51, MacArthur Memorial & Archives, Norfolk, VA. Also see Muto,
"Memoirs," p. 1.
[24]For a discussion of the initial confusion, see Muto, "Memoirs." Also see Saburo
Hayashi, *KOGUN* (Quantico: Marine Corps Association, 1959).

in choosing his own staff members, was not only following a common military practice but also was carrying out the express wishes of the Southern Army. In his request in August to the Imperial General Headquarters to relieve Kuroda, Terauchi had requested the removal of Kuroda's staff as well. Indeed, without waiting for Yamashita to arrive, the field marshal already had begun transferring members of the 14th Area Army staff.

The chaotic conditions surrounding the transfer of command, coupled with the imminence of an American invasion, forced Yamashita to deal only with the most important army matters, the most vital of which was a workable plan of defense.[25] Within days of his arrival, therefore, he called a conference of his division commanders to outline his defensive ideas. "Our forces," he informed the officers of his new command, "will be mainly deployed on Luzon where the invading forces will be repulsed and annihilated." We will, he continued, occupy three major regions on Luzon—the mountains east of Manila, the mountains west of Clark Field, and the mountains around Baguio. From those positions "the oncoming enemy must be destroyed by suicidal combat methods in order to assure the successful termination of this decisive battle."[26] Given the increasing American air attacks, the dramatic increase in the loss of ships ferrying supplies to the Philippines, the presence of only partially trained divisions, and the confusion inherent in a new command assumed under these circumstances, a decisive defensive operation on Luzon seemed eminently preferable to the shuttling of troops to the central and southern Philippines, where the U.S. attack might first come.

Although the American decision to invade Leyte on 20 October had been made on 15 September, before Kuroda's removal, the timing was perfect for MacArthur but disastrous for Yamashita. Had Yamashita implemented his plan to defend Luzon and not Leyte, however, the American invasion could have been useful to the Japanese general. While U.S. forces battled in the central Philippines, he could have used the additional time to coordinate Luzon's defenses and to retrain his own men. But Yamashita did not implement his plan. Two days after the invasion of Leyte, Field Marshal Terauchi ordered his new commander to cooperate with the Japanese navy and air force in destroying the enemy at Leyte and not Luzon.[27] Clearly the count had not budged from his August decision to

---

[25]Yamashita testimony, "Before the Military Commission Convened by the Commanding General, U.S. Army Forces Wes. Pac. . . . Yamashita, Tomoyuki," p. 3537, RG 153, Records of the Judge Advocate General, U.S. Army, Washington National Records Center (hereafter cited as Transcript).

[26]JMS 4, pp. 24, 31–32; A.T.I.S., Southwest Pacific Area, Current Translations No. 66: "Combat Regulations of 14th Area Army, 15 Oct. 44," box 2001, RG 331.

[27]CMH Interrogations, Colonel Kobayashi, 1:432; Muto, "Memoirs," pp. 5, 7; JMS 4, p. 30; JMS 24, p. 118.

carry the struggle, if necessary, into the central and southern Philippines.

The order caught Yamashita by surprise. Since Kuroda and his staff had not been convinced of the wisdom of Terauchi's decision in August, they had continued to plan for a decisive battle on Luzon. Therefore, based on his briefings and discussions with members of his new command and based on file records, Yamashita had decided to continue with Kuroda's basic defensive arrangements. Any doubts that he may have had about adopting the plan of an ousted officer were probably eased by briefings he had received from Imperial General Headquarters as he journeyed through Tokyo to Manila. Both the chief and deputy chief of the General Staff had informed Yamashita that "if American forces invaded the southern part of the Philippine islands, our operation would call for a showdown battle by the Naval and Air Forces, with an active participation and cooperation *of only those army troops located in the vicinity of the landings.*" Upon arrival in the Philippines, Yamashita naturally predicated his plans on those instructions which, based on his observations, also coincided with the policies previously adopted by the 14th Area Army Headquarters.[28]

Terauchi's order of 22 October, therefore, came, in the words of Chief of Staff Muto, as "a bolt from the blue."[29] Perhaps Terauchi assumed Yamashita knew of, and would naturally feel bound by, the strategic decisions reached at the August conference. Perhaps Yamashita assumed that the plan outlined by the chief and deputy chief of the General Staff accurately reflected the wishes of Terauchi's Southern Army. Why Yamashita adopted a measure that Terauchi had scrapped two months earlier was especially puzzling since the headquarters of both men were in Manila until mid-November. Whatever occurred to cause such a remarkable breakdown in communication, Terauchi's 22 October order left no doubt that the decisive battle would be on Leyte.

Yamashita and Muto questioned that order, informing Terauchi and his staff that the transportation system between Leyte and Luzon was "almost impossible"; that Leyte had not been prepared as the site of a major battle; that without heavy weapons, bunker systems, and other crucial defenses a "mere increase of personnel would do little toward gaining victory"; and that success would hinge on Japan's fragile control of the sea and air, which, they argued, seemed unlikely to last.[30] Nevertheless, Terauchi was adamant: they must begin transferring troops and vital materiel to Leyte at once. Lest his new commander turn to the Imperial

---

[28]Emphasis added. Muto, "Memoirs," p. 5.

[29]Ibid.

[30]See the following CMH Interrogations: Major Yorio Ishikawa, staff officer, 14th Area Army, 1:249, 257–58; LTG Seizo Arisue, chief of army intelligence, Imperial General Headquarters, 1:18; Colonel Kobayashi, 1:433; and Major Masaaki Kawase, supply staff officer, 14th Area Army, 1:336. Also see Muto, "Memoirs," p. 7; and JMS 24, p. 118.

General Headquarters for support, Terauchi informed the Tokyo generals of his decision and received their assurances that they would not attempt to second-guess Southern Army Headquarters. Terauchi left Yamashita no alternative but to comply with the disagreeable order.

A series of naval engagements commonly called the Battle for Leyte Gulf on 24 and 25 October confirmed Yamashita's fear that Japanese forces could not contain America's naval might. Surface units of the U.S. Pacific Fleet, engaging four separate Japanese battle formations, sank four carriers, three battleships, six cruisers, three light cruisers, and ten destroyers.[31] That grievous defeat, Yamashita realized, dangerously compromised any possible maritime resupply effort to Leyte.

Ignoring those defeats, Terauchi on 11 November reaffirmed that "the Leyte battle will be carried on as before.... Luzon must be strengthened," Terauchi conceded, "but this must in no way interfere with the execution of the Leyte battle."[32] Bound by this reaffirmation, Yamashita, between 23 October and 11 December, coordinated the reinforcement and resupply of army forces on Leyte. During those seven weeks 14th Area Army, in cooperation with the Southwest Area Fleet, dispatched nine convoys to Ormac on the northwest coast of the beseiged island. Of those nine, only the first two, arriving on 26 October and 1 November, respectively, were unharmed. Convoy three, sailing on 10 November, was totally destroyed, as was convoy five a week later. Convoys four and nine, sailing on 9 November and 11 December, respectively, survived with only light to moderate damage. Convoys six, seven, and eight, sailing on 28 and 30 November and on 7 December, respectively, were severely damaged and unable to carry out further resupply operations. Convoy nine was forced to abandon Ormac when it fell to the U.S. Army on 10 December and fled to Palompon, which itself fell within two weeks.[33] General MacArthur's announcement on 25 December that the campaign against Leyte was complete, despite a few scattered pockets of Japanese defenders still resisting throughout the island, served official notice that the Japanese resupply effort had failed.

By complying with Southern Army orders, Yamashita had successfully transferred to Leyte more than forty-five thousand men and over ten thousand tons of materiel. The cost of that success had been high. He had lost well over two thousand men and more than seven thousand tons of equipment in transit. Futhermore, the Southwest Area Fleet had lost at

---

[31]Samuel Eliot Morison, *History of United States Naval Operations in World War II: Leyte, June 1944–January 1945*, 15 vols. (Boston: Little, Brown & Co., 1966), 12:91–94.

[32]JMS 24, p. 125.

[33]Cannon, *Leyte*, pp. 99–102; Morison, *Leyte*, chaps. 15, 16; "Philippines Area Naval Operations, Part II," JMS 84, p. 108; George C. Kenney, *General Kenney Reports* (New York: Duell, Sloan & Pearce, 1949), pp. 482–83.

least eleven transports, six destroyers, and numerous smaller craft.[34] Yamashita attributed the loss of men and materiel to foolish Southern Army policies. Convinced by late November that sending more men and materiel to Leyte was useless, and well aware that America's submarine fleet and carrier aircraft were slowly strangling Luzon, he secretly decided to disobey Terauchi's 11 November order.[35] Meeting with a few trusted staff members, he emphasized his commitment to defending Luzon by concentrating his forces east of Manila, west of Clark Field, and in the vicinity of Baguio. Rather than fight a decisive battle to defeat the enemy, he explained, they would fight a defensive battle to stave off their own quick annihilation. At the conclusion of the mutinous meeting, Yamashita instructed his trusted coconspirators to commence the transfer of units into the mountains, to launch immediately the rehabilitation and construction of roads necessary to his defensive strategy, and to begin the surveying and charting of the mountainous terrain in each of his three defensive sectors. In profound understatement, one of Yamashita's staff officers later observed: "As it was considered both unnecessary and undesirable to inform either higher headquarters or subordinate units of these activities, strict secrecy was preserved."[36] With the departure in early December of one of Terauchi's staff officers, a man who had been attached to Yamashita's headquarters to ensure that he complied with Southern Army's decision to wage a decisive battle on Leyte, Yamashita began to operate more openly.[37]

By mid-December, Yamashita decided to forego all pretense of compliance with Terauchi's Leyte order. On 14 December he informed Lieutenant General Sosaku Suzuki, commander of the 35th Army, that he would hereafter have to rely on his own resources rather than on those of Luzon. Five days later the 14th Area Army Headquarters formally issued its new operational policy.[38] That army would concentrate its forces in the

---

[34]Cannon, *Leyte*, pp. 99–102.

[35]Statements, MG Toshio Nishimura, assistant chief of staff, 14th Area Army, p. 677; CMH Interrogations, Colonel Kobayashi, 1:424, 436–37; JMS 4, p. 31; "Philippine Operations Record, Phase III," JMS 7, p. 3.

[36]Statements, MG Nishimura, p. 679.

[37]CMH Interrogations, Major Kawase, 1:336.

[38]A discussion of Yamashita's defensive plans may be found in the following: "Outline of Operational Policy for Luzon Island," 19 December 1944, Shobu Group Operational Department, CMH Translations; JMS 24, pp. 127–28; JMS 7, p. 4; and the following CMH Interrogations: LTG Shuichi Miyazaki, chief of operations, Army Section, Imperial General Headquarters, 1:524; Colonel Naokata Utsunomiya, assistant chief of staff, 14th Area Army, 2:553; Colonel Katsusaburo Nakazawa, supply staff officer, 14th Area Army, 2:39; and Major Ishikawa, 1:257. Also see Muto, "Memoirs"; RG 243 Interrogations, Commander Moriyoshi Yamaguchi, commander in chief, First Combined Air Force, Luzon; Statements, Colonel Kobayashi, p. 242; and testimony of Colonel Yoshiharu Kumegawa, senior staff officer, Tactical Affairs Section, 14th Area Army, contained in *Proceedings of the International Military Tribunal for the Far East* (IMTFE), p. 33071.

three mountain ranges designated by Yamashita at his earlier secret conference. Yamashita himself would directly control the 152,000 troops in northern Luzon, which would be designated Shobu Group. Lieutenant General Shizuo Yokoyama's 70,000-man Shimbu Group would be located in the mountains east and south of Manila, while Major General Rikichi Tsukada's 40,000-man Kembu Group would defend the Bataan Peninsula-Clark Field area.[39] Furthermore, the orders read: "All elements will prepare for self-sufficiency, independent fighting and extended resistance and will cooperate to check and contain the main body of the American Forces on Luzon Island and to crush the enemy's fighting strength."[40] Such a strategy not only failed to call for major opposition to the Americans on the beaches of Luzon but also failed to call for a "decisive" battle anywhere. Clearly Yamashita anticipated no quick victory but rather a protracted campaign that would tie up large numbers of U.S. soldiers and large quantities of American materiel.

These directives, blatantly at odds with the wishes of Terauchi and Imperial General Headquarters, remained in effect despite the sudden appearance in Manila of Lieutenant General Jo Iimura, chief of staff, Southern Army, and Major General Shuichi Miyazaki, chief of operations, Army Section, Imperial General Headquarters. While both generals, reflecting the views of their superiors in Saigon and Tokyo, urged Yamashita "to seize any opportunity he might have for carrying out decisive engagements," they declined to order the 14th Area Army commander to fight a decisive battle, either on Leyte or on Luzon. Both realized that with the rapidly changing military situation and the nearness of the powerful American foe, Yamashita, and Yamashita alone, must assume the ultimate responsibility for the tactics and strategy used in the defense of the Philippines.[41]

While Yamashita argued with his superiors and hastened defensive preparations in the fall of 1944, General MacArthur considered the final plans for his return to Luzon. Of all the Philippine islands, Luzon was special to MacArthur. His father had gained fame there as a brigadier general in 1898 and as military governor in the early years of the twentieth century. He himself, upon graduating from West Point, had traveled there in 1903 on his first assignment. He had returned to the island to serve a second tour between 1922 and 1925 and a third tour between 1928 and 1930. "No assignment," he had noted in response to his orders to Manila in 1928, "could have pleased me more."[42] Writing in late December 1934

---

[39]See maps, pp. 14, 18, 20.

[40]CMH Translations, "Outline for Operational Policy for Luzon Island," p. 16.

[41]CMH Interrogations, LTG Miyazaki, 1:522, 524; Muto, "Memoirs," p. 10; JMS 24, p. 127; JMS 7, p. 3.

[42]Douglas MacArthur, *Reminiscences* (1964; reprint ed., Greenwich, CT: Fawcett Publications, 1965), p. 96. Also see pp. 25, 36–37, 43, 91–92, 284.

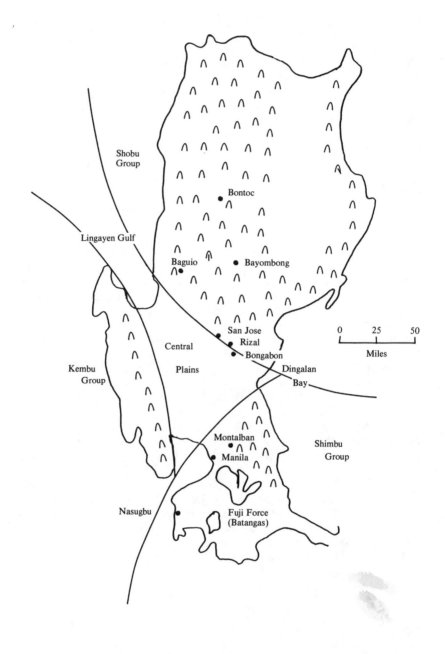

to Manuel Quezon, anticipated winner of the upcoming Philippine presidential campaign, MacArthur reaffirmed his ties to the Philippines and to Luzon: he agreed that, upon his retirement as chief of staff in the summer of 1935, he would journey to Manila and assist, at a \$33,000 per year salary, in upgrading the islands' defense.[43]

Memories of the last decade must have flooded MacArthur's consciousness in the fall of 1944 as he recalled his former relationship to Luzon, the Philippines, and Quezon.[44] As he had promised, he had traveled to Manila in 1935 as a U.S. military adviser to President Quezon. Viewing MacArthur's advisory duties as in the best interests of the United States, President Roosevelt and Secretary of War Harry Woodring had allowed him to remain in the U.S. Army while assuming his new role. In August 1936, Quezon had appointed him field marshal of the Philippines, that nation's highest military officer. But marring that pleasant memory was his recollection that serving two masters, the U.S. Army and the Philippine Army, had proven impossible. That had become only too clear by August 1937 when he had learned that the U.S. War Department planned to transfer him back home as soon as he had completed the normal two-year tour of overseas duty. Realizing that he could not avoid such an order and desiring to remain in the Philippines as head of its army, he had submitted his resignation to Washington.

MacArthur's resignation had severed his direct tie to the U.S. government and, as a result, had lessened his influence with the Quezon administration. Despite the fact that the Philippine president and his wife were the godparents of his only child, relations between the two men deteriorated in 1938 and 1939. His relations with the Philippine National Assembly also had deteriorated as that legislative body became increasingly skeptical of large military budgets and of his assertions that, with larger military appropriations, the Philippines could be successfully defended. Indeed, that political controversy almost led to a request from Quezon asking for MacArthur's resignation. Instead, the Philippine president had replaced his chief of staff in late 1938 with Major General Basilio Valdes who was clearly not a "MacArthur man." Furthermore, Quezon shattered their former cordiality and cooperation by forcing him to deal with an intermediary—the presidential secretary—rather than

---

[43]Ibid., p. 112; William Manchester, *American Caesar: Douglas MacArthur, 1880–1964* (New York: Dell Publishing Co., 1979), pp. 176–77.

[44]The following paragraphs are based on MacArthur, *Reminiscences;* D. Clayton James, *The Years of MacArthur*, vol. 1 (Boston: Houghton Mifflin Co., 1970); Frazier Hunt, *The Untold Story of Douglas MacArthur* (New York: Devin-Adair Co., 1954); Charles Willoughby and John Chamberlain, *MacArthur: 1941–1951* (New York: McGraw-Hill, 1954); Theodore Friend, *Between Two Empires: The Ordeal of the Philippines, 1929–1946* (New Haven: Yale University Press, 1965); and Carlos Quirino, *Quezon: Paladin of Philippine Freedom* (Manila: Filipiniana Book Guild, 1971).

dealing directly with the president. But perhaps most illustrative of their strained relations, and certainly one of his bitterest memories, was Quezon's decision to establish, with the National Assembly's backing, the Department of National Defense in May 1939. That department reduced MacArthur's authority as field marshal. Its establishment stripped him of his power to order munitions, enroll soldiers, or build new military facilities without the express permission of Quezon and the secretary of defense.

As MacArthur reflected over the preceding years, however, he recalled the change in his fortunes. On 26 July 1941, Roosevelt had formally incorporated the Philippine force into the U.S. Army. At the same time he also had reactivated MacArthur and given him control of the U.S. Far Eastern Command. Unluckily, the subsequent months had allowed him very little time to prepare a force capable of more effectively resisting Lieutenant General Homma's 14th Army as it invaded Luzon in December 1941. That invasion led to bitter reverses: MacArthur's forced flight to Australia, the subsequent loss of his command under Wainwright, and the fall of his beloved Philippines to the Japanese empire in those dark days of early 1942.

Not surprisingly, such memories gave MacArthur special incentive to wrest control of Luzon from Yamashita. Journeying northward along the west coast of Luzon in January 1945 aboard the light cruiser *Boise*, flagship of his invasion fleet, MacArthur, gazing at the rugged terrain of the familiar Philippine coastline, discovered that he "could not leave the rail. . . . At the sight of those never-to-be-forgotten scenes of my family's past, I felt an indescribable sense of loss, of sorrow, of loneliness, and of solemn consecration."[45]

Adopting a page from Lieutenant General Homma's 1941 tactics, MacArthur had decided to invade Luzon at Lingayen Gulf.[46] Attacking on 9 January, his forces, encountering no Japanese beach defenses, advanced south through the Central Plains toward the airfield complex at Clark Field and the dock facilities at Manila. Within three days MacArthur, displeased with the speed of that advance, began pressuring General Walter Krueger, commander of the Sixth Army.[47] Krueger, while realizing

---

[45]MacArthur, *Reminiscences*, p. 278

[46]The following discussion of American tactics relies heavily upon Robert Ross Smith's *Triumph in the Philippines* (Washington: Government Printing Office, 1963), which is one of the excellent volumes in the *U.S. Army in World War II* series.

[47]James, *MacArthur*, 2:629, 631. Also see MacArthur, *Reminiscences*, p. 280; Walter Krueger, *From Down Under to Nippon: The Story of the Sixth Army in World War II* (1953; reprint ed., Washington: Zenger Publishing Co., 1979), p. 228; and Samuel Eliot Morison, *History of United States Naval Operations in World War II: The Liberation of the Philippines: Luzon, Mindanao, the Visayas, 1944–1945*, 15 vols. (Boston: Little, Brown & Co., 1965), 13:184. As field commander, Krueger and not MacArthur was directly

that MacArthur wanted to capture Manila by 26 January, his birthday, pointed out to his superior that such a reckless dash without adequate flank protection would be unwise. "Though it was obvious," Krueger later wrote, "that General MacArthur did not share my views, he did not direct me to change my dispositions or plans."[48]

Despite Krueger's caution the American forces still moved south rather quickly. By 11 January, they were ten miles south of the invasion area; by 17 January, twenty-six miles; and by 31 January, eighty-three miles. By the end of January, therefore, not only had Clark Field been secured but American units also had advanced to within twenty-one miles of the city limits of Manila. Nevertheless, MacArthur was still impatient with Krueger's "slow" approach to the capital. Lieutenant General Robert L. Eichelberger, commanding officer of the Eighth Army, whose forces on 31 January would invade Nasugbu Bay forty miles south southwest of Manila, wrote his wife on 23 January: "The Big Chief [MacArthur] has served an ultimatum on your palsy-walsy [Krueger] that he must be in our old home town [Manila] by the 5th of February." Writing again on 2 February, after his invasion force had advanced inland fifteen miles to the Tagaytay Ridge, Eichelberger noted that MacArthur was "very impatient" to reach Manila and wanted him to try to arrive there ahead of Krueger.[49]

It appeared that Eichelberger, charging north on 4 February, might indeed reach Manila by MacArthur's rumored 5 February deadline. By nightfall units of his 511th Infantry had reached Parañaque four miles south of Manila. But while the rapid advance initially had caught the Japanese by surprise, they were able at Parañaque to stop Eichelberger's forces temporarily.

On 2 February, General Krueger, reacting to MacArthur's pressure and thinking that his flank was secure now that Yamashita was on the defensive at San Jose, ordered his XIV Corps "to drive on Manila with all possible speed."[50] Within XIV Corps a friendly rivalry between 37th Infantry and 1st Cavalry Division prompted a race by those units to see who would "open Manila" first. Foregoing sleep on the night of 2 February, 1st Cavalry seized crucial bridges, enabling it to enter Manila on the night of 3 February. The 37th Division entered the city twenty-four hours later on 4 February. Within a week the American units, without

---

responsible for Sixth Army's survival. Unless MacArthur was willing to assume that direct responsibility by countermanding Krueger's orders, the Sixth Army commander would continue to determine the rate of advance.

[48]Krueger, *Down Under*, pp. 227–28, 234.

[49]Jay Luvaas, ed., *Dear Miss Em: General Eichelberger's War in the Pacific, 1942–1945* (Westport, CT: Greenwood Press, 1972). Also see James, *MacArthur*, 2:623–28.

[50]Smith, *Triumph*, p. 217.

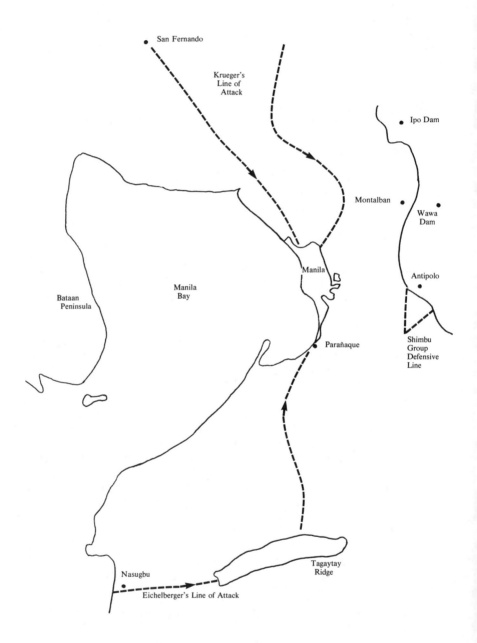

meeting major opposition, had secured all of Manila north of the Pasig River. But even before that area had been totally cleared of the enemy, units of the 37th Division and the 1st Cavalry Division had crossed on 7, 8, and 9 February to the south side of the Pasig. Within twenty-four hours of that crossing, units of the 37th Division south of the river had effectively cleared the Pandacan District and were moving westward toward coastal Manila.

While the infantry cleared the northern sections of the city, on 8 and 9 February the 1st Cavalry Division on the 37th Infantry's left flank began to encircle Manila, using its 5th and 8th Cavalry regiments. On late 9 and early 10 February, the 8th Cavalry curved through the western suburbs of Manila, crossing the Pasig River at the Philippine Racing Club, only one-quarter mile from the Manila city limits. Moving simultaneously, but following a wider arc around Manila, was the 5th Cavalry. While its sister unit crossed the Pasig at the Racing Club, the 5th began crossing one mile to the southeast at the suburb of Makati. When that crossing was completed on 11 February, the 5th Cavalry joined the 8th Cavalry to form a continuous line of American fighting men east of the city. At the same time the 8th Cavalry also joined on its right flank with units of the 37th Division. By the evening of 11 February, therefore, the American forces had blocked any Japanese escape either to the north or to the east.

In the south, units of Eichelberger's 11th Airborne Division had broken through at Parañaque on 5 February and battled slowly northward. By 12 February they had seized Nichols Field and penetrated to within one and one-half miles of the Manila city limits. The only gap in the American lines on the night of 11 February, therefore, was that between the 5th Cavalry and the 11th Airborne Division. But by 1100 hours on 12 February that gap had disappeared as the 5th Cavalry, moving at day-break, pushed west and successfully completed the American encirclement of Manila. To maximize coordination between the three major divisions in these operations, Generals Krueger and Eichelberger had established direct communication between their headquarters on 8 February. To assure unified command as the units embraced Manila, two days later MacArthur detached 11th Airborne Division from Eichelberger's command and placed it under Krueger's control.

Even before the 37th and 1st Cavalry divisions crossed the Pasig, MacArthur believed his victory in Manila was assured. He, or at least his staff, anticipated a grand victory parade through the Manila streets, perhaps by 11 or 12 February. On 10 February, Lieutenant General Eichelberger had received his invitation to participate in that gala event. But writing to his wife four days later, he noted that MacArthur's headquarters had informed him the night before "that the parade into Manila has been put off indefinitely."[51] The days in mid-February, which the

---

[51]Luvaas, *Miss Em*, pp. 214–16.

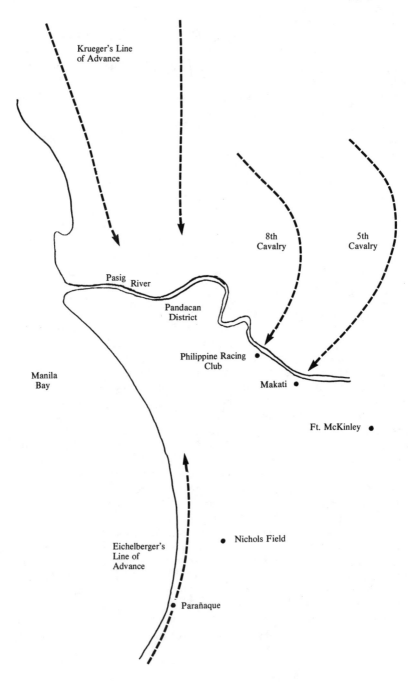

American officers hoped would be marked by a joyous liberation cele-
bration, instead were marked by some of the most vicious killing in the
Pacific War.

Yamashita was as surprised as MacArthur that the Americans
had not achieved a quick victory in the capital. He had neither anticipated
nor prepared for a major battle in Manila.[52] In formulating his defensive
strategy for Luzon in mid-December, he had been more concerned with
deploying his forces where the terrain would most effectively aid sustained
defensive operations. The loss of ships, men, and materiel destined for the
Leyte campaign, together with the American seizure of both Leyte and
Mindoro by mid-December, had helped convince Yamashita that a
decisive campaign aimed at annihilating MacArthur's forces on Luzon's
beaches would be suicidal for his command.

Knowledge that American air and naval operations had dramatically curbed the movement of men and supplies to Luzon from Japan had
further reinforced Yamashita's decision for a mountain defensive. Indeed,
as Japanese naval statistics would later reveal, American aircraft and
submarines had sunk, in the waters surrounding Luzon alone, twenty-nine
Japanese ships in October 1944, thirty-nine in November, and eighteen in
December.[53] While perhaps not knowing these precise figures, Yamashita
knew that the fate of one convoy, which carried the 23d Infantry Division
to Luzon from Manchuria, had not been unusual. Hit repeatedly by the
Americans on 15, 17, 18, and 21 November, two of the seven troop
transports in that convoy had been sunk as well as the convoy's only
escort carrier.[54]

Yamashita clearly realized that interdiction of naval convoys not
only deprived him of new soldiers and new equipment but also denied him
vital spare parts.[55] How could he fight a decisive battle on the beaches
when so many planes, needed to provide air cover, and so many trucks and

---

[52]For a discussion of Yamashita's decision not to defend Manila, see Muto
testimony (p. 3018) and Yokoyama testimony (p. 2664), Transcript; Muto testimony, pp.
33141–142, IMTFE; Muto, "Memoirs"; "Philippine Operations Record, Phase III," JMS
8, pp. 2–3; RG 243 Interrogations, MG Nishimura, pp. 1–2; CMH Interrogations, Major
Sato, 2:178; and Interrogation of LTC Tsuginori Kuriya, assistant operations officer, 14th
Area Army, contained in 201 Yamashita File, box 1217, p. 4, RG 331. Also see statements, Colonel Kenichiro Asano, chief of staff, 8th Division and assistant chief of staff,
41st Army, p. 91; Colonel Niroshi Hashimoto, chief of staff, Manila Defense Force,
p. 278; Rear Admiral Kaoru Arima, chief of staff, Southwest Area Fleet, p. 55; and
MG Nishimura, p. 691. For orders dated 20 December 1944 urging a more forceful
resistance in Manila, see "Outline of Operations Policy in South and Central Luzon,"
3:app. 1, CHM Translations.
[53]"The Imperial Japanese Navy in World War II," JMS 116, pp. 204–21.
[54]Morison, *Leyte*, pp. 409, 413.
[55]RG 243 Interrogations, Commander Yamaguchi and Colonel M. Matsumae,
senior staff officer, 4th Air Army.

locomotives, needed to transport men and materiel, were idled by lack of spare parts? How could he be expected to transport men and supplies to the points of an American invasion when the earlier decision of Southern Army and the Imperial General Headquarters to rely heavily on air power as the major method of defeating MacArthur had denied him fuel for his trucks? Much to Yamashita's chagrin, when he needed regular gasoline he discovered the 14th Area Army had stockpiles of high octane aviation gasoline that were useless for his more vital motor transport.[56] How could he jeopardize his command in any decisive battle when the Americans, after mid-December 1944, intensified their fighter and bomber attacks to the point where those trucks and locomotives still operational could travel only at night? To answer this last question, for example, Yamashita only needed to examine his position during the first week of January. He had lost his air cover by 2 January. As a result, American aircraft bombed and strafed almost at will. Yamashita's examination of his dismal situation merely confirmed an evaluation made by Lieutenant General George Kenney, commander of MacArthur's air arm. Succinctly summarizing the situation as of 9 January, Kenney later explained that "the air combat days [over Luzon] were over."[57]

Lacking air cover, deprived of naval support, and without a reliable means of transportation, Yamashita believed that he could not defend the Central Plains of Luzon, extending from Lingayen Gulf to Manila, despite the fact that the major roads, railroads, and communication facilities were located there.[58] To fight in that vital region would give MacArthur the tactical advantages that would enable him to use his firepower, mobility, and air superiority to overcome quickly the Japanese defenders. In deciding to abandon the Central Plains, to divide Luzon into three military sectors, and to fight the campaign only in the mountainous regions of the island, Yamashita simply chose a military strategy that MacArthur himself had discussed in an address to the Command and General Staff School of the Philippines in August 1936. "The mountainous terrain, the primeval forests, and the lack of communications," MacArthur informed his assembled Filipino officers, "combine to create a theatre of operations in which a defensive force of only moderate efficiency

---

[56]Muto, "Memoirs," p. 13. For additional comments on the difficulties plaguing motor transportation, including guerrilla activities, also see RG 243 Interrogations, MG Nishimura and LTC Toyama Yahei, a 14th Area Army shipping officer stationed in Manila.

[57]Kenney, *General Kenney Reports*, pp. 502, 512. For comments on the devastating impact of American air power, see RG 243 Interrogations, MG Nishimura, LTC Yahei, and Colonel Matsumae; and Muto, "Memoirs," pp. 13–14, 31–32. Also see JMS 24, p. 141.

[58]For maps and an evaluation of roads, railroads, and the terrain of the Central Plains, see OSS reports 121724, "Terrain Study 94: Central Luzon, I"; and 94381, "Report on Railroads of the Philippine Islands, October 1943," RG 226.

and strength could test the capabilities of the most powerful and splendidly equipped army that could be assembled here."[59] Yamashita's decision to fight a defensive rather than a decisive battle, therefore, while not original, theoretically would enable him to utilize his men to best advantage. An obvious corollary to his retreat to the mountains and the surrender of the Central Plains was a similar evacuation of Manila.

Nevertheless, while Yamashita planned no major battle for the capital, he refused in January or February 1945 to declare it an open city as MacArthur had done in December 1941. Tactical matters precluded that option. Manila had been the hub of Japanese resupply efforts until the Americans gained air and sea control of the Philippine waters. Japanese ships naturally had carried their cargo to the best port on the islands, and many of those supplies had been stored in the city's warehouses awaiting transit inland. Since General MacArthur had banned any aerial bombing of Manila, for fear of destroying the capital, those warehouses had remained safe throughout the winter of 1944. Yamashita, therefore, could not declare Manila an open city without sacrificing 13,000 metric tons of supplies that his forces would vitally need in the months to come. Nor was he able to transfer those supplies quickly. In December, for example, he was able to remove only about six hundred metric tons daily. Even that amount had fallen as American aircraft made daylight movement impossible in early January.[60] But so long as even a trickle of supplies continued to flow out of Manila, Yamashita could not—would not—abandon the city or declare it outside the battle zone.

Although Yamashita had decided not to hold the city, he had created a special Manila defense unit in the fall of 1944 to maintain order there, to supervise the security of the stockpiled supplies, to protect transportation units from guerrilla attack, and to guard against a surprise Allied raid. On 19 December he had made it clear, however, that that unit, after wiping out the fighting strength of the advancing enemy from its prepared positions around Manila, would be expected to fall back in the face of a vigorous enemy attack to the mountains east of Manila. His orders on or about 23 December and 1 January instructed most of the unit in Manila to establish a defensive position at Wawa fifteen miles northeast of the city. A skeleton force remaining in the city was to guard and to destroy critical bridges over the Pasig when the enemy approached. It was also to protect the remaining transportation columns departing Manila and maintain order among the civilian population until the last Japanese soldiers had withdrawn.[61]

---

[59]Vorin E. Whan, Jr., ed., *A Soldier Speaks: Public Papers and Speeches of General of the Army Douglas MacArthur* (New York: Praeger, 1965), p. 103.

[60]10th I & H, "Staff Study of Japanese Operations on Luzon," sec. 1, pp. 12–13.

[61]Colonel Hashimoto testimony, Transcript, p. 3114.

Chart 1. Japanese Command Structure, December 1944

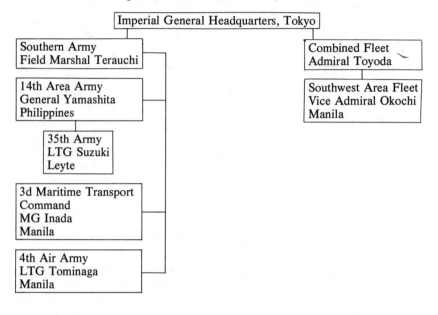

As Yamashita implemented these plans, the 4th Air Army and the Southwest Area Fleet, also headquartered in Manila, had created their own defensive plans for the city. Though aware of Yamashita's plan to evacuate, the commander of the 4th Air Army, according to one of his senior staff officers, "thought it impractical to shift the concentration of our forces into Northern Luzon, the results of which might be disastrous to the morale of the men at that important time. Consequently, [the 4th Air Army] endeavored to fight to the utmost to hold Manila and Clark [Field]."[62] Since 4th Air Army was not under Yamashita's command in December 1944, he could only advise and not order the air army's evacuation. Six days after Yamashita received control of the air army on 1 January, however, he ordered that unit from Manila to Echuague. Since Yamashita's control of the air unit was complete, senior air officers had no choice but to obey.[63]

Unfortunately for Yamashita, for 16,000 naval personnel, and for the citizens of Manila, the general's control over the navy was not as clearly stated. Like the air army, the command of the Southwest Area

---

[62]"Philippine Operations Record, Phase III," JMS 12, p. 65; Muto, "Memoirs," pp. 17, 26.

[63]JMS 12, p. 77.

Chart 2. Japanese Command Structure, January 1945

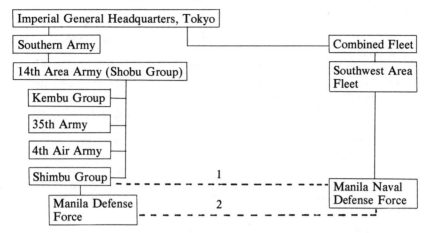

1. Shimbu Group assumed control on 6 January 1945 of the Manila Naval Defense Force "in regard to land operations."
2. By 21 January 1945 the Shimbu Group placed that section of its Manila Defense Force still remaining in the capital under the control of the Manila Naval Defense Force.

Fleet had initially favored defending Manila and, like the air army, it was initially independent of Yamashita's command. In the fall of 1944, while the 14th Area Army had created the Manila Defense Force, the navy had likewise created its own Manila Naval Defense Force.[64] Given a traditional rivalry between the Japanese army and navy, cooperation was by no means assured. Yamashita, hoping to coordinate his evacuation and defense policies with the Southwest Area Fleet, instructed Muto to inquire of the navy's plans for Manila. Southwest Area Fleet informed Muto in late December that, once its surface units had departed, it planned to leave only 4,000 men in Manila.[65] Understanding that those men might have to evacuate into the Shimbu defensive sector, the navy then asked Muto that if an evacuation of the Manila Naval Defense Force proved necessary, to what position would the army send the unit? Colonel Shujiro Kobayashi, 14th Area Army's liaison, responded that naval personnel should fall back

---

[64] An "Organization Chart of the Manila Naval Defense Force" with the names of all officers is in World War II Operation Reports, A.T.I.S. 389: Enemy Publications, box 1255, RG 407, Records of the Adjutant General's Office, Washington National Records Center.

[65] Statements, Colonel Kobayashi, p. 243.

to Antipolo. Then, allowing his antinavy bias to surface, he added: "We place little hope on the fighting power of the naval forces since they are not used to land fighting."[66] Such a remark, although not surprising given the rivalry between the services, may have unnecessarily raised the ire of the naval command.

Perhaps disturbed by Kobayashi's attitude, the Manila Naval Defense Force launched an investigation of its proposed defensive sector. Lieutenant Commander Koichi Kayashima, one of the staff officers who had discussed evacuation with Kobayashi, later explained: "Early in January, the Manila Naval Defense Force, after compiling various reports of topographical reconnaissance of Antipolo and its vicinity, concluded that since that area was an open terrain with its southern part utterly defenseless, it was unsuitable for defense. . . ." Naval officers further concluded "that by establishing positions in Manila they would be able to resist longer." Based on those findings and conclusions, according to Kayashima, "the Manila Naval Defense Force abandoned all considera-tion of Antipolo."[67] The navy did not notify Yamashita of its decision. Nor did it notify him that the naval forces remaining in Manila would number 20,000 rather than 4,000.[68] Therefore, when on 2 January Yamashita moved north to Baguio to control the Shobu Group, he believed that the navy had only 4,000 men in Manila and that even those planned to evacuate into the Shimbu Group area after completing their demolitions in the city.

On 5 January, when the headquarters of Southwest Area Fleet decided to accompany Yamashita into the mountains around Baguio, it issued the following order to its Manila forces: "Subsequent to 0000 hours 6 January 45, the 31 Special Base Force [Manila Naval Defense Force] commander will receive instructions from the Shimbu Group commander *in regard to land operations*." The order, according to Rear Admiral Kaoru Arima, chief of staff of the Southwest Area Fleet, did not mean that naval units remaining in the city would be farmed out piecemeal to individual army commands. Rather, it meant that while Lieutenant General Yokoyama would give orders relating to land operations to Rear Admiral Sanji Iwabuchi, Iwabuchi alone would control his officers and men.[69] Since

---

[66]Ibid., p. 244. Also see JMS 114, p. 4.

[67]Statements, Lt. Commander Koichi Kayashima, staff officer, Manila Naval Defense Force, p. 168.

[68]Statements, Rear Admiral Arima, p. 55, and Commander Shigeichi Yamamoto, staff officer, Southwest Area Fleet and army-navy liaison between 5 and 25 January 1945, p. 487.

[69]Emphasis added. Statements, Rear Admiral Arima, p. 56, and Commander Yamamoto, p. 488. Yamashita's control was limited to the actual employment of naval personnel in land operations. He could not promote, demote, remove, or court-martial any naval person. Testimony of Vice Admiral Denshichi Okochi, commanding officer, South-west Area Fleet, Transcript, pp. 2545–46.

the precise distinction between land operations and naval operations was left to Iwabuchi's discretion, Yokoyama's control of the navy remained ill-defined. A second problem facing the Shimbu Group leader was the size of the navy contingent. Basing his calculations for the eventual withdrawal and integration of Japanese personnel in Manila into his sector on a navy contingent of 4,000, Yokoyama was astonished to discover on 8 January that the navy had 20,000 personnel in Manila, all of whom were still theoretically engaged in naval operations.

Until he could meet personally with Rear Admiral Iwabuchi, Yokoyama instructed the Naval Defense Force, probably on 8 January, to continue its current duties relating to the defense of Manila and the demolition of naval facilities.[70] He then quickly arranged for a conference to be held at Montalban on 14 January. In the interim, members of Iwabuchi's staff began pressuring Yokoyama to transfer to the admiral direct control of those army units still remaining within the city.[71]

At their mid-January meeting, Yokoyama discovered that Iwabuchi had no intention of making a last-ditch stand in Manila, but that he thought he could not depart until he had fulfilled his orders and destroyed the strategic value of the city by mining the harbor and destroying naval installations.[72] Only after he had completed his naval mission would he be willing to bow to Yokoyama's wishes and retire to the mountain defenses. If the enemy attacked early, he had no choice but to resist until his duties were fulfilled. Colonel Kenichiro Asano, who was present at the meeting, later observed: "The Shimbu Group . . . was forced by the Navy's demand to alter existing plans so as to adopt a policy of slightly more vigorous defense of the city than was originally planned." Yokoyama, aware that Iwabuchi was acting under naval directives, which pertained to "naval business" and not "land operations," thought that he "could not but accept" Iwabuchi's decision. The "slightly more vigorous defense" agreed upon by Yokoyama and Iwabuchi, however, implied that both officers still planned no decisive battle in Manila.[73]

Further complicating the chain of command in the capital was a contingent of Southwest Area Fleet staff officers who were responsible to neither Iwabuchi nor Yokoyama but to the Southwest Area Fleet Headquarters at Baguio.[74] They were to supervise the departure of any

[70]Statements, Colonel Kobayashi, p. 245, and Lt. Commander Kayashima, p. 158.

[71]Statements, Commander Yamamoto, pp. 489–90.

[72]Statements, Colonel Asano, p. 93. For comments on naval orders to Rear Admiral Iwabuchi relating to Manila, see Statements, Commander Yamamoto, p. 488, and Rear Admiral Arima, p. 54; Muto, "Memoirs," p. 29; and testimony of Vice Admiral Okochi, pp. 2546–50, and LTG Shizuo Yokoyama, commanding officer, Shimbu Group, Transcript, p. 2693.

[73]Statements, Colonel Asano, p. 92.

[74]Statements, Rear Admiral Arima, pp. 55–56, and Commander Yamamoto, p. 488.

remaining operational naval craft and to expedite the movement of noncombat naval units out of the city of Bayombong. Not only did some of those officers favor a stubborn defense of Manila, but they also sought to impress their ideas on both Iwabuchi's and Yokoyama's staffs. One of that group, Commander Shigeichi Yamamoto, naval liaison to Yokoyama, argued at the end of the war that the staff officers succeeded in influencing "the defense ideology and fighting spirit of the key members of the Manila Naval Defense unit," although not that of staff members of Yokoyama's Shimbu Group. "Some staff officers of the Southwest Area Fleet who remained in Manila," he recalled, "were impressed by the Battle of Stalingrad, and were strongly of the opinion that although the Manila Naval Defense Unit was poorly armed, it would be able to repulse the U.S. forces if so determined, because the battle in and around Manila was street fighting, and that for this reason it should wage battle with firm resolution."[75] If Yamamoto's assessment was correct, Southwest Naval Fleet staff officers were blatantly attempting to undercut the efforts of both Yamashita and Yokoyama to evacuate the Philippine capital.

Colonel Kobayashi, who had been 14th Area Army's chief of operations and liaison officer with the navy in Manila in late 1944, and who had joined Yokoyama's staff with the same liaison duties when Yamashita's headquarters moved to Baguio on 5 January, found naval arguments for a determined battle in Manila to his liking. Kobayashi, in November 1944, had disagreed with Yamashita and Muto's decision to retreat into the mountains and adopt a passive defense. He had favored an active defense—launching attacks on the enemy from the mountain positions.[76] Initially skeptical of the navy's fighting abilities, Kobayashi reevaluated its usefulness in light of their ideas about vigorous resistance. In discussions with Commander Yamamoto, he indicated that if the decision were his, "he would let the Army forces remaining in Manila defend the city to the last." Taking advantage of Kobayashi's more favorable perception of the navy, Yamamoto quickly requested that those 1,800 army personnel in the city be placed under the command of the navy. "It would not be amiss," he added, "for them to carry out a determined defense."[77]

Kobayashi may well have influenced Yokoyama, for during the third week of January those men were indeed transferred to Iwabuchi's command. Colonel Asano's observations, however, indicate Kobayashi

---

[75]Statements, Commander Yamamoto, pp. 489–91, and Lt. Commander Kayashima, p. 169; Muto, "Memoirs," p. 17.

[76]CMH Interrogations, Colonel Kobayashi, 1:437; Muto, "Memoirs," pp. 11–12.

[77]CMH Interrogations, Colonel Kobayashi, 1:436. Field Marshal Terauchi also had favored a battle for Manila but deferred to Yamashita who directed the actual defense. CMH Interrogations, Major Sato, 2:180. Also see Statements, Commander Yamamoto, p. 490.

had not convinced Yokoyama to adopt the navy's defensive ideas. Asano later argued that Yokoyama agreed to transfer the men only after Iwabuchi promised to "eventually have those units withdrawn to the main positions east of Manila."[78] But while Yokoyama apparently refused to approve a final stand in the city, he failed to establish a timetable for withdrawal and failed to have Iwabuchi define just what "eventually" meant. Since withdrawal hinged on when the admiral believed that he had carried out his naval responsibilities, the decision for decisive battle still rested less with Yokoyama than with his naval counterpart.

Iwabuchi, too, was unsure about how to handle the battle for Manila.[79] He could not evacuate to the east until he had made Manila port facilities useless to the Americans. But his own staff, and at least some of the Southwest Area Fleet staff who had remained in Manila until 25 January, opposed any withdrawal, favoring instead a decisive stand. In addition, his forces were becoming restless. If he informed them of any withdrawal plans, they might offer only token resistance and withdraw prematurely, jeopardizing his command and his mission.[80] Iwabuchi died in the subsequent struggle for the city and his reasoning in late January remains unknown. Colonel Asano, however, observed navy personnel constructing strong positions in the city.[81] Whether that symbolized a tangible decision to fight and die in the capital or merely a precaution to cover a naval withdrawal is unclear.

One thing is certain. On 19 January, Lieutenant General Yokoyama warned Iwabuchi of an American attack and instructed him to "halt [the] advance in prepared positions." Yokoyama later explained that he meant his orders to apply only to those army and navy forces guarding strategic areas and not to all military personnel in Manila. "It was my desire," he noted, "to withdraw all other troops in the city of Manila to the hills. However, with respect to those naval forces who were along the

---

[78]Statements, Colonel Asano, p. 93.

[79]Statements, Rear Admiral Arima, p. 57.

[80]Statements, Colonel Kobayashi, p. 242. In this statement Kobayashi indicated that in December this had been of concern to the 14th Area Army with its own Manila Defense Force. To avoid a problem, Kobayashi verbally informed the commanders of the Manila Force that they were "ordered to be resolved to fight to the last." He justified that decision later by noting: "Of course, if the intention were made known to the units that retreat was contemplated after some minor battles, it would be natural for the units to withdraw hastily. Especially since the Shimbu Group was a combination of miscellaneous units, need was taken to show the units in general that a resolute will to fight to the finish existed, to induce units to fight with resolution."

[81]Statements, Colonel Asano, p. 92. Despite the presence of some strong defensive emplacements, a XIV Corps after-action evaluation concluded that "Japanese defenses within the city were characterized by improvisation." "Japanese Defense of Cities as Exemplified by the Battle for Manila," Yamashita Trial, Prosecution Exhibit 404, p. 3. Also see OSS 121724, "Terrain Study 94: Central Luzon," 1:4, RG 226.

shore line, who were placed there for purely naval duties, my orders did not include them."[82] Presumably, Yokoyama explained his reasoning carefully to Iwabuchi when they toured Manila the following day. Whether it was on that occasion or later in the week, Iwabuchi and Yokoyama decided to authorize their operations officers to meet on 27 January at Montalban.

Here, inexplicably, there was also no discussion of withdrawal.[83] Indeed, the decisions reached by Kobayashi, Kayashima, and other staff officers present implied that Manila was to be defended to the last. According to Kayashima's recollection, the officers decided that, while Shimbu Group would concentrate east of Manila, "the Manila Naval Defense Force will remain in its present position and destroy the enemy forces." Colonel Kobayashi, recalling the same meeting, later recorded that the decision was as follows: "The city of Manila and Fort McKinley are to be stubbornly defended and secured so as to deny to the enemy their effective use. . . . The Duty of the Manila Naval Defense Force . . . shall [be to] destroy the enemy fighting power from positions already pre-pared." Perhaps Kobayashi's desire for strong resistance in the city, as well as the impact of opinions held by staff members of the Southwest Area Fleet who advocated the same plan, bore fruit at Montalban. The operations officers may have decided to implement the policy most in accord with their own views. Or perhaps both sides were aware of Iwabuchi's and Yokoyama's earlier statements that the forces would be "eventually" withdrawn and decided nothing further needed to be said about the matter. Or perhaps the discussions were shaped by a combina-tion of both factors. By not discussing withdrawal, Kobayashi could emphasize resistance over retreat, and the naval operations staff could ensure that they would not be bound by either a timetable or set pro-cedures of withdrawal.

Failure to discuss the awkward issue of retreat, then, may have been deemed by both staffs as in their own best interests. Whatever the logic, Kobayashi later noted that at this meeting "the Shimbu Group commander's intention of having the Manila Naval Defense Force evacu-ate from Manila after engaging in fighting to some extent was never set forth."[84] The last opportunity to discuss jointly planned, orderly with-drawal had passed. American forces, urged on by MacArthur, would penetrate Manila's city limits exactly one week later.

The American forces arrived at Manila ten days earlier than Yamashita had anticipated in his preinvasion planning. He would argue in late 1945 that the failure of the Kembu Group to delay the American

---

[82]Testimony of LTG Yokoyama, pp. 2672–73, Transcript.

[83]The following discussion of the 27 January conference is based on Statements, Colonel Kobayashi and Lt. Commander Kayashima.

[84]Statements, Colonel Kobayashi, p. 246.

forces effectively in the Clark Field area enabled the XIV Corps to take Iwabuchi and his naval forces by surprise before they could withdraw. Vice Admiral Denshichi Okochi, commanding officer of the Southwest Area Fleet, and Lieutenant General Yokoyama also both believed that Iwabuchi had tried desperately to conclude his destruction of harbor facilities and had indeed planned to flee east. Like Yamashita, they thought that Iwabuchi had miscalculated the speed with which the Americans would encircle the city.[85]

Whatever motivated Iwabuchi, it is clear he did not attempt an evacuation immediately upon learning of the nearness of XIV Corps. His effort to complete the demolition work and maintain order in the city may have been seriously complicated and slowed by Filipino guerrillas. Anticipating victory and emboldened by the nearby American forces, guerrillas blew munitions dumps, cut communication lines, and attacked Japanese forces within the city, only to fade back among many civilians.[86] Their tactics may have delayed the navy just long enough for MacArthur to entrap the city.

By 9 February, Rear Admiral Iwabuchi moved his headquarters to Fort McKinley, thereby acknowledging that he and his forces would have to retreat soon if they were to do so at all. But he had waited too long. The 5th and 8th Cavalry regiments arrived at the Pasig River the next day. Crossing it early on 11 February, they threatened to isolate Iwabuchi from his men in Manila. Abandoning any hope that he personally would be able to escape to the east, Iwabuchi returned to the city around noon.[87] It was his last chance to join Yokoyama in the mountains. Within twenty-four hours all remaining escape routes were clamped shut: the Manila Naval Defense Force was trapped. Whether it had planned to fight a decisive battle for the city or not, it no longer had a choice.

In Baguio, 125 miles to the north, Yamashita did not have sufficient knowledge of American troop disposition to understand Iwabuchi's critical situation on 9 February. Indeed, when Shimbu Group notified him that Iwabuchi had transferred to Fort McKinley, Yamashita and Muto apparently believed that the evacuation of the city had finally begun. They were astonished a few days later to learn that Iwabuchi and his men were still in the city. On 13 February, Yamashita specifically ordered Yokoyama to evacuate the naval and army forces remaining in Manila.[88] Yokoyama immediately ordered Iwabuchi to retreat. Similarly,

---

[85]Statements, Yamashita, p. 500; testimony of Vice Admiral Okochi, p. 2553, Transcript; Yamashita Interrogation, box 79, p. 2, RG 5; Muto, "Memoirs," p. 29.

[86]Statements, Yamashita, p. 499; 10th I & H, "Staff Study of Japanese Operations on Luzon," sect. 2, p. 2; JMS 114, pp. 13–14.

[87]Statements, Lt. Commander Kayashima, pp. 159–60.

[88]Testimony of LTG Yokoyama, pp. 2683, 2686, and Akira Muto, p. 3062, Transcript; Muto, "Memoirs," p. 29.

Vice Admiral Okochi, breaking his self-imposed silence in Baguio, informed Iwabuchi on 15 February that he should "speedily withdraw in compliance with the order of the Army."[89] Communicating to Yokoyama's headquarters, Iwabuchi revealed around 15 February that he had unsuccessfully tried to establish ground contact with Fort McKinley. "Escape," he reported, "is believed impossible." And, almost as if pleading, he added: "Will you please understand this situation?"[90]

Yokoyama now had little hope of rescuing Iwabuchi, although on 17 February his forces made a half-hearted effort to break the American encirclement, an attempt that was neither well planned, well coordinated, nor well executed.[91] When that effort failed, Yokoyama virtually wrote off his Japanese colleagues in the city. As for Iwabuchi, in one of his last important transmissions to Yokoyama on the day of the counterattack he explained that he would not be able to extract all his men in one single breakout: "It is very clear that we will be decimated if we make an attempt." He reminded the Shimbu Group leader, however, that "we can hold out another week if we remain entrenched as we are. What is vitally important now is to hold every position and inflict severe losses on the enemy by any means. Fixed positions are our strong advantage. If we move, we will be weak. Therefore, we will hold out as long as possible and then make a desperate charge with our entire strength."[92] That concisely summarized his unfortunate position on 17 February. Thereafter, his situation would deteriorate further. Encircled, without hope of escape, bombarded by American artillery, and harassed by urban guerrillas, Iwabuchi, his staff, the Manila Naval Defense Force, and the 1,800 army personnel in the city would fight a vicious defensive action for two more weeks. By 3 March all were dead.

The forces of MacArthur and Yamashita had waged a bloody, devastating battle in Manila which neither had wanted nor anticipated. The murky lines of authority between Rear Admiral Iwabuchi and Lieutenant General Yokoyama, the preexisting antagonism of the two rival services, and the rapidity of the American advance contributed to that clash. Ironically, the full responsibility for the city's destruction and the thousands of civilian deaths rested most heavily on the two who had sincerely wished to spare the capital.

With the collapse of Japanese resistance in Manila, the threat

---

[89]Statements, Commander Tadao Kusumi, staff officer, Southwest Area Fleet, p. 387. For comments on Okochi's silence, see Statements, Rear Admiral Arima, pp. 55–57, and Commander Yamamoto, p. 490; and testimony of Vice Admiral Okochi, Transcript, p. 2544.

[90]JMS 114, p. 18; CMH Interrogations, Colonel Kobayashi, 1:438.

[91]Smith, *Triumph*, pp. 272–73; Statements, Lt. Commander Kayashima, pp. 161–62, and Colonel Hashimoto, pp. 279–80.

[92]JMS 114, p. 19.

that prepared Shimbu positions faced from Krueger's Sixth Army dramatically intensified.[93] It was probably the presence of the Sixth Army, in fact, that had convinced Yokoyama to launch only a half-hearted counterattack to save Iwabuchi. To have ordered his men into an offensive strike against U.S. forces surrounding Manila would have presented the Americans a golden opportunity to eliminate easily crucial elements of Shimbu's strength. Additionally, of no consolation to those trapped in Manila, Yokoyama's decision to continue fortifications in the mountains, rather than commit his men to a risky rescue venture, coincided more clearly with his orders to resist and inflict maximum injury on the enemy from his fortified positions. Even in those mountainous bastions, Yokoyama and his army were mauled by Krueger's command when, only three days after the Manila rescue effort, Sixth Army launched attacks against Shimbu's northern front just south of Montalban. By early March it had captured Montalban and was driving toward the strategically important Wawa Dam. Simultaneously, along the southern front of the Shimbu line, the Americans had launched a drive toward Antipolo, which finally fell on 11 March. Slowly and methodically, infantry and cavalry units continued to chip away at the Shimbu defenses east of Manila. By the end of May they had eliminated that Japanese force as an effective fighting command, even though Lieutenant General Yokoyama, when he surrendered in August 1945, still had 6,300 men in his unit.

While the Philippine capital lay in ruins, devastated by artillery blasts, demolitions, and ferocious combat, and while MacArthur wore down Yokoyama's forces east of the city, XIV Corps advanced against the Fuji Force under Colonel Masatoshi Fujishige—a force created by Yokoyama in early January to prevent the Americans from moving east of Laguna de Bay and outflanking his fixed positions. To meet the American offensive, Fujishige had only 10,000 soldiers, three-quarters of whom were not trained combat troops but merely men assembled from service units. Although the Fuji Force south of Laguna de Bay faced no concerted American attack before early March, it had not been idle. Fujishige had discovered the power of a determined Filipino guerrilla movement in southern Luzon during that period. According to one U.S. military historian, "southern Luzon had become a veritable hornet's nest of guerrilla activity."[94] Nor had that activity just emerged. When American ships and aircraft wreaked havoc on Japanese resupply efforts to Leyte in October and November 1944, Yamashita's staff had tried two alternate plans, on

---

[93]For a detailed discussion of Sixth Army's operations against the Shimbu Group, see Smith, *Triumph*, pp. 361–445.

[94]Ibid., p. 427. For activities of Filipino guerrillas before October 1944, see A.T.I.S. Enemy Publications, "Guerrilla Warfare in the Philippines," pts. 1, 2, box 1253, RG 407.

which Filipino guerrillas had had a major impact. Major General Toshio Nishimura, the aide to Chief of Staff Muto responsible for keeping abreast of supply problems, later recounted what had occurred:

> First we shipped goods by rail down the Legaspi Peninsula then by ship across to Leyte. The railroad was frequently bombed and the guerrillas greatly interfered with the movement of trains. We tried to send truck convoys along with the rail shipments, but they were often captured by natives. The second plan was the transporting of supplies to Batangas and then sending them on to Leyte by means of small boats in a series of shuttle hops at night. We planned to establish about ten bases along this route and sent twenty-five to thirty men to each place to set them up. However, the natives learned of our intention and killed all of the personnel at these spots.[95]

The problem Nishimura faced in October and November 1944 was that shared by Fujishige after January 1945. The further the Americans forced their way down the Central Plains of Luzon, the greater the guerrilla activity became in the Fuji Force sector.

In considering operational orders to Colonel Fujishige, who was operating 100 to 200 kilometers to Shimbu's south, Yokoyama decided to issue only general guidelines, leaving the formulation of specific details to his commander in the field.[96] Exercising his discretionary powers, Colonel Fujishige on or about 17 January called his battalion commanders together to discuss the military situation and the anticipated American attack. After discussing troop dispositions and sectors of responsibility, Fujishige turned to the problem of guerrillas. Obviously, he noted, past antiguerrilla policies had failed. Given the increase in local resistance, resulting in the destruction of Japanese supplies, the disruption of Japanese transportation, and the death of fellow soldiers, it was clear that the guerrilla issue had to be resolved before the Americans launched an attack. "Therefore," he concluded, "the suppression of guerrillas must be carried out thoroughly and resolutely."[97] Meeting shortly thereafter with company commanders in the vicinity of Santa Clara, he repeated those instructions. Lieutenant Yuzo Sakata, recalling that meeting after the war, testified that Fujishige had wanted guerrillas aggressively "subjugated" without trial. He said, Sakata continued, "all the civilians have now turned into guerrillas; therefore, kill all of them."[98] Realizing that women

---

[95]RG 243 Interrogations, MG Nishimura, p. 4

[96]Testimony of LTG Yokoyama, box 1678, 11:1103, 1109, RG 331.

[97]Testimony of Major Zenichi Uehara, chief of staff, Fuji Force, box 1678, 13:1286–87, and 14:1318, RG 331; 11th Airborne Division, "Report of Atrocities . . . Batangas," box 2001, RG 331. The 11th Airborne Division report includes extracts of interrogations and captured diaries.

[98]Testimony of Lt. Yuzo Sakata, company commander, Fuji Force, box 1678, 1:67–68, RG 331. Using almost identical words, 2d Lt. Bunji Kanto testified how his

might pose a special problem, Fujishige also informed the battalion commanders and at least one company commander that women too should receive no mercy "if they are guerrillas or anti-Japanese."[99]

Fujishige's action, taken without consulting Shimbu Group, made civilians "fair game" in southern Luzon.[100] A selection of diary extracts from soldiers in that area reveals what those orders meant in actual practice:

> February 1945: Every day is spent in hunting guerrillas and native inhabitants. The killings I have done already exceed well over one hundred in number.
>
> 10 February: By order of the Army, we began punitive operations against Filipino terrorists and killed 500 of them.
>
> 13 February: For security reasons, all inhabitants of the town [TN: presumably Anilao] were killed. . . .
>
> 17 February: Because 90% of the Filipino people did not feel pro-Japanese but on the contrary are anti-Japanese Army Hq issued orders on the 10th to punish them. In various sectors we have killed several thousand. . . .[101]

Despite reports of large guerrilla deaths and concern by staff members that there was overzealous interpretation of the earlier orders, Fujishige refused to curb antiguerrilla activities.[102] Consequently, an estimated twenty-five thousand civilians died before American forces, launching an offensive in early March, could liberate the area. Not until 30 April, when the Americans had effectively destroyed the Fuji command as an organized military force, were civilians in southern Luzon really safe. Although Fujishige and his 2,000 remaining soldiers held out until August 1945, they posed little threat after April.

Even while Shimbu units in Manila, in the mountains east of the city, and in the Fuji Force sector struggled to withstand American assaults, Yamashita and his Shobu Group had their hands full in northern Luzon. Between 1 and 3 February, Yamashita had fought to hold San Jose, a critical supply storage depot and his last land link with the Shimbu Force. By early morning of 3 February, Yamashita had finally been forced

---

battalion commander interpreted Fujishige's orders: "He said that all the natives have turned into guerrillas, therefore to kill them." Box 1678, 5:557–58, RG 331.

[99]Testimony of Lt. Mikio Taneichi, company commander, Fuji Force, box 1678, 4:418–20, 428, and of Major Uehara, box 1678, 13:1286–87, RG 331.

[100]Testimony of Major Uehara, box 1678, 14:1323, and of LTG Yokoyama, box 1678, 11:1088, 1096, RG 331.

[101]11th Airborne Division, "Report of Atrocities . . . Batangas," box 2001, RG 331.

[102]Testimony of Major Uehara, box 1678, 13:1296–99, 1303, RG 331.

to retreat northward, having successfully removed most of his supplies.

The withdrawal from San Jose starkly illustrated the nature of Yamashita's communications link with units directly under his own command as well as with Shimbu and Kembu groups. Citing a critical shortage of batteries, a staff officer of the 2d Tank Division, entrenched south and west of San Jose, recalled that by 1 February communications with the 14th Area Army Headquarters "were extremely poor." He continued: "Liaison between units was kept by the use of messengers who had to move under the cover of darkness."[103] Given this rather crude method, the Ida Detachment of the 2d Tank Division not surprisingly failed to receive promptly Yamashita's order to retreat, which was issued in the early hours of 4 February despite the fact that Yamashita's headquarters was less than fifty miles away. When the order did get through on 6 February and the unit attempted to escape, it was destroyed by American units.

Yamashita's communications with Shimbu and Kembu groups were almost as severely hampered. Indeed, after mid-January Yamashita had no communication with Kembu at all. As for land communication with General Yokoyama and Shimbu, that had been cut when San José fell in early February and when American forces seizing Rizal, Bongabon, and Dingalen Bay physically separated the Shimbu and Shobu armies. Furthermore, by early February Yamashita's radio communication with Yokoyama was often broken or distorted. That problem was due in part to the loss of vital, but heavy, communication equipment that had been left behind as Yamashita was forced to shift his headquarters from Fort McKinley to Ipo in December, from Ipo to Baguio in January, from Baguio to Bambang in April, and from Bambang to Kiangan in May. In addition, the lack of batteries, replacement tubes, and heavy oil for the generators made long-distance communication exceedingly precarious, even early in the defense of northern Luzon.[104] It was these foreseeable obstacles to communication that had prompted Yamashita's decision in December to create three separate armies on Luzon and to delegate command of two of those units to Major General Tsukada and Lieutenant General Yokoyama.

---

[103] 10th I & H, sec. 4, p. 8, "Staff Study of Japanese Operations on Luzon."

[104] Muto, "Memoirs," pp. 28, 49; Interrogation of LTC Kuriya in 201 Yamashita File, box 1217, p. 3, RG 331; Statements, Yamashita, p. 497; 10th I & H, "Staff Study of Japanese Operations on Luzon," sec. 1, p. 13; JMS 7, p. 112; Yamashita Interrogation, box 79, pp. 1–2, RG 5; Lt. Commander Samuel S. Stratton, "Tiger of Malaya," *U.S. Naval Institute Proceedings* 80 (February 1954): 136–43. For other comments on the poor communications among Japanese units, see CinCAFPAC Advance to CinCAFPAC, 5 November 1945, box 763, 00.5 Yamashita, RG 331; and CMH Interrogations, LTC Yorio Ishikawa, 1:252.

Isolated from the Shimbu and Kembu groups, Yamashita, withdrawing to the north in February, created an iron triangle within which he planned to concentrate his forces. The cities of Baguio, Bontoc, and Bambang formed the three apexes of that triangle. From that defensive position, Yamashita resisted American assaults from February to August 1945. When he marched out of the mountains in August, he still had an army of 50,500 men out of an original 152,000.

General MacArthur's victory over Yamashita had been costly. By the end of the war Yamashita's Shobu Group alone still tied down three reinforced U.S. divisions, one Filipino regiment, and thousands of guerrillas. Shobu Group had inflicted 16,190 battle casualties on U.S. Army ground combat forces; Shimbu Group, 6,340 casualties, excluding Manila, which accounted for 6,575 more; and Kembu Group, 6,730 casualties. In comparison, however, Japanese losses were staggering because the figures included not only battle casualties but also deaths due to starvation, exhaustion, and disease. In Shobu Group, 63% of the defenders died; in Shimbu Group, 86%; and in Kembu Group, 93%. As for Filipino civilians, tens of thousands had died as a result of the Japanese-American conflict. Between thirty and forty thousand of them had been slain by the Japanese during the struggle for Manila and for southern Luzon.[105]

While Yamashita's resistance had tied up thousands of American soldiers and tons of American equipment, it had not prevented the Allies from humbling Japan and forcing it to accept an unconditional surrender. In August 1945, therefore, MacArthur was clearly the victor in the Philippines; Yamashita, the loser. But for MacArthur the thousands of lives lost and the millions of dollars in damage on the islands made his victory bittersweet.

---

[105]These figures are based on data contained in Smith, *Triumph*, app. H, pp. 692–94.

CHAPTER TWO
WAR-CRIMES POLICYMAKING: EUROPE

News filtering out of Europe and the Far East as early as 1942 alerted Allied leaders to the barbarous behavior of the enemy toward civilians and prisoners of war. Such reports prompted President Franklin D. Roosevelt in August 1942 to warn the perpetrators of such acts that they would be held accountable "in courts of law" by the nations whose citizens they had maltreated.[1] Seven weeks later on 7 October the president, reaffirming his commitment to prosecute war criminals, announced that the United States would cooperate with other Allied governments in establishing a special war-crimes commission. Rather than awaiting defeat of the Tripartite powers, that organization would begin the collection and assessment of evidence against war criminals during the actual hostilities. To assuage fears that the Allies might launch a series of mass reprisals against the enemy as repayment for past atrocities and violations of the law of war, Roosevelt declared that the United States and its wartime associates intended to impose a "just and sure punishment" on "the ringleaders" who had authorized or permitted "the organized murder of thousands of innocent persons and the commission of atrocities which [had] violated every tenet of the Christian faith."[2]

Roosevelt was not alone in viewing enemy actions with grave concern and in condemning the violators of the law of war. The U.S. Senate and the House of Representatives, by concurrent resolution in March 1943, characterized Nazi actions as "brutal and indefensible outrages against millions of helpless men, women and children." Both legislative units (the House by a unanimous vote) also demonstrated their

---

[1]Samuel I. Rosenman, *The Public Papers and Addresses of Franklin D. Roosevelt*, 13 vols. (New York: Harper & Brothers, 1950), 11:330.

[2]Press release, 7 October 1942, ASW 000.51, War Crimes Working File, RG 107, Records of the Office of the Secretary of War, National Archives, Washington, DC. Also see Rosenman, *Public Papers*, 11:410. For statements by Winston Churchill emphasizing the same sentiment, see Robert Rhodes James, ed., *Winston S. Churchill: His Complete Speeches, 1897–1963*, 8 vols. (London: Chelsea House Publishers, 1974), 6:6498, 6675. For the Russian position, see Molotov to Fierlinger et al., 14 October 1942, U.S., Department of State, *International Conference on Military Trials* (Washington: Government Printing Office, 1945), p. 17; and "Russia's Declaration for War-Crimes Trials," *New York Times*, 16 October 1942, p. 8.

concern by resolving "that those guilty, directly or indirectly, of these criminal acts shall be held accountable and punished in a manner commensurate with the offenses for which they are responsible."[3]

Following that congressional statement, which had been directed specifically at Germany, the State Department considered dispatching a pointed reminder to Japan, lest its leaders mistakenly assume that the Nazis alone bore the wrath of the American government. On 12 April, Secretary of State Cordell Hull instructed the U.S. minister in Geneva to transmit a warning to Japan, using the neutral Swiss government as an intermediary. That message, which the Swiss obligingly communicated, warned the Hideki Tojo cabinet not to permit war crimes against American prisoners of war. Hull cautioned that if captured U.S. military personnel were mistreated, abused, or handled in any way contrary to the law of war, "the American government [would] visit upon the officers of the Japanese Government responsible for such uncivilized and inhumane acts the punishment they deserve."[4] By the summer of 1943 the secretary's message, coupled with the congressional resolution and Roosevelt's declaration, served notice on both the Japanese and the Germans that the United States took the war-crimes issue seriously.

Not surprisingly, given the international scope of the fighting in 1943 and the increasingly frequent Allied discussions of wartime strategy, the United States, the United Kingdom, and the Soviet Union began to search for a common solution that might dissuade the enemy from committing further violations of the law of war. In the fall of 1943 the three governments agreed at Moscow to issue a joint statement on war crimes. Although aimed specifically at Germany, since the Soviet Union was not at war with Japan, the 1 November release by President Roosevelt, Prime Minister Winston Churchill, and Marshal Joseph Stalin clearly indicated the attitude of the three Allied governments toward war criminals wherever found. Not only did the three leaders pledge the punishment of those who already had violated the law of war, but they also issued a somber warning to those of the enemy who might commit violations in the future. "Let those who have hitherto not imbrued their hands with innocent blood," they cautioned, "beware lest they join the ranks of the guilty, for most assuredly the three Allied Powers will pursue them to the uttermost ends of the earth and will deliver them to their accusors in order that justice may be done."[5] Had the Japanese and Germans been unsure about joint Allied

---

[3]U.S., Congress, *Congressional Record*, 78th Cong., 1st sess., 89, pp. 1723, 2184. The resolution passed the Senate on 9 March 1943 and the House on 18 March 1943.

[4]Hull to Minister Leland Harrison, 12 April 1943, U.S., Department of State, *Foreign Relations of the United States, 1943* (Washington: Government Printing Office, 1963), 3:981–82 (hereafter cited as *FRUS*).

[5]For a copy of the 1 November 1943 declaration, see ASW 000.51, War Crimes Working File, RG 107, or Rosenman, *Public Papers*, 12:498–99. The Moscow Declaration

reaction to war crimes and war criminals in October, that firm statement should have significantly clarified the Allies' position.

The joint declaration at Moscow not only revealed Allied intent but also helped crystallize policy on the technical process of reaching judgment. Even though each government had previously issued public statements on the matter, neither Moscow, London, nor Washington had clearly enunciated in 1942 or 1943 a specific, detailed, workable plan to ensure justice. In his August 1942 pronouncement, Roosevelt had envisioned war trials conducted by those governments under whose jurisdiction the atrocities had occurred. But neither in his August speech nor in his October press release had he elaborated further. The British had been equally vague. In London, Prime Minister Churchill, in a message to the House of Commons in early September 1942, had merely affirmed, without specifics, that war criminals would "have to stand before tribunals in every land" where atrocities had occurred.[6] Nor were the Soviets any clearer. In a communiqué to Czechoslovakian diplomat Zdenek Fierlinger on 14 October 1942, which they had released to the press, Foreign Minister Vyacheslav Molotov had suggested that major Nazi leaders be tried "without delay" by special international tribunals.[7] But, like Churchill and Roosevelt, he left undefined the nature and responsibilities of such courts. Until the release of the Moscow Declaration, therefore, there had been no general Allied agreement as to a uniform method of judgment.

The 1 November announcement erected an Allied framework, an outline of a plan where only vague national pronouncements had existed before. Under that framework war criminals would be divided into two distinct categories. Major malefactors guilty of atrocities over wide geographic areas and wanted by two or more of those countries struggling against the Germans would be "punished by joint decision of the Governments of the Allies." Lesser criminals whose illegal activities had been directed against a single ally would be returned "to the countries in which their abominable deeds [had been] done in order that they [could] be judged and punished according to the laws of those liberated countries. . . ." The announcement still left unresolved the exact nature of the national and international judicial tribunals that would try these two categories of war criminals. Indeed, by stipulating that the major malefactors would be "punished," whereas the lesser criminals would be "judged and punished,"

---

initially had been proposed by Churchill. See Churchill to Roosevelt, 12 October 1943, in Francis Loewenheim, Harold Langley, and Manfred Jonas, eds., *Roosevelt and Churchill: Their Secret Wartime Correspondence* (New York: E. P. Dutton, 1975), pp. 375–76.

[6]James, *Churchill: Complete Speeches*, 6:6675.

[7]Department of State, *International Conference*, p. 17; "Russia's Declaration for War-Crimes Trials," *New York Times*, 16 October 1942, p. 8.

the Allies implied that archcriminals might even be denied a judicial hearing altogether.

Since the creation of a general structure satisfied immediate wartime demands in November 1943, the Allies were in no mood to rush into technical war-crimes policy formulation or to clarify further some of the intriguing questions left unsettled by the Moscow statement. None of them wanted hastily formulated technical procedures that might even remotely lead to a repetition of that judicial fiasco at the conclusion of the First World War known as the Leipzig trials.[8]

By the Versailles settlement in 1919 the victors, including the United Kingdom, France, and the United States, had dutifully pledged themselves to try before Allied military tribunals those who had violated the traditional law of war. Additionally, they had pledged to try by a special international tribunal Kaiser Wilhelm II, former German emperor, for his "supreme offenses against international morality and the sanctity of treaties." But the Allies had failed to create a structure that assured the operation of the trials as they had envisioned. The refusal of the Netherlands, which had granted Wilhelm political asylum in November 1918, to accede to Allied demands for the kaiser's extradition had forced the cancellation of the special international tribunal. And when shortly thereafter the prostrate Weimar government, emboldened by the action of the Netherlands government and capitalizing on the waning interest of Allied civilians, refused to extradite those war criminals in Germany sought by the Allies, the original war-crimes structure collapsed completely. Trying to salvage something of their war-crimes policies and anxious lest they appear to have abandoned judgment of the defeated Germans, the embarrassed Allies lamely agreed to a suggestion from the Weimar government that Germany try its own war criminals. Assuming—hoping—that the defeated nation would act in good faith, the Allies had submitted to it the names of forty-five individuals (pared down from an original list of over nine hundred) who, in their opinion, certainly ought to face trial for their crimes. Of the forty-five, only twelve were ever tried, six of whom were acquitted. On the six found guilty, the Leipzig court had imposed only minimum sentences.

Evaluating the Leipzig trials in January 1922, an Allied commission of jurists had concluded that the Germans not only freed individuals who should have been convicted but also sentenced those found guilty to unacceptably lenient prison terms. The commission also had decided to

---

[8]The following discussion of the Leipzig trials and the Treaty of Versailles is based on *FRUS: The Paris Peace Conference, 1919*, 13:271–80; William J. Bosch, *Judgment on Nuremberg: American Attitudes Toward the Major German War-Crimes Trials* (Chapel Hill: University of North Carolina Press, 1970), p. 6; and Robert K. Woetzel, *The Nuremberg Trials in International Law* (New York: Praeger, 1962), pp. 27–36.

recommend that further trials be conducted by the Allies themselves. Although a number of Allied leaders would have personally preferred more rigorous judgment at Leipzig, and although the Versailles settlement clearly granted the Allies the right to retry any war criminal, regardless of the outcome of proceedings in German courts, the victorious powers had decided to neither reopen the cases nor to devote more time and money to the war-crimes issue. The memory of that distasteful episode still lingered twenty-three years later as the United States, the Soviet Union, and Great Britain considered war-crimes policy during a second worldwide conflagration. They had no desire to repeat in 1943 the mistakes that had led to the judicial charade at Leipzig two decades earlier.

In the United States the responsibility for formulating a policy that would avoid a repeat of past failures and at the same time achieve some semblance of Allied consensus fell to Secretary of War Henry Stimson. Knowing that a general international debate on war crimes and war criminals was virtually inevitable and desirous of being prepared for that eventuality, Stimson on 1 October 1943 ordered Brigadier General T. H. Green, acting judge advocate general, to prepare a policy memorandum on the issue. Stimson set specific parameters for the study. He wanted the judge advocate general's investigation and recommendations to focus on the legal aspects of trying war criminals before military commissions rather than civilian courts. He also notified Green that he need only discuss the issues, procedures, and problems involved in the trial of enemy nationals and should not consider the problems involved in the trial of Allied and/or American personnel. Having restricted the nature of the inquiry by those two provisions, Stimson then ordered Green to concentrate his research on seven important issues. He was to evaluate the authority needed to establish the military tribunals; the jurisdiction of those tribunals once established; the type of criminal offenses those tribunals could hear; the qualifications and selection of court personnel; the legal procedure needed to regulate pretrial hearings, the trial, and the appellate process; the types of sentences the tribunal could legally impose; and the nature and place of punishment if defendants were found guilty.[9]

On 30 October, General Green submitted a preliminary memorandum to the War Department. Citing relevant precedent he informed Stimson and the War Department General Staff that clear authority existed for trials by both national and international military tribunals.

---

[9]Green, who was the assistant judge advocate general, assumed the title acting judge advocate general during the absence of his boss Myron Cramer. This and the following paragraphs are based on Green's memorandum entitled "Trial of War Criminals," 30 October 1943, file 103-1-book 3, box 1602, RG 153. Stimson and Green channeled their exchanges through the chief of the Civil Affairs Division, Office of the Chief of Staff, War Department General Staff.

Neither judicial body, he reported, would be restricted in its jurisdiction by territorial limitations. An individual suspected of committing war crimes against an American, for example, could be tried by a U.S. military commission, whether the violation had actually occurred within territory controlled by American forces or whether it had occurred in distant theaters of operation. The nationality of the victim, he observed, was much more important than the physical location of the war crime. The greatest obstacle to the trial of the lesser war criminals by national military tribunals, Green further explained, would not be territorial limitations but whether or not the Allied state whose citizens had been maltreated actually had physical custody of the accused. If a defendant had been captured by another power, then the aggrieved nation could only request, not force, his transfer to its own military and judicial jurisdiction.

Despite that one drawback, Green was convinced that national military tribunals offered an attractive method for trying war-crimes cases. Not only were they the logical bodies to try cases during the actual conflict, but they also could even legally retain their jurisdiction over war criminals upon cessation of hostilities. Indeed, they could retain control at least until a formal peace had been signed and perhaps beyond. Nor would staffing of such courts pose a problem. While war-crimes cases in the United States had customarily been tried by military tribunals staffed by army or navy personnel, Green explained that the War Department was under no legal obligation to so staff upcoming war-crimes courts. Should it choose to do so, the department could legally appoint civilians to sit on the military tribunals. Nor was there a legal rule forcing the department to place a specific number of judges on national military commissions. Membership in the past had varied in number from as few as three to as many as thirteen. Legal precedent, Green continued, also enabled the Washington government, if it chose, to appoint a military court without appointing either a lawyer or someone proficient in law who was capable of ruling on technical and procedural issues. In staffing, therefore, the War Department would have great flexibility. Moreover, as Green's report demonstrated, the department would have equally wide latitude in imposing and implementing sentences.

National military tribunals even had a specific advantage over international military tribunals, the acting judge advocate general argued. National military courts, working with familiar precedent, could start operations quickly.[10] That would not be true of international courts, which would have to agree on a common set of rules and procedures before they could try their first defendant. Such a process, Green believed, would be

---

[10]Despite his assertions that national courts would be more desirable and could follow familiar precedent, Green acknowledged that his office had not yet agreed on a procedural framework that would guide U.S. military courts.

very "time consuming," causing unnecessary delay in the prosecution of war-crimes cases. Therefore, while the United States could legally try war crimes in either type of court, the acting judge advocate general clearly favored the use of national military tribunals over international ones.

While the judge advocate general and the secretary of war considered the use of national and international military tribunals, 4,900 miles to the east, in Moscow, Secretary of State Hull met on 23 October 1943 with Anthony Eden and Molotov, his English and Soviet counterparts. Unlike his War Department colleague, Hull favored the quasi-judicial disposition of major war criminals. "If I had my way," he informed Eden and Molotov, "I would take Hitler and Mussolini and Tojo and their arch accomplices and bring them before a drumhead court-martial. And at sunrise the following day there would occur an historic incident." Under ideal circumstances, he opined, the trial should be based on incriminating documents and evidence captured by the Allies, but as he later emphasized, "I did not want [the lack of such data] to disturb the prompt disposition of those bandit chiefs." Summary execution of the ringleaders would not only prevent Hitler, Tojo, and their cohorts from using a trial for propaganda purposes, but Hull thought it also would serve notice to future would-be aggressive dictators of the fate awaiting them if they followed in Germany's and Japan's footsteps. Once the ringleaders had been hanged, Hull indicated, he would then be willing to deal with the remaining criminals in a less drastic manner, punishing them only if they were found guilty by military courts-martial.[11]

The secretary thought it unfortunate that Roosevelt, Churchill, and Eden, while still uncommitted in October 1943, tended to favor "a formal trial under some form of international law" rather than his "execution at sunrise" approach.[12] Nor could Hull convince the Soviets of the propriety of summary executions in cases involving the arch criminals. Therefore, Allied policymakers at the close of the Moscow Foreign Ministers Conference only issued a general framework for war-crimes trials and did not settle on a specific policy regarding the fate of top Axis leaders. Nor would they do so until the summer of 1945, when their three countries would finally adopt a unified, detailed war-crimes strategy.

In Washington, from fall 1943 until spring 1945, Stimson's War Department and the Joint Chiefs continued to favor judicial proceedings before military commissions, preferably national.[13] Departmental pride

---

[11]Cordell Hull, *The Memoirs of Cordell Hull* (New York: Macmillan Co., 1948), 2:1289–91.

[12]Ibid., 2:1291.

[13]The War Department in the summer of 1944, before any policy had been adopted by the Roosevelt administration, informed its training officers that it opposed shooting or hanging criminals without trial. See War Department Education Manual EM-11, "What Shall Be Done With the War Criminals," 2 August 1944, 000.5 (6-21-44), box

played a role in that advocacy. The adoption of their policy would reaffirm the military's traditional jurisdiction over violators of the law of war. Furthermore, the use of military commissions seemed only natural, Stimson had argued, since U.S. personnel on the battlefield would be collecting much of the evidence and since U.S. military officers already would be in the occupied areas where the trials would be held. Coordinating the exchange of evidence and prisoners of Allied units, they also would be in the most advantageous position to initiate the trial process, ensuring that Leipzig would not be repeated. Indeed, the operation should run so smoothly and efficiently, he had asserted, that there would be only a very limited need for an international military court.[14]

On 6 September 1944 a third cabinet member joined Stimson and Hull in the war-crimes debate. On that date Secretary of the Treasury Henry Morgenthau, eager to formulate postwar strategies toward a defeated Germany, transmitted to his two colleagues and to presidential adviser Harry Hopkins a lengthy memorandum on postwar policies. In an appendix to his primary proposals, Morgenthau urged the United States and its allies to compile a list of archcriminals, who, he suggested, upon capture and positive identification should be immediately executed "by firing squads made up of soldiers of the United Nations." Lesser criminals whose war crimes had caused the death of any individual should be tried, he conceded, by Allied and/or national military commissions, the procedure Stimson favored. Morgenthau calmly noted in his memorandum that, in order to expedite matters and to inflict such punishment on war criminals, there would be only one sentence for those found guilty by the courts—immediate execution. Although he did acknowledge that the military commissions might, under extremely unusual circumstances, impose a lighter sentence, he clearly anticipated little use of that judicial discretion.[15] Secretary of State Hull had found an ally.

Concerned lest Hull and Morgenthau convert the president, Stimson drafted a memorandum that he hoped would undermine their arguments favoring the summary execution of archcriminals. He warned that the Roosevelt administration must move cautiously and not precipitiously in formulating war-crimes procedures. Stimson wrote:

> Such procedure must embody, in my judgment, at least the rudimentary aspects of the Bill of Rights, namely, notification to the

---

314, RG 165, Records of the War Department General Staff, Washington National Records Center, Suitland, MD. Also see data in CCS 000.5 (3-8-44), RG 218, Records of the Joint Chiefs of Staff, National Archives.

[14]Stimson to Hull, 13 March 1944, 000.5 (3-8-44), RG 218.

[15]For a copy of the Morgenthau Plan, see *FRUS: Quebec, 1944*, pp. 101–6; and Henry Morgenthau, *Morgenthau Diary (Germany)* (Washington: Government Printing Office, 1967), 1:547–52. Also see John Morton Blum, ed., *From the Morgenthau Diaries: Years of War, 1941–1945* (Boston: Houghton Mifflin Co., 1967), p. 397.

accused of the charge, the right to be heard, and, within reasonable limits, to call witnesses in his defense. I do not mean . . . to introduce any cumbersome machinery but the very punishment of these men in a dignified manner consistent with the advance of civilization, will have all the greater effect upon posterity. Furthermore, it will afford the most effective way of making a record of the Nazi system of terrorism and of the effort of the Allies to terminate the system and prevent its recurrence.

The secretary of war again stressed, as he had in a letter to Hull in March, that most war criminals should be tried by national military commissions, the only exceptions being the few high-ranking enemy prisoners whose crimes had been so widespread that they would probably have to be tried by an international military tribunal.[16]

Alarmed because Prime Minister Churchill, in his consultations with the president at Quebec in late September, also favored the summary handling of major German war criminals, and because Secretary Morgenthau had been called to that Canadian city to explain his entire plan to the British, Stimson redoubled his efforts to formulate an acceptable war-crimes policy.[17] He promptly directed Assistant Secretary of War John McCloy to assemble experts on military law and have them formulate a specific, detailed recommendation. Meeting with that war-crimes working committee on 24 October, Stimson encouraged its members to continue their efforts in hammering out a workable proposal.[18] Writing to Hull three days later, Stimson reemphasized the need for prompt punishment "by fair judicial means" so that the Allies would not appear to be as barbarous as the Germans. The Allies have an opportunity, he noted, to use the trial as a means of educating mankind on the evils of totalitarianism. "Punishment is essential, not as retribution, but as an expression of civilization's condemnation of the Nazi philosophy and aggression. . . . That condemnation must be achieved in a fair manner which will meet the judgment of history."[19]

---

[16]Memorandum to president, 9 September 1944, reel 110, Papers of Henry Stimson (microfilm), Library of Congress Manuscript Division; Stimson to Hull, 13 March 1944, box 1674, RG 153.

[17]Stimson had reason to worry. Roosevelt agreed with Churchill and Lord Simon on 15 September to send proposals to Stalin, provided the State Department approved, calling for the political disposition of major war criminals. The message was never sent when Churchill, following talks with Stalin in Moscow, requested that it be shelved. See *FRUS: Quebec, 1944*, pp. 91–93, 467, 489–90.

[18]Stimson Diary, 22 October 1944, reel 9, p. 179; Henry Stimson and McGeorge Bundy, *On Active Service in Peace and War* (New York: Harper & Brothers, 1948), p. 585. For information relating to the Quebec conference, see *FRUS: Quebec, 1944*, esp. pp. 91–93, 467, 489–91. Also see Cramer's memorandum to McCloy, 27 September 1944, entitled "Trial of War Criminals," for an idea of proposals then under discussion.

[19]Stimson to Hull, 27 October 1944, 000.5 (9-12-44), box 313, RG 165.

Despite Stimson's commitment to judicial proceedings, the secretary had no intention of extending to any of the criminals—not even those tried by U.S. personnel—the full legal safeguards granted either to civilians or to the military personnel of the United States. In a telephone conversation of 5 September with Major General Myron Cramer, the judge advocate general, Stimson supported the use of military commissions in war trials because they made their own rules.[20] That power would enable members of the court to eliminate trial delays by avoiding debates over legal technicalities, which might arise if prosecution occurred in either civilian courts or in trials by court-martial, where clearly defined procedures already prevailed. Stimson also wondered aloud whether war criminals should be allowed legal counsel and whether they should even be allowed to call witnesses in their defense.[21] Acceptable judicial procedures, as he defined them, need only ensure war criminals of "the skeleton of what we call the requisitional fair trial," which included the right for defendants to know the charges against them and to have "some sort of opportunity" to respond to those charges. Stimson's conversation with Cramer revealed a secretary much more interested in the appearance of a judicial process than in the process itself, a secretary determined to establish a simplified legal mechanism that would record Nazi atrocities and excesses, reveal the dangers inherent in totalitarian governments, and quell possible angry demands for summary treatment. To accomplish these goals with minimum delay, the legal process, he notified Cramer, "has got to be cut down to its bare bones."

Having delegated in September specific policy formulation to Assistant Secretary McCloy and his committee of able advisers, Stimson waited for their first report. McCloy, the judge advocate general, and the director of the War Department's War Crimes Office, together with members of the G-1 Section of the War Department General Staff, the U.S. deputy representative to the United Nations War Crimes Commission in London, and other assorted officials, conferred frequently between September 1944 and January 1945. In the midst of those conversations the assistant secretary invited the Navy and State departments to join the regular War Department gathering for a briefing and discussion of the war-crimes issues. On 9 November 1944, therefore, three naval representatives, together with the U.S. ambassador to Great Britain and the legal adviser to the U.S. State Department, participated in the dialogue at the War Department. The ensuing debate revealed that Stimson's per-

---

[20]For a record of the calls between Stimson and Cramer, see file 103-3-book 2, box 1603, RG 153.

[21]Cramer believed that they should be able to call witnesses. Four days later Stimson conceded that war criminals could "within reasonable limits" do so.

sistance had paid off.[22] All conferees agreed that a judicial disposition of war criminals, even the archcriminals, would be superior to a political one. They also agreed with Stimson and the authors of the Moscow Declaration that individual war criminals should be transferred whenever possible to the nations against whom they had committed their offenses. They clearly realized the truth of an observation made by General Green in his memorandum to Stimson in 1943: that national trials were more practical than international ones and could eliminate Allied squabbling over procedures, powers, and punishments.

Quickly accepting the judicial handling of prisoners of war, the conferees considered a second Stimson-McCloy recommendation calling for the addition of a new violation—conspiracy—to the traditional list of war crimes. Not only would this concept enable the Allies to prosecute the leaders of Nazi organizations that had conspired both before and during the war to violate international law and the law of war, but it also would make it easy to prosecute and convict every member of those organizations. Under this new concept, rank-and-file members of an organization were just as guilty as the leaders. Once group leaders had been found guilty, the Allies could then try all other members of those organizations for the same violations of the law of war even though they had no evidence connecting individual members of those bodies to a specific atrocity. One could be found guilty of conspiracy merely by belonging to an organization whose leaders had been previously convicted of conspiracy. Such a proposal clearly enabled the Allies, if they so desired, to cast a wide net for war criminals without having to research and document isolated atrocities by individual members of a Nazi organization.

The consensus of those present at the 9 November conference favored adopting conspiracy as a war crime. Having reached that decision, they focused attention on the type of tribunal that would try conspiracy cases. Such cases could be brought before military courts appointed by military commanders, or before an international court established by a formal treaty among the Allies. Unsure of the reaction of the U.S. Senate to the creation of an international court and fearful that such a judicial body, even if created, would be composed of civilian jurists who would

---

[22]The discussion of this conference is based on "Memorandum of Conference on War Crimes Procedure," 9 November 1944, ASW 000.51, War Crimes Working File, RG 107. Also see "Punishment of War Criminals, Agenda for 9 Nov 44 Conference," ibid.; and Bradley F. Smith, *The Road to Nuremberg* (New York: Basic Books, 1981).

Secretary Hull, who had earlier disagreed with Stimson over war-crimes policies, did not influence the November proceedings. An ill man, he had spent much of October at home trying to regain his strength. When that failed, he entered the naval medical center at Bethesda, Maryland, on 20 October and remained there until his resignation on 30 November.

adopt a technical, deliberate, and slow pace, Green Hackworth, State Department legal adviser, favored the utilization of military tribunals. On the other hand, McCloy, Lieutenant Colonel Frederick Wiener of the Judge Advocate General's Department, and Colonel Robert W. Berry of the War Department General Staff favored a treaty court.

Assistant Secretary McCloy endorsed the use of an international treaty court as a facile way of firmly establishing conspiracy as a war violation. While unconvinced of the absolute need for such an Allied court for the trial of archcriminals for regular war crimes, he did believe that such a prestigious body, by designating Nazi organizations guilty of conspiracy, could expedite the entire process of trying members of those organizations in national military courts. In McCloy's estimation that international judicial body would complete its main task once it designated those organizations guilty of conspiracy. As soon as it had completed that job, he expected it to dissolve, leaving to national military courts the conduct of all remaining trials.

Lieutenant Colonel Wiener also supported a treaty court but not for the same reasons as McCloy. Less concerned with expediency, he wondered whether the whole question of conspiracy might not be too important an issue to leave to a panel of army officers appointed by a single army commander. Observing that the trial and conviction of Nazis on the new charge of conspiracy ought to rest on "the most secure foundation possible," he favored using a more dignified and prestigious court created by the highest Allied officials.

Sympathetic to the arguments presented by McCloy and Wiener, Lieutenant Colonel Murray Bernays of the War Department General Staff and R. Keith Kane of the Navy Department also favored the creation of a treaty court. But in order to circumvent the obstacles Hackworth and others feared, they suggested that the Allies write a charter in which the rules clearly limited technical delays and the staff would be military officers rather than civilian justices. With that practical suggestion, the debate over treaty and military courts ended. Having reached general agreement on the judicial disposition of war criminals, the addition of conspiracy to the list of war crimes, and the creation of a treaty court to hear the conspiracy arguments, those present at the 9 November conference decided to adjourn, but not before they had instructed the War Department, in consultation with the State and Navy departments as appropriate, to prepare a specific written policy memorandum that could be submitted to the president for his approval.[23]

Based on previous War Department discussions, as well as on the interdepartmental meeting of 9 November, General Cramer submitted just such a draft proposal to McCloy on 13 November. On 19 January 1945,

---

[23]Ibid.

Cramer submitted to the assistant secretary his final draft, entitled "Trial and Punishment of Nazi War Criminals." Satisfied with that last draft, McCloy conferred with Stimson and, upon securing his approval, instructed Brigadier General John Weir, assistant judge advocate general, and Lieutenant Colonel Bernays to confer with Hackworth at State and with Attorney General Francis Biddle at Justice. Weir and Bernays quickly discovered that those men and their departments were satisfied with the War Department's final proposal.[24]

Even before McCloy could prepare and circulate a formal copy of the document for the signatures of the attorney general and the secretaries of war and state, Stimson journeyed to the White House to confer with Judge Samuel Rosenman, the president's special war-crimes adviser, and with Roosevelt himself. Recording his meeting with Roosevelt, Stimson revealed that he urged a "state trial with records" rather than a purely political solution to the war-crimes problem. But as his next diary entry demonstrated, he was unsure whether the president firmly supported his argument. "He assented to what I said," Stimson wrote, "but in the hurry of the situation I am not sure whether it registered."[25]

By January 1945, however, Stimson faced no major opposition from his cabinet colleagues. Hull's resignation as secretary of state in November had removed one potential opponent. The only other cabinet officer who might oppose the Stimson-War Department plan was Secretary Morgenthau, whose department had not been represented at the November meeting. But by 19 January even the treasury secretary realized that Stimson had won their long-standing disagreement over war-crimes policies. While grudgingly conceding defeat, Morgenthau cautioned Rosenman on 19 January that the judicial proceedings must use "the most simple and expeditious procedure that can be devised." Indeed, the Allies, he emphasized, "should be completely unrestricted by rules of evidence and other technicalities" when they begin prosecution of the Nazis.[26]

Although Roosevelt had discussed the memorandum with Stimson on 19 January, he did not receive the formal memorandum signed by his secretary of war, Secretary of State Edward Stettinius, Jr., and Attorney

---

[24]For a fuller discussion of action on the memorandum, see 000.5 (12-1-44 to 12-15-44), box 312, RG 165. Also see memorandum to General Berry from M. C. Bernays, 27 December 1944, 000.5 (9-12-44), box 313, RG 165; "Trial of War Criminals," 27 September 1944, ASW 000.51, War Crimes Working File, RG 107; and Smith, *Road to Nuremberg*, chaps. 2, 3, 4.

[25]Stimson Diary, 19 January 1945, reel 9, pp. 57–58. Stimson also discussed war-crimes policy with Judge Rosenman on 18 January. Ibid., p. 53. On 22 January, Hackworth sent the president a memorandum explaining the State Department's support of the war-crimes memorandum. See *FRUS: Malta/Yalta*, p. 405.

[26]Morgenthau to Rosenman, 19 January 1945, folder 4: War Crimes File, box 9, Papers of Samuel Rosenman, Harry S Truman Library, Independence, MO (hereafter cited as Rosenman Papers).

General Biddle until 22 January.[27] All three secretaries, the document disclosed, formally favored the judicial handling of war criminals. Such a policy, they argued, would "command maximum public support," provide a terrifying record of Nazi criminality, and "receive the respect of history." Reflecting the agreement reached on 9 November, they also recommended to the president that the United States adopt conspiracy as a war crime. In resolving the question of whether the government should favor national or international courts, they suggested that an international military tribunal chosen by the Allied governments try the highest ranking German leaders and identify those groups and organizations guilty of conspiracy. In order to avoid Senate scrutiny, they suggested that the international tribunal ought to be established by executive agreement and not by a treaty. As one of the stipulations of that executive document, they recommended adopting the Bernays compromise: that judges chosen for the court be military officers rather than civilian judges. Military personnel, they argued, would be "less likely to give undue weight to technical intentions and legalistic arguments."

While an international tribunal should handle cases involving the highest ranking enemy and those involving the conspiracy concept, national military tribunals, according to the secretaries, should perform the bulk of all war-crimes trials. Those tribunals, as McCloy had envisioned on 9 November, should try all subordinate members of Nazi groups and organizations found guilty of conspiracy by the international court. They also should try those individuals charged with committing regular war violations against a particular nation.

Roosevelt's acceptance of the 22 January memorandum signified a bureaucratic victory for Stimson and his War Department. Together with Assistant Secretary McCloy, Stimson had steered Roosevelt away from Hull and Morgenthau's nonjudicial punishment toward a more respectable process. Retaining firm control of the decision-making machinery, Stimson also ensured that American war-crimes policies incorporated safeguards against obstructionist tactics and undue technical delays in the upcoming judicial proceedings. Adoption of his policy not only avoided a potentially cumbersome judicial process but also provided an effective forum where barbaric enemy practices could be revealed, while doing so in "a dignified manner consistent with the advance of civilization."

Even the sudden death of President Roosevelt on 12 April posed no threat to Stimson's war-crimes policy. Harry S Truman, a man who had served only eight weeks as vice-president, informed Judge Rosenman on the seventeenth that, like Stimson, he too opposed the political dis-

---

[27]"Trial and Punishment of Nazi War Criminals," 22 January 1945, ASW 000.51, War Crimes Working File, RG 107.

position of the archcriminals.[28] And in a message to Associate Justice of the U.S. Supreme Court Robert Jackson in late April, the new president affirmed his support of the statement approved on 22 January by the attorney general and the secretaries of state and war.[29]

Confirming the direction of America's war-crimes policy, Truman wasted little time in presenting its position to the Allies. Deciding to take advantage of the UN conference that convened in San Francisco on 25 April, he authorized the presentation of written arguments favoring the judicial treatment of Nazi criminals to the foreign ministers of the Soviet Union, the United Kingdom, and France. Additionally, he authorized the presentation of a formally drafted executive agreement which, by closely following the suggestions set forth by the Stimson-Stettinius-Biddle memorandum, would transform, if accepted, Washington's goals into Allied goals.[30]

Because of earlier conversations between Judge Rosenman and British officials in London, Washington expected no resistance from that crucial ally to the proposal that each nation return regular criminals to the countries against whom the crimes had been perpetrated.[31] That idea, after all, had been a part of the 1943 Moscow Declaration. The Truman administration and particularly War Department officials, however, had anticipated significant resistance from the British to its proposed judicial resolution of cases involving the archcriminals. Despite the famous incident at Tehran in 1943, when Stalin had suggested the execution of 50,000 German war criminals and army personnel and an infuriated Churchill had vigorously protested such "mass executions," the Americans were far more worried over the possibility of British acceptance of a political solution than they were over the Soviet position. Roosevelt in 1943 had not taken Stalin's 50,000 quip very seriously; he himself had suggested perhaps killing only 49,500! And even Churchill later grudgingly conceded that Stalin had taken him aside at Tehran and assured him

---

[28]Rosenman to General Weir, 17 April 1945, folder 7: War Crimes File, box 9, Rosenman Papers. Also see McCloy to Eisenhower, 28 April 1945, file 103-1a-book 1, box 1603, RG 153.

[29]For other examples of the president's commitment clearly to punish war criminals and to do so by judicial means, see Rosenman memorandum to Truman, 19 April 1945, General File: UNWCC, Harry S Truman Papers, Harry S Truman Library (hereafter cited as Truman Papers); and Truman's "Address Before a Joint Session of Congress," 16 April 1945, Public Papers, 1945, Truman Papers.

[30]For copies of both papers, see Department of State *International Conference*. In March, John Weir, assistant judge advocate general, had suggested an international conference on war crimes and had outlined some of the issues needing resolution. See "War Crimes Conference," 22 March 1945, ASW 000.51, War Crimes Working File, RG 107.

[31]The British had agreed to this on the day Roosevelt died. See Rosenman memorandum to Truman, 19 April 1945, General File: UNWCC, Truman Papers.

that he had been "only playing."[32] Whatever happened at Tehran, Stalin, by conducting a military trial of three suspected German war criminals at Kharkov in December 1943, had helped dispel any lingering doubts in Washington that he might shoot on sight suspected violators of the law of war.[33] A communiqué from Churchill, who visited Stalin in Moscow in October 1944, had reassured the Americans even more. On the question of major war criminals, "Uncle Joe took an unexpectedly ultrarespective line," Churchill reported. Stalin indicated that "there must be no executions without trial otherwise the world would say we were afraid to try them. I pointed out the difficulties in international law," Churchill wrote, "but he replied if there were no trials there must be no death sentences, but only life-long confinements."[34] While Stalin's observations disturbed the British prime minister, they clearly pleased Stimson and McCloy.

During the winter of 1944 and the spring of 1945, Churchill and the British, not Stalin and the Soviets, favored the adoption of nonjudicial punishment in certain war-crimes cases. Writing to President Truman on 19 April 1945, Judge Rosenman, in London to discuss Anglo-American war-crimes policy, reported that "their unanimous view was that [the top six German war criminals] be not given a trial, but that they should be dealt with politically by agreement of the four major powers and that they be shot forthwith." He also informed the president that Churchill had even recalled, in the midst of their conversations, Stalin's insistence at Moscow on a judicial rather than a political process, a solution that the prime minister still could not accept.[35] Four days later on 23 April Rosenman received an aide-mémoire from the British, which reiterated His Majesty's government's belief that in regard to the archcriminals "execution without trial is the preferable course."[36]

---

[32]Winston S. Churchill, *The Second World War: Closing the Ring* (Boston: Houghton Mifflin, 1951), pp. 373–74. Churchill argued in his study that he did not believe Stalin was "only joking." For another account of the Tehran episode, see Elliott Roosevelt's *As He Saw It* (New York: Duell, Sloan & Pearce, 1946), pp. 188–91. Roosevelt recalls that Stalin's comment followed a good deal of drinking by all heads of state.

[33]For information on the Kharkov trials and the Soviet Union's attitude toward war crimes, see R & A 1988.1 and 1988, RG 59, Records of the U.S. Department of State, National Archives. Foreign Minister Anthony Eden confirmed Stalin's opposition to summary executions when meeting with Secretary of State Stettinius in February 1945. See *FRUS: Malta/Yalta*, p. 507.

[34]Churchill to Roosevelt, 22 October 1944, *FRUS: Malta/Yalta*, p. 400.

[35]Rosenman memorandum, 19 April 1945, General File: UNWCC, Truman Papers. Also see Churchill's comments relating to war criminals in *FRUS: Quebec, 1944*, pp. 91–93, 467, 489–90; and diary entry of 9 October 1944, in Lord Moran, *Winston Churchill* (London: Constable & Co., 1966), p. 194. For a fuller discussion of Rosenman's trip to London, see Smith, *Road to Nuremberg*, chapt. 5.

[36]Aide-mémoire, Sir Alexander Cadogan to Judge Rosenman, 23 April 1945, Department of State, *International Conference*, pp. 18–19; Sir Llewellyn Woodward, *British Foreign Policy in the Second World War* (London: Her Majesty's Stationery Office,

Not without reason had the War Department and Judge Rosenman expected major opposition from Foreign Minister Eden at San Francisco to their proposal for trials. Fear of British obstinacy had prompted McCloy to send to Rosenman on 23 April the memorandum for distribution to the foreign ministers explaining the rationale behind the proposed American draft. He had done so, McCloy informed Stimson, "in the event the English come through with their impending opposition to the trial method." Rosenman, who had quickly transmitted a revision of that memorandum to the appropriate delegations, emphasized the American commitment to the judicial process. His comments, together with the explanatory memorandum, left little doubt about the American position. "It may be argued," Washington observed in its brief, "that the Axis leaders should be dealt with politically rather than judicially and that, without trial, by joint action of the Allies they should be put to death upon capture. The United States is vigorously opposed to any such political disposition."[37] To further emphasize the American commitment to judicial trials, President Truman, in a statement to the press on 2 May, proclaimed that "it is our objective to establish as soon as possible an international military tribunal and to provide a trial procedure which will be expeditious in nature and which will permit no evasion or delay—but one which is in keeping with our tradition of fairness towards those accused of crime."[38] He went on to announce that he was designating Associate Justice Jackson as chief U.S. prosecutor in the upcoming trials.[39]

The refusal of the United States and the Soviet Union to accept summary executions and Truman's obvious determination to hold trials convinced the British to alter their policy. On 3 May an elated Judge Rosenman reported to the president that Foreign Minister Eden had finally agreed that the fate of the archcriminals should be determined by a

---

1962), pp. 573–74; David Dilks, ed., *The Diaries of Sir Alexander Cadogan* (New York: G. P. Putnam's Sons, 1972), pp. 731–32. For further confirmation of the British-Churchill policy of political disposition, also see *FRUS: Malta/Yalta*, pp. 849, 854, 938; and U.S. negotiators in London to War Department, 17 April 1945, folder 7: War Crimes File, box 9, Rosenman Papers.

[37]For a rough draft of the proposals, see McCloy to Stimson, 23 April 1945, ASW 000.51, War Crimes Working File, January–April 1945, RG 107; and McCloy to Rosenman, 23 April 1945, folder 7: War Crimes File, box 9, Rosenman Papers. For the revised draft, which was actually submitted to the Allied delegations, see "Memorandum of Proposals for the Prosecution and Punishment of Certain War Criminals and Other Offenders," 30 April 1945, ASW 000.15, War Crimes Working File: San Francisco Papers, RG 107; and folder 8: War Crimes File, box 9, Rosenman Papers.

[38]General File: War Crimes Trials, 1945, Truman Papers.

[39]Jackson strongly favored a trial rather than political disposition (Stimson Diary, reel 9, p. 87) and found the Stimson-Stettinius-Biddle draft perfectly acceptable (Jackson to Truman, 29 April 1945, in Eugene Gerhart, *America's Advocate: Robert H. Jackson* [New York: Bobbs-Merrill, 1958], pp. 309–10).

trial, and that such trials should be conducted by an international military tribunal.[40] One of the most crucial obstacles to Allied agreement on war-crimes policy had been overcome at last.

Despite the reaffirmation at San Francisco of the Moscow Declaration and the general acceptance of judicial proceedings, the Allies still had no detailed war-crimes policy. Not until Allied delegations arrived in London in June 1945 did it appear that the major governments were actually ready to hammer out specific details. While neither Stimson nor McCloy headed the American delegation to that conference, their presence was clearly felt. In accepting the British invitation to the meeting, each of the Allies had agreed to consider an American proposal dated 14 June as the basis for discussion.[41] That proposal, with only slight modifications, was the same one that Rosenman had carried to San Francisco from the War Department, and that McCloy had justified in the explanatory memorandum that Rosenman had handed to each of the foreign ministers in San Francisco.

Even Justice Jackson's speech to the assembled delegations on the first day of the conference smacked of Stimson's rhetoric and reasoning.[42] The American proposal, Jackson argued, tried to incorporate the varied legal traditions of the four nations, rather than relying heavily on American jury trial procedure. He also observed that the incorporation of those varied legal procedures did not deprive defendants of a fair trial. The American proposal not only assured suspected criminals of reasonable notice of the charges against them in their own language but also assured them of an opportunity to present a defense aided by legal counsel. On the other hand, the American draft enabled an international military tribunal to adopt "to the greatest extent possible expeditious and non-technical procedures." It allowed that body to admit evidence "which it [deemed] to have probative value," and to prevent any unreasonable trial delay by confining trials "to an expeditious hearing of the issues raised by the charges." As Stimson desired, there would be no "cumbersome machinery" to slow the trial of suspected criminals, and yet the process, sanctioned by the major Allied powers and utilizing legal procedures, allowed for the punishment of those found guilty in such a way so as to "meet the judgment of History."

The debates that followed Jackson's opening address clearly revealed that Stimson's and McCloy's extensive efforts in formulating U.S.

---

[40]Rosenman to Truman, 3 May 1945, folder 8: War Crimes File, box 9, Rosenman Papers. Also see Dilks, *Cadogan Diaries*, p. 738; Woodward, *British Foreign Policy*, p. 574; and Smith, *Road to Nuremberg*, pp. 218–44.

[41]"Executive Agreement Relating to the Prosecution of European Axis War Criminals," 14 June 1945, Department of State, *International Conference*, pp. 55–60.

[42]Gerhart, *Jackson*, pp. 325–27; "Minutes of Conference Session, 26 June 45," Department of State, *International Conference*.

policy had not been in vain.[43] As the Allies debated the American definition of war crimes, especially the new conspiracy concept, and as they discussed the precise powers residing in Allied judges, they found most of the U.S. proposals acceptable. Having fine-tuned the American draft, rather than creating a whole new structure, the delegations finally affixed their signatures to a charter that established an international military tribunal. They also signed a companion agreement that pledged the return of lesser criminals to the countries where they had committed their crimes.

The charter creating the international military tribunal stipulated that four civilian and/or military judges, one each from the major Allied governments, would sit in judgment.[44] It confirmed their right to try individuals who had committed regular war crimes, crimes against humanity, and crimes against peace, which included the concept of conspiracy. It granted them discretion in formulating the rules that would govern the operation of their tribunal, provided that they remain within the structural and procedural framework stipulated in the charter. It also conferred on the justices full authority to free, imprison, or execute defendants. And with a note of finality, it allowed for no appeal.

The procedural safeguards granted defendants by Article 16 and the powers granted to the tribunal in Articles 18, 19, and 21 closely resembled those formulated by Stimson, McCloy, and the U.S. government during the spring and summer. As the Americans had proposed in June, defendants would receive the right to a fair trial. They would be informed a reasonable time in advance of the trial of the charges against them in their own tongue or in a language they could understand. They would have the right to legal counsel and also would have the right to present evidence in their own defense.

The tribunal, on the other hand, had full authority to "confine the trial strictly to an expeditious hearing" of the charges. Nor would it be bound by technical rules of evidence. "It shall adopt and apply to the greatest possible extent," the charter ordered, "expeditious and non-technical procedure, and shall admit any evidence which it deems to have probative value."[45]

---

[43]For a full discussion of the conference and of the proposed drafts and counter-drafts, see Department of State, *International Conference*; and Gerhart, *Jackson*. For earlier drafts leading to the American 14 June revision, see "War Crimes Prosecutions: Planning Memorandum," 17 May 1945, file 103-0, box 1602, RG 153; draft of an "Executive Agreement Relating to the Prosecution of European Axis War Criminals," 21 May 1945, file 103-la-book 3, ibid.; and "Memorandum on Trial Preparation," 16 May 1945, box 1719, RG 153. Also see the sections on war crimes in *FRUS: Conference of Berlin (Potsdam), 1945*, vols. 1, 2.

[44]Department of State, *International Conference*, pp. 420–28.

[45]Ibid.

The War Department and the Jackson delegation had done their homework well. As a result, they had a profound impact in authoring a charter that successfully incorporated the varied legal traditions of the United Kingdom, France, the Soviet Union, and the United States.

CHAPTER THREE
WAR-CRIMES POLICYMAKING: THE FAR EAST

During the negotiations in London that led to the signing of the Allied war-crimes agreement on 8 August 1945, the Soviet Union was at peace with Japan.[1] Despite the Soviets' declaration of war against the Japanese on the same day they signed that charter, the policies and procedures adopted at London to govern the trial and punishment of war criminals still applied only to the European theater. Germany's surrender in May and the Soviet Union's neutrality in the Far Eastern conflict had so focused British and American attention during the summer of 1945 on a European war-crimes policy that they failed to formulate simultaneously a policy toward the Far Eastern foe. Confirming that rather dramatic oversight, the director of the State Department's Office of Far Eastern Affairs revealed to Assistant Secretary of State Archibald MacLeish on 8 August that the United States had no policy whatsoever for handling war criminals in the Pacific. He assumed that the London agreement, perhaps modified to meet special circumstances arising in the Pacific theater, would be the basic guide for future war-crimes planning in that region.[2]

The War Department also was unprepared in August to offer a policy. On 17 August the department's General Staff merely affirmed MacArthur's authority to continue the apprehension of suspected war criminals. As soon as it developed more precise guidelines regarding war-crimes policies, it added, he would be notified.[3] Such information was not immediately forthcoming, even though the war-crimes section of the department's Office of the Judge Advocate General transmitted to MacArthur a list of suspected Japanese war criminals on 28 August.[4]

Since MacArthur would be primarily responsible for the execution of all policies adopted in the Far Eastern theater, the War Department

---

[1]The Soviet Union had signed a neutrality agreement with Japan in April 1941.

[2]U.S., Department of State, *Foreign Relations of the United States: The British Commonwealth: The Far East, 1945*, vol. 6 (hereafter cited as *FRUS*): 591–92.

[3]WARCOS to CinCAFPAC, 17 August 1945, file 000.53 #1, box 763, RG 331. Also see Personnel Division, War Department General Staff to CinCAFPAC, 16 August 1945, 000.5 (4-16-44), box 314, RG 165.

[4]A copy of that list—"Japanese War-Crimes Suspects: List A"—may be found in box 1739, RG 153, Washington National Records Center, Suitland, MD.

decided to seek its prestigious general's opinion on the war-crimes question. Rather than receiving a departmental directive defining war-crimes policies and procedures as promised, on 31 August MacArthur learned that Washington wanted to know his plans for the trial and punishment of the Japanese. Reacting to that surprising request, Colonel Alva Carpenter, chief of MacArthur's War Crimes Branch and acting theater judge advocate general, wanted MacArthur to stall for time. He suggested that Washington be notified that the Pacific command already had formulated such plans—even though it had not—but would be unable to communicate the precise details until 10 September.[5] That postponement would allow at least a few additional days during which an acceptable response could be drafted.

That MacArthur had the right to establish whatever rules, regulations, and procedures he desired for military commissions within his jurisdiction was virtually unquestioned. The flexibility of military commanders in this regard had been a major argument utilized throughout 1944 and 1945 by Secretary Stimson and Assistant Secretary McCloy as they lobbied for judicial proceedings before military commissions.[6] The War Department's own field manual, which outlined army and navy policies in occupied territory, also clearly recognized the right of a theater commander to establish military commissions, including his right to determine "their numbers, types, jurisdictions and procedure."[7] Furthermore, the powerful and influential Joint Chiefs of Staff in March 1944 had affirmed its opposition to any decision that might limit the power of military officers over war-crimes prosecution. "Military commanders," the Joint Chiefs had argued, "must retain the power to try and punish, at their discretion, all offenders who are subject to their jurisdiction."[8] The arguments of Stimson, McCloy, and the Joint Chiefs received legal support from Charles Fairman's highly regarded and frequently cited *Law of Martial Rule*. Military commissions, Fairman had written, are "agencies of the commander in doing what may be necessary and proper for him to

---

[5]WARCOS to CinCAFPAC, 31 August 1945, file 000.5 #1, box 763, RG 331; Carpenter (CinCAFPAC) to MacArthur (CinCAFPAC Advance), 31 August 1945, ibid. Assistant Secretary of War McCloy clearly explained to Undersecretary of State Dean Acheson that the War and Navy departments felt "very strongly" that MacArthur have the power to establish war-crimes courts and prescribe their rules and procedures. Acheson, even before receipt of McCloy's letter, was inclined to grant MacArthur such authority. See Acheson to the director of the Office of Far Eastern Affairs, 6 September 1945; and McCloy to Acheson, 7 September 1945, *FRUS: The British Commonwealth*, 6:921–22.

[6]See Chapter Two.

[7]*U.S. Army and Naval Field Manual of Military Government and Civil Affairs (FM 27-5)*, (Washington: Government Printing Office, 1945), p. 50.

[8]See JCS 752 contained in Colonel A. J. McFarland to JCS, 9 March 1944, 000.5 (3-8-44), RG 218. The Joint Chiefs of Staff approved JCS 752 on 13 March. See William D. Leahy to secretary of war and secretary of navy, 13 March 1944, ibid.

do."[9] Other legal support also came from Major General Myron Cramer, the judge advocate general, who in early 1944 observed that an integral part of the military's wartime function was the seizure and trial of enemies who had violated the law of war. Cramer informed a colleague in February 1944 that "there are no limitations of the jurisdiction of a military commander in the field to try and punish, by military tribunals, offenses against the law of war which affect the interest of his nation and which are committed by enemy personnel . . . who come under his control by reason of capture."[10] But perhaps the greatest affirmation of the acceptability, even desirability, of utilizing military commissions to try suspected violators of the law of war occurred in the summer of 1942.

In mid-June 1942 eight German saboteurs, under cover of darkness, emerged from a German submarine and slipped ashore, four landing on the coast of New York, four landing on the coast of Florida. Trained in the use of explosives at a facility outside Berlin, they had orders to commit sabotage against the war industries of the United States. Their ill-fated mission ended abruptly, however, when agents of the Federal Bureau of Investigation seized them before they had an opportunity to impair industrial output.[11]

The arrest of those eight German saboteurs in late June raised legal questions within the Roosevelt administration over their disposition. In a brief note to Attorney General Biddle on 30 June, the president favored trial by military court-martial. Roosevelt did not doubt the nature of the punishment such a tribunal should impose. "The death penalty," he wrote, "is called for. . . ."[12] Although Roosevelt was probably unaware, the issue of whether to try the eight by court-martial had been discussed the day before on 29 June by Biddle, Stimson, and Cramer, among others. Stimson recorded in his diary that Biddle had at that meeting favored the use of a military commission rather than a court-martial. It was a

---

[9]*The Law of Martial Rule* (1930; reprint ed., Chicago: Callaghan and Company, 1943), p. 250. Fairman, a graduate of Harvard Law School, served in the army from 1942 to 1946 as chief of the International Law Division, Office of the Theater Judge Advocate and Legal Adviser, G-5 Section (Civil Affairs), Allied Force Headquarters, European Theater of Operations.

[10]Cramer to assistant chief of staff, Operations Division, War Department General Staff, 22 February 1944, 000.5 (3-8-44), RG 218. Also see Cramer to McCloy, memorandum entitled "Trial of War Criminals," 9 October 1944, ASW 000.51, War Crimes Working File, RG 107; and Cramer's address to the Washington State Bar Association, 25 September 1942, entitled "Military Commissions: Trial of the Eight Saboteurs," *Washington Law Review* (November 1942): 247–55.

[11]This paragraph is based on a brief factual review of the case written by Chief Justice Harlan Fiske Stone in *ex parte* Quirin, 317 U.S. 20-22.

[12]Roosevelt to Biddle, 30 June 1942, President's Secretary's File (PSF), Justice Department, box 76, Papers of Franklin D. Roosevelt, Franklin D. Roosevelt Library, Hyde Park, NY (hereafter cited as FDR Papers).

suggestion that Stimson and the other conferees could enthusiastically support.[13]

On the date the president dispatched his note to Biddle, the attorney general had completed his own memorandum to the president. That document, which he "carefully explained" to Roosevelt on the telephone on the first day of July, outlined the thinking of the members present at the 29 June conference. Attached to it, he notified Roosevelt, was a proposed press release that he hoped the president would distribute for publication, and a proposed proclamation denying the saboteurs access to U.S. civil courts, which he hoped the president would issue. Following their conversation, those documents were routed by air to Roosevelt at Hyde Park.[14]

Biddle's oral and written presentations were convincing. On 2 July, Roosevelt signed Biddle's proclamation as written:

> All persons who are subjects, citizens or residents of any nation at war with the United States or who give obedience to or act under the discretion of any such nation, and who during time of war enter or attempt to enter the United States or any territory or possession thereof . . . and are charged with committing or attempting or preparing to commit sabotage, espionage, hostile or warlike acts, or violations of the law of war, shall be subject to the law of war and the jurisdiction of military tribunals; and that such persons shall not be privileged to seek any remedy or proceeding sought on their behalf, in the courts of the United States, or of its States, territories, and possessions, except under such regulations as the Attorney General, with the approval of the Secretary of War, may from time to time prescribe.[15]

Having specifically deprived the Germans of access to the civil court system, the president, acting in his role of commander in chief of the

---

[13]Stimson Diary, 29 June 1942, reel 7, p. 131. In addition to Biddle, Cramer, and Stimson, the other conferees were: Oscar Cox, assistant solicitor general; Wendell Berge, assistant attorney general; Colonel Archibald King, chief, War Plans Branch, Judge Advocate General's Office; Robert Patterson, undersecretary of war; and General George Strong, assistant chief of staff, G-2, War Department General Staff. Also see memorandum to attorney general from Oscar Cox, 29 June 1942, German Saboteurs folder, box 61, Papers of Oscar Cox, Franklin D. Roosevelt Library (hereafter cited as Cox Papers); a memorandum entitled "History of the Proceedings," ibid.; and Louis Hecker to Cox, 30 June 1942, ibid.

[14]Biddle to Roosevelt, 1 July 1942, No. 5036, Official File, FDR Papers. The enclosed memorandum is dated 30 June. Also see Biddle to Marvin McIntyre, Roosevelt's private secretary, 1 July 1942, ibid.; and Cox's marginal notations dated 1 July on his copy of Biddle's memorandum. German Saboteurs folder, box 61, Cox Papers.

[15]For the text of the official proclamation, entitled "Denying Certain Enemies Access to the Courts of the United States" and dated 2 July 1942, see German Saboteurs folder, box 61, Cox Papers.

armed forces, then considered issuing a special order appointing a military commission to try the saboteurs' case.[16]

Attorney General Biddle obviously reassured Roosevelt with his arguments that military commissions would provide the prisoners "a full and fair trial."[17] By avoiding the civil courts and by establishing a military commission, Biddle emphasized, the president could not only "minimize the delays incident to any obstructionist proceedings which may be brought by the prisoners" but also could "save a considerable amount of time" by avoiding technical rules of evidence and judicial procedure. Avoiding the more legally circumscribed civil courts and military courts-martial also would allow the government to convict and sentence defendants more easily. By utilizing a military commission, a two-thirds vote of the court would be sufficient to find any one of the saboteurs guilty and to impose whatever judgment, including the death penalty, the court members believed appropriate. Furthermore, the attorney general continued, trial by military commission enabled the president to adopt a flexible review process. As commander in chief, Biddle explained that the president could rule as inapplicable the normal appellate processes for those found guilty and sentenced. Indeed, if the president adopted the current proposals, Biddle concluded, an appeal would be forwarded directly to the president, another example of how military commissions could avoid prolonged delays in both the trial and the appellate process.[18]

Again Roosevelt was convinced. He adopted without alteration the Biddle order establishing a military commission to try the saboteurs. That commission, Roosevelt declared, "shall have power to and shall, as occasion requires, make such rules for the conduct of the proceedings, consistent with the powers of military commissions under the Articles of War, as it shall deem necessary for a full and fair trial of the matters before it." Following his attorney general's suggestion, the president also ordered that "such evidence shall be submitted as would, in the opinion of the President of the Commission, have probative value to a reasonable man."[19]

Any doubts that may have existed in 1942 about the constitutionality of the president's actions in depriving the saboteurs of access to civil courts and in ensuring their trial before a military commission had

---

[16]Biddle also had sent Roosevelt a proposed draft creating just such a commission. See Biddle to Roosevelt, 1 July 1942, German Saboteurs folder, box 61, Cox Papers.

[17]Memorandum to president, 30 June 1942, No. 5036, Official File, FDR Papers.

[18]Ibid.

[19]For Biddle's proposal and the official order, see German Saboteurs folder, box 61, Cox Papers. Also see No. 5036, Official File, FDR Papers; and W. D. Hassett's Diary, 2 July 1942, Franklin D. Roosevelt Library.

been largely erased by the U.S. Supreme Court's ruling in *ex parte* Quirin in July 1942.[20] In reviewing the judicial process by which the saboteurs had been judged and sentenced, the nation's highest court upheld the president's power as commander in chief to establish a military commission, together with its own rules, procedures, and appellate process in cases involving violations of the law of war. Chief Justice Harlan Fiske Stone, speaking for the court, stressed that the powers upon which the president had based his actions had been specifically granted to him by Congress under the articles of war, especially Article 38. The military commission, Stone and his colleagues therefore concluded, had been lawfully appointed and legally empowered to judge and sentence violators of the law of war.[21]

MacArthur's staff, reviewing these presidential pronouncements, bureaucratic arguments, and legal precedents, discovered one more re-affirmation of the right of military authorities to try violators of the law of war before military commissions. Roosevelt, they found, had reaffirmed his 1942 declarations on 11 January 1945.[22] On that date he granted the various commanding generals within the nation's continental defense and service commands unquestioned authority to establish, at their discretion, military commissions to try all who illegally entered the United States in order to commit hostile acts against the nation. That reaffirmation in 1945, coupled with the earlier arguments and proclamations, convinced Carpenter's War Crimes Branch that it could constitutionally formulate whatever rules and procedures it thought necessary for trials before military commissions.

Under pressure from Washington and reassured by past precedent, Carpenter and his staff in September 1945 endeavored to create a single plan that would cover all war-crimes violations. That would be

---

[20]317 U.S. 1. The case was argued on 29 and 30 July 1942 during a special session of the Court. Desiring not to delay such a sensitive case, the Court announced its opinion, without explanation, on 31 July. Not until 29 October 1942 did the Court render its substantiated decision.

[21]Ibid. For the articles of war, see U.S. Army, *A Manual for Courts-Martial* (Washington: Government Printing Office, 1943), pp. 203–30. For further legal discussion of the rights and powers of military commissions, see the following reports contained in boxes 1853 and 1854, RG 331: "Military Commissions Are Not Bound By Rigid Rules of Procedure or Evidence," file 46c; "Procedural Law Applied By Military Commissions," file 46; "The Military Commission," file 54; "War Crimes and the Punishment of War Criminals," file 87; and "Trial of War Criminals by Military Commission," file 88.

[22]"Military Order Governing the Establishment of Military Commissions for the Trial of Certain Offenders Against the Law of War, and Governing the Procedure for Such Commissions," *Code of Federal Regulations: Title 3 (The President, 1943–1948 Compilation)* (Washington: Government Printing Office, 1957); and ASW 000.51 #58, War Crimes Working File, RG 107.

much quicker than the production of two separate documents, one governing trial before an international military court and the other governing trial before national military commissions. Within twenty-four hours of receipt of Washington's request for MacArthur's policy proposals, Captains Robert Kerr and M. D. Webster, members of Carpenter's War Crimes Investigation Detachment in Manila, had produced a workable draft reply.[23] Reminding Carpenter of the determination of the United States to pursue war criminals, they noted Roosevelt's past proclamations promising retribution to those guilty of barbarous behavior and Truman's approval of the Potsdam Declaration only six weeks earlier. As Carpenter realized, that latter document, issued jointly by Truman, Churchill, and Chiang Kai-shek, had conveyed a terse warning to Japan concerning the terms for peace. "[The] following are our terms," the heart of the declaration began. "We will not deviate from them. There are no alternatives. We shall brook no delay."

Affirming Allied commitment to the establishment of democratic principles in a postwar Japan, the three men then warned:

> There must be eliminated for all time the authority and influence of those who have deceived and misled the people of Japan into embarking on world conquest, for we insist that a new order of peace, security and justice will be impossible until irresponsible militarism is driven from the world. . . . We do not intend that the Japanese shall be enslaved as a race or destroyed as a nation, but stern justice shall be meted out to all war criminals.[24]

After recapitulating these former presidential directives, Kerr and Webster proceeded to discuss the organization, the powers, and the procedures of military commissions. In formulating and in presenting their recommendations, they made the same assumption as had the State Department's director of the Office of Far Eastern Affairs: policy guidelines for all trials, including those occurring before both national and international tribunals, should closely follow those formulated in London. Apparently the fact that the earlier document applied only to trials before an Allied judicial tribunal did not disturb the two captains.

While the draft submitted to Carpenter by Kerr and Webster on 1 September could have formed a justifiable foundation for the establishment of a war-crimes structure in the Far East, it was preempted by a proposal emerging from representatives of the U.S. War Crimes Office in early September. That office, created in October 1944 within the Office of the Judge Advocate General and under the direct control of Brigadier

---

[23]Kerr-Webster memorandum to Carpenter, "A Draft Plan for Trial of War Criminals in the Far East," 1 September 1945, box 2003, RG 331.

[24]Potsdam Declaration, 26 July 1945, *FRUS: Potsdam*, 2:1474–76.

General John Weir, assistant judge advocate general, had dispatched four officers to Japan to assist MacArthur and Carpenter in the formulation of war-crimes policies and procedures.[25] Heading the delegation was naval Captain James J. Robinson, deputy director of the War Crimes Office. Assisting him were Commander George Brereton, Weir's administrative assistant, and two other War Crimes Office staff members, Colonel Frederick Bradshaw and Lieutenant Colonel Charles Warren.

On 3 September these four men, on behalf of the War Crimes Office, submitted to Carpenter their own ideas for war-crimes trials.[26] Obviously more conversant with previous decision making and policies than were Kerr and Webster, their draft reflected a more sophisticated and international flavor. Citing the London Charter, Roosevelt's saboteur proclamations, the Supreme Court's ruling in the Quirin case, the army and navy's field manual entitled *Military Government and Civil Affairs* (FM27-5), and other U.S. military documents, together with the war-crimes procedures adopted by the British in June 1945, they presented their suggestions to the Pacific command.[27]

But neither Carpenter nor MacArthur had the luxury of formulating policy at a relaxed, deliberate, and unhurried pace. On 6 September, Truman informed his Pacific commander for the second time in nine days that those persons already charged with war crimes by either American or UN agencies were to be "arrested, tried, and if convicted, punished."[28] On that same date the president informed Admiral William D. Leahy, his

---

[25]Brigadier General Weir had fully participated in the war-crimes policy discussions in the War Department in 1944 and 1945. For an evaluation of the functions and operations of the War Crimes Office, see "A History of the War Crimes Office," prepared by the Office of the Judge Advocate General, box 1709, RG 153. By July 1945 the authorized strength of that office was 79 army officers; 95 civilians employed by the army, and/or enlisted army personnel; 8 naval officers; and 7 civilians employed by the navy, and/or enlisted naval personnel. On 25 September 1944, Stimson ordered Cramer to create the War Crimes Office so that it could collect evidence on war crimes and coordinate and arrange the arrest, trial, and punishment of war criminals. Stimson ordered Cramer to report directly to him. He added, however, that at some point in the future he may have the judge advocate general report to his personal representative.

[26]For a copy of the War Crimes Office proposal, see Robinson-Brereton-Bradshaw-Warren memorandum to Colonel Carpenter, Miscellaneous Yamashita file, box 2003, RG 331. One year earlier Major General Cramer had prepared his own proposals. See "Trial of War Criminals," 9 October 1944, ASW 000.51, War Crimes Working File, RG 107; Cramer to McCloy, 9 December 1944, file 103-8, box 1604, RG 153; and "Executive Order Governing the Rules of Procedure for Military Commissions in the Trial of Offenses Against the Law of War," drafted by the Judge Advocate General's Office, file 103-8, box 1604, RG 153.

[27]For a copy of the British policies, see "Royal Warrant, Regulations for the Trial of War Criminals," 18 June 1945, file 89, box 1853, RG 331.

[28]"U.S. Initial Post Surrender Policy for Japan," U.S. Department of State *Bulletin* 13 (1945): 423–27. These instructions originated from consultations between the departments of State, War, and Navy.

personal chief of staff, that MacArthur *"be directed to proceed, without avoidable delay* with the trial by court martial and the punishment of such Japanese war criminals as have been appprehended or as may be apprehended."[29] Since that directive was routinely routed to MacArthur's superiors, the Joint Chiefs of Staff, the Far Eastern commander would not immediately learn of Truman's wishes. On 10 September the Joint Chiefs finally authorized the transmission of Truman's instructions to General MacArthur.[30]

Upon receipt of that order, MacArthur, who already had examined the Robinson-Brereton draft proposals, sent those two officers and their U.S. War Crimes Office colleagues to Manila.[31] There they were to confer with Carpenter on the actual drafting of charges against Japanese war criminals. To coordinate that consultative process was MacArthur's own deputy chief of staff, Major General R. J. Marshall. It was Marshall, therefore, who convened on 14 September in Manila a major war-crimes conference composed of the War Crimes Office representatives, Colonel Carpenter and members of his staff, and selected officers from MacArthur's personnel and military intelligence sections.

The conference, Marshall observed, need not consider the formulation of a judicial framework.[32] Colonel Carpenter, upon careful consideration of the Robinson-Brereton memorandum, already had issued a plan that the deputy chief of staff and his superiors were convinced would provide a sound basis for orchestrating war-crimes proceedings in the Pacific. The purpose of this conference, Marshall notified the assembled officers, was to brief them on the types of issues and questions that the supreme commander in Tokyo wanted them to consider. The conferees, excluding Marshall, upon receipt of that information would adjourn into full-scale working sessions. The officers would then reassemble to report their findings to the deputy chief of staff and to discuss as appropriate the specific war-crimes issues.

---

[29]Emphasis added. Leahy memorandum to JCS, 6 September 1945, miscellaneous memorandum, 1945–46, Leahy file 136, box 21, RG 218, Records of the U.S. Joint Chiefs of Staff, National Archives.

[30]The message was not actually transmitted to MacArthur until 12 September 1945. See memorandum to secretary, JCS from Lieutenant Colonel F. T. Newsome, assistant secretary, General Staff, 10 September 1945, 000.5 (3-13-45) War Criminals, sec. 1, RG 218; and JCS to MacArthur, 12 September 1945, 000.5 War Criminals, sect. 1, box 763, RG 331.

[31]Robinson to Weir, 12 September 1945, file 103-1B-Japan, book 1, box 1603, RG 153. Hereafter, the Robinson-Brereton-Bradshaw-Warren memorandum will be referred to in the text as the Robinson-Brereton draft or the U.S. War Crimes Office draft.

[32]For a record of the conference, broken into morning and afternoon sessions, see "Report of Preliminary War Crimes Conference, 0830–0900," and "Report of Second War Crimes Conference, 1540–1630," Miscellaneous Yamashita file, box 2003, RG 331. The following paragraphs are based on those records.

There seemed to be no doubt on that mid-September day that Marshall spoke for MacArthur. At numerous points in his briefing, he attributed his remarks directly to his commander in chief.[33] In addition, comments by other speakers clearly indicated that MacArthur also had personally discussed the war-crimes questions in some detail with others present, especially those from the U.S. War Crimes Office. Despite any such earlier conversations with MacArthur, however, all recognized that Marshall was clearly in charge of the Manila sessions and spoke with his commander's authority.

The "top men" in both Japan and in the Philippines would need to be charged as soon as possible, the deputy chief of staff asserted in his briefing. The "first trial," he added, would be against General Tomoyuki Yamashita, commander of the 14th Area Army.[34] Since he was already in U.S. custody in the Philippines and the evidence needed in his case could be readily obtained in that occupied American territory, it was logical to launch judicial proceedings against him first. Although the conference also would develop charges against former Prime Minister Hideki Tojo, his trial would come later. While Marshall did not fully explain the delay in trying the powerful and influential Tojo, the decision was again a logical one. Since many of the charges against Tojo would fall under the crimes against peace category rather than the regular war-crimes category, MacArthur could not try him without first securing the express permission of the War Department.[35] Furthermore, the War Department favored the use of an international military tribunal to judge Tojo, while MacArthur preferred dropping the crimes against peace charges and trying the former Japanese leader immediately for regular war crimes before an American military commission. Until the War Department adopted MacArthur's logic, however, the decision to try Tojo rested in Washington and not Tokyo. And if, as the War Department wished, Tojo faced trial before an

---

[33]The use of the term commander in chief to denote MacArthur is Marshall's.

[34]As late as 4 September, Kerr and Webster, who had drafted the 1 September memorandum, were uncertain about disposition of the Yamashita case. At that time they still were undecided whether to recommend trial before an American tribunal for Japanese offenses in the Philippines or trial before a British tribunal for offenses in Malaya. On 14 September, however, Marshall ruled out any possibility of granting the British jurisdiction or of even consulting with them on the Yamashita case.

[35]MacArthur was still trying to secure permission in November to try Tojo. For a discussion of War Department policy, see "Policy of the United States in Regard to the Apprehension and Punishment of War Criminals in the Far East," SWNCC 57/1, 57/3, 000.5 (3-13-45) War Criminals, sec. 1, RG 218; memorandum by H. Freeman Matthews, 3 October 1945, *FRUS: The British Commonwealth; The Far East, 1945,* 6:938–39; and Report by SWNCC, 12 September 1945, ibid., pp. 926–36. Also see War Department to MacArthur, 4 October 1945; MacArthur to War Department, 7 October 1945; JCS to MacArthur, 10 November 1945; and MacArthur to War Department, 12 November 1945. Each of these cables may be found in 000.5 (3-13-45) War Criminals, sec. 1, RG 218.

international tribunal, the proceedings would have to be postponed until the Allies hammered out all the details and appointed all the officials. His prosecution might be even further delayed since the Japanese had only formally surrendered on 3 September, providing the prosecution insufficient time for the collection of evidence in Japan.

Yamashita's case was different. Charged with more traditional war crimes, he could be tried quickly by an American military commission established by MacArthur without the necessity of Washington's imprimatur. No new procedural delays would be necessary since the Carpenter-Robinson-Brereton procedures seemed satisfactory. Nor would collection of evidence hinder a speedy trial. Since the major battles in the Philippines had ended in late spring and since MacArthur's staff, following standard War Department procedures, had begun immediately collecting information on war crimes, prosecution in the archipelago could move forward rapidly.[36] Given the president's message of 12 September, which ordered MacArthur to "proceed without avoidable delay," the Yamashita case seemed an ideal and rather uncomplicated one with which to start.

Having earmarked the issues that he and MacArthur had wanted discussed at the working sessions, Marshall completed his briefing. Before formal adjournment, however, he reminded the conferees that "speed is the essence in bringing the 'big' criminals to trial."[37] When the conferees reassembled with Marshall later in the day, the Yamashita case was the focus of conversation.[38] Indeed, as the deputy chief of staff learned, his subordinates had devoted so much of the day to the case that they had barely discussed the specific charges to be levied against Tojo. In the Yamashita discussions, the impact of Marshall's remarks in the morning session was obvious. At that meeting he had notified his officers and the War Crimes Office advisers that the charges against the 14th Area Army commander "should indicate that he failed to exercise proper control over his troops and that he permitted the sacking of Manila." However, as the minutes of that meeting indicate, he had acknowledged "that there was no precedent here for charging a Field Commander with the negligence of duty in controlling his troops." The lack of such precedent neither deterred Carpenter nor the other officers at the conference. In reporting their conclusions to Marshall, Carpenter emphasized that Yamashita would be charged, as the deputy chief of staff had instructed, with "negligence in allowing his subordinates to commit atrocities." They agreed he had failed to exercise adequately his command responsibility.

---

[36]MacArthur received orders from the War Department, dated 25 December 1944, to establish a war-crimes office to investigate war crimes. See ASW 000.51, War Crimes Working File, January–April 1945, RG 107.

[37]"Report of Preliminary War Crimes Conference 0830-0900," Miscellaneous Yamashita file, box 2003, RG 331.

[38]"Report of Second War Crimes Conference 1540-1630," ibid.

Examining sample charges drafted by the conferees, who according to Captain Robinson had "tried to incorporate . . . what we thought
General MacArthur meant when he talked to us [in Tokyo]," Marshall
lamented the absence of a general all-inclusive charge. In addition to
identifying specific atrocities to be levied against Yamashita's command,
Marshall warned his colleagues: "You should also submit an alternative
charge which will be of a more general nature which will NOT include
naming specific atrocities."[39] That, he informed those present on two
separate occasions, was what MacArthur desired. Those comments,
combined with his emphasis in the morning session, left little doubt that
command responsibility would provide just such an ideal general charge.

Anxious to launch the trials as quickly as possible, Marshall
instructed Colonel Carpenter during the afternoon session to submit to
MacArthur within three days a formal set of charges against Yamashita
and four other leading Japanese generals. "Nothing," he enjoined, "must
be placed in the charges that cannot be proved." Marshall also notified
Carpenter that by the next day he would be expected to prepare for
submission to Marshall himself his recommendations relating to the
number of men to be appointed to military commissions, his recommendations relating to any final procedural matters, and his recommendations
relating to where headquarters might find military defense counsel for the
accused Japanese.

MacArthur's personal representative then warned the conferees
that the commander in chief in Tokyo wanted to ensure that no suspected
war criminal utilized his trial as a forum for a "philosophic discussion" of
the Japanese cause. To assist the military commission "in keeping out
extraneous material," the commander in chief also favored the presence of
judge advocate general "observers" during the trial.[40] These observers
would be allowed to raise objections over matters that might enable the
trial to "get out of line." Elaborating on this issue, Marshall announced
that it might even be necessary to brief the president of the military
commission so that he would be particularly careful to keep the proceedings within the desirable limits. Colonel S. F. Cohn, Carpenter's
executive officer, immediately expressed reservations over that idea. Such
briefings were irregular and questionable and, in Cohn's view, "may be
going too far." In responding to Cohn, Marshall extricated himself neatly
by transferring the responsibility for keeping both the defendants and the
commission in line to Colonels Carpenter and Cohn and their subordinates in the theater Judge Advocate General's Office. Shortly after that

---

[39]Marshall's emphasis.
[40]During the conference, Marshall never precisely defined the role or character of
"observers."

exchange the deputy chief of staff brought the conference to a close. Before adjournment, however, Marshall reiterated the same admonition with which he had closed the morning session: "Remember that speed of action is the essence in handling these cases."[41]

Marshall's general emphasis on haste, together with his specific order to complete the drafting of charges within seventy-six hours, prompted Colonel Carpenter to produce eight and one-quarter legal-size pages of charges against Yamashita on 17 September. Having received the charges, MacArthur's headquarters immediately notified Lieutenant General Wilhelm D. Styer, commanding general, U.S. Army Forces, Western Pacific, that he henceforth had the power to establish military commissions. Those commissions, the message continued, would try suspected war criminals "as designated by [MacArthur's] headquarters."[42] In a second message that same day, Styer learned that three junior officers in Colonel Carpenter's office, who had heretofore been investigating atrocities in the Philippines, would now be made available to him for selection as members of the prosecuting teams he would soon have to create. Two of those officers, Major Kerr and Captain Webster, were the same men who had originally drafted the war-crimes policy proposal submitted to Carpenter on 1 September.[43]

Discussing the state of MacArthur's recent preparations relating to war-crimes policy and their own role as advisers, Colonel Bradshaw and Lieutenant Colonel Warren briefed Brigadier General Weir and other War Crimes Office personnel in a "top secret" telephone conversation to Washington on 21 September.[44] During that dialogue the two officers reviewed the decision-making process at the recent 14 September sessions in which they, Robinson, and Brereton had fully participated. Explaining that they would be departing Manila the next day on their return trip to the States, they indicated that Robinson and Brereton would leave at a later date. They added, by way of explanation, that "Robinson is advising very closely with Carpenter on the technical forms of the procedures and Carpenter desired him to remain a few days longer."

Reflecting upon their most recent observations and conversations with the general in Tokyo, Bradshaw and Warren discussed MacArthur's categorization of war criminals. He had, they revealed, divided war

---

[41]"Report of Second War Crimes Conference 1540-1630," Miscellaneous Yamashita file, box 2003, RG 331.

[42]Carpenter's charges and MacArthur's orders to Styer are found in ibid.

[43]GHQ, USAFPAC to Styer, 17 September 1945, ibid. Kerr had only recently been promoted to Major.

[44]"Conference Between B. Gen. Weir and Colonel Bradshaw," 21 September 1945, ASW 000.51, War Crimes Working File, Japan, RG 107. Eight officials participated in that conversation.

criminals into three groups: the major instigators of the war, the field and area commanders, and the lesser malefactors.[45] In discussing those three categories with them, MacArthur, in their view, had given it "a great deal of thought." The first trials, they reported, probably would be those of Yamashita and Homma, representing the field- and area-commander category. While they had not been informed of any specific date by which any of the trials would begin, MacArthur's evident intention, they contended, was to begin judicial proceedings "as soon as possible."

Warren and Bradshaw continued by noting MacArthur's evaluation of the Yamashita and Homma cases. Those leaders, he had argued, may have been ignorant of some of the atrocities committed by their forces, but "they were certainly aware of a certain portion of them." Because those two Japanese officers had neglected their command responsibility, the general had observed, the commission of such acts occurred. Somewhat later in their conversation with Washington, Lieutenant Colonel Warren notified his superiors that MacArthur's headquarters, hoping to found the concept of command responsibility firmly in law, wanted the War Crimes Office in Washington to prepare "a brief of legal points and legal history" on that issue.[46]

Whether Warren realized it or not, Carpenter's office had just forwarded a similar request to the War Department.[47] That cable had served notice to Washington of MacArthur's intention to try commanders who failed to restrain their men. It also had requested "a comprehensive legal brief" that could support the concept of command responsibility, including the trial and punishment of those who had failed to do their duty, either because they neglected to see a "series or pattern" of violations of the law of war, or because they had knowledge of, and yet did nothing to prevent, war crimes.

Without waiting for Washington's legal analysis, MacArthur on 24 September ordered Lieutenant General Styer to "proceed immediately" with the trial against Yamashita.[48] To assist in the prosecution, MacArthur's staff added two other names to that earlier list of prospective prosecutors, which had included Kerr and Webster. Since the five names recommended by MacArthur's headquarters were listed in the sentence immediately following Styer's notification that Yamashita should be tried, Styer probably took the recommendation as seriously as an order. What-

---

[45]For the categorization of war criminals by the London conferees and by the UN War Crimes Commission, see Department of State, *International Conference*, p. 423; *FRUS: The British Commonwealth*, 6:915.

[46]"Conference Between B. Gen. Weir and Colonel Bradshaw," ASW 000.51, War Crimes Working File, Japan, RG 107.

[47]CinCAFPAC to WARTAG, 19 September 1945, 000.5 #1, box 763, RG 331.

[48]USAFPAC to USAFWESPAC, 000.5 Yamashita, box 763, RG 331.

ever his rationale, on 1 October those five men were named as the Yamashita prosecuting team. By that same order, Styer, in compliance with his instructions to proceed immediately, also appointed the members of the defense and the members of the military commission.[49]

Styer's authority, however, did not include formulating the charges against Yamashita or establishing the rules governing the judicial proceedings. Both came from MacArthur's staff. But only the charges were original creations of MacArthur and his subordinates. The same could not be said for the "Regulations Governing the Trial of War Criminals," which MacArthur's headquarters had dispatched to Styer on 24 September and which would govern the proceedings against Yamashita.[50]

Although MacArthur authorized the issuance of those 24 September regulations and ordered Styer to base Yamashita's prosecution upon them, the rules and procedures were in large measure those proposed on 3 September by Captain Robinson, Commander Brereton, Colonel Bradshaw, and Lieutenant Colonel Warren.[51] Since MacArthur later would be soundly lambasted for originating that document, and since its rules would cause a legal controversy among justices on the U.S. Supreme Court, a closer examination of its most important sections is in order.

Section 1 merely affirmed the right of MacArthur as commander in chief, U.S. Army Forces, Pacific, to appoint military commissions to try those suspected of violating the law of war. It was a right affirmed by President Roosevelt in the saboteurs' case, by Congress in the articles of war, and by the army and navy in their field manual 27-5. As worded, it also closely paralleled the Robinson-Brereton draft.

Sections 3 and 4, also following the Robinson-Brereton draft, limited a commission's jurisdiction to those lands and those persons subject to the authority of MacArthur's own command. In Section 5, which defined the crimes over which the commission had authority, Carpenter, as MacArthur's chief legal adviser, had clearly rejected the vague U.S. War Crimes Office wording in favor of the more precise terminology of the London Charter.[52] He and his staff also had added a

---

[49]Special Orders #112, USAFWESPAC, 1 October 1945, 000.5 Yamashita, ibid. On 9 October 1945, Styer notified MacArthur's headquarters that there was a "shortage of personnel of right rank and qualifications" to sit on other military commissions. See Styer to DC/S for administration, Radios file, box 1945, RG 331. On 26 October two Yamashita commission members were replaced. See Special Orders #134, USAFWESPAC, 000.5 Yamashita, box 763, RG 331.

[50]AG 000.5 (9-24-45) JA, "Before the Military Commission Convened by the Commanding General United States Army Forces, Western Pacific: Yamashita, Tomoyuki," pp. 6–16, Washington National Records Center (hereafter cited as Transcript).

[51]Robinson-Brereton memorandum, Miscellaneous Yamashita file, box 2003, RG 331.

[52]Carpenter formally becomes the official war-crimes adviser to MacArthur on 2 October. See SCAP, "History of the Non-military Activities of the Occupation of Japan,

stipulation found neither in the London Charter nor in the Robinson-Brereton draft: "The convening authority may specify particular offenders to be tried before any commission appointed by him." That sentence merely reaffirmed a right MacArthur had reserved to himself on 17 September in his instructions to Styer.[53] While this addition may appear original, it was not. General Dwight D. Eisenhower on 25 August 1945 had similarly notified his subordinates that "no case" would be tried "except when directed by this headquarters."[54] Indeed, while MacArthur simply reserved the right to order the trial of particular individuals, he did not formally reserve the right of ultimate approval of all cases.

Relying on the Robinson-Brereton draft, the articles of war, field manual 27-5, the saboteurs' rulings, and the London Charter, MacArthur's Sections 6–10 discussed the membership of the military commission. The commander in chief either would appoint all members or he would authorize his commanding generals to assume that task. The limitations imposed upon the selection process were minimal, requiring only that the appointees be competent to perform such duties and not be prejudiced or personally involved in the cases before them. Conviction and sentence would be by a two-thirds vote, a policy earlier favored by President Roosevelt, Secretary of War Stimson, and Attorney General Biddle.

Sections 13–18, which established the powers and procedures of the military commissions, were the most controversial of MacArthur's 24 September regulations. Section 13 read: "A Commission shall: a) Confine each trial strictly to a fair, expeditious hearing on the issues raised by the charges, excluding irrelevant issues or evidence and preventing any unnecessary delay or interference. b) Deal summarily with any contumacy or contempt, imposing any appropriate punishment therefor." While perhaps controversial because it appeared to undermine traditional American legal procedures, MacArthur's draft was less strident than either the Robinson-Brereton draft or the London Charter. Those documents had granted the commissions the right to "prevent *by strict measures* any unreasonable delay or interference."[55] They also had specifically allowed, as "appropriate punishment" for contumacy, a commission to exclude either the defendant and/or his counsel from all future proceedings. That specific delegation of authority, together with the "strict measures" wording, had been excised in the MacArthur orders.

Section 14 enumerated the rights of the accused, including his

---

Trials of Class 'B' and 'C' War Criminals," Historical Manuscript file, 8-5AA-2-C-1, Office of the Chief of Military History, Washington, DC.

[53]Miscellaneous Yamashita file, box 2003, RG 331.

[54]Eisenhower to his commanding generals (AG 250.4JAG-AGO), box 1717, RG 153.

[55]Emphasis added. Contumacy implies stubborn disobedience and/or resistance to authority.

right to counsel, to cross-examine prosecution witnesses, and to have all proceedings translated into a language he could understand. The 24 September document also stipulated that the defendant receive "in advance of trial a copy of the charges and specifications, so worded as clearly to apprise the accused of each offense charged."[56] In adopting that wording MacArthur's staff dropped the War Crimes Office proposal that the defendant not only receive the offenses with which he was charged, but that he also receive "the essential facts constituting each offense." Likewise MacArthur's staff dropped that portion of the Robinson-Brereton draft that allowed the defendant to apply for an extension of time in which to prepare his defense.[57] This omission may well have been symptomatic of the sense of urgency felt in Tokyo and Washington and the result of a decision not to emphasize, or draw attention to, this prerogative. As the Yamashita court later would demonstrate, the omission did not prohibit a commission from granting extensions when its members believed it necessary.

MacArthur's additions and omissions in these sections do not indicate that he was "stacking the deck" against Japanese war criminals. Indeed, in Section 15 he virtually guaranteed defendants the right to refuse to testify without such a decision adversely affecting the court. He had done so by failing to adopt a Robinson-Brereton proposal that allowed the court to interrogate any defendant "whether or not he elects to testify in his own behalf," and that allowed it to "draw such inferences as the circumstances justify from the answers of the accused or from his refusal to answer pertinent questions." He also had done so by declining to adopt the even vaguer phrasing of the London Charter, which allowed the court "to interrogate any defendant."

Nor were MacArthur's rules related to the admission of evidence uniquely arbitrary. In giving the commission the right to "admit such evidence as in its opinion would be of assistance in proving or disproving the charge, or such as in the commission's opinion would have probative value in the mind of a reasonable man," he simply followed guidelines and ideas already set forth by the U.S. War Crimes Office draft, President Roosevelt, Stimson, McCloy, Biddle, Eisenhower, and the Allied delegations at the London conference.

In stipulating the specific kinds of evidence that would be admissible, MacArthur adopted the work of others. The acceptance of Allied, civilian, and military documents "without proof of the signature or of the

---

[56]The London Charter had stipulated that the defendant receive the charges "at a reasonable time before the trial." Neither Eisenhower, MacArthur, nor the U.S. War Crimes Office included that phrase in their proposals and policies.

[57]The Eisenhower orders also failed to include phrasing that specifically allowed for an extension of time.

issuance of the document"; the acceptance of reports by the International Red Cross, by doctors, or by any other person the court determined had prepared them "in the course of his duty"; the acceptance of any diaries and letters; and the acceptance of copies of documents if the original was unavailable or "[could] not be produced without undue delay" were all ideas contained in the Robinson-Brereton draft. Indeed, those U.S. War Crimes officers had simply taken as their own the rules of evidence adopted by the British government in June 1945.[58] The only major addition MacArthur made to the Robinson-Brereton draft concerning this specific list of valid evidence permitted the admission of "affidavits, depositions, or other statements taken by an officer detailed for that purpose by military authority." By adding that sentence he simply included a section of the British rules that the War Crimes officers had deleted. MacArthur, following the London Charter and not the War Crimes Office proposal, also granted the courts the right to take judicial notice of commonly known information, official government documents, and "the proceedings, records and findings of military or other agencies of any of the United Nations." Continuing to follow the London document, he also allowed the commission to require both the defense and the prosecution to explain the nature of their evidence before actual presentation so that the court could rule on its admissibility.

Just as MacArthur generally followed the work of others in relation to the admission of evidence, so too did he follow their lead in other sections of his rules and procedures. His discussion of the conspiracy concept, the trial format, maintenance of records, and of the rules for passing judgment closely followed suggestions made by the U.S. War Crimes Office.

MacArthur's draft differed substantially, however, in its appellate-review procedures. Under the London Charter no formal appeal existed, although the Allied Control Council could lower, at its discretion, the sentences. Under the Robinson-Brereton draft the judgment and sentence were "subject to approval" or alteration downward by the convening authority. In sentences of death, however, review was mandatory. In order to provide guidance to the reviewing authorities, the War Crimes Office draft also had adopted the clear intent of Article of War 37. "The judgment and any sentence which a commission has jurisdiction to impose," its proposal read, "shall be valid notwithstanding any defect or variation from these rules in the proceedings unless it appears that a substantial miscarriage of justice has actually occurred." Not only did MacArthur's staff reject that wording, but it also altered the "subject to approval" proposal. Under the 24 September procedures, no sentence could be

---

[58]"Royal Warrant, Regulations for the Trial of War Criminals," file 89, box 1853, RG 331.

implemented until the officer convening the commission had approved it. And in cases where a commission had imposed the death penalty, MacArthur himself had to review and approve. The phrasing, reminiscent of Article of War 37, was omitted altogether.[59]

Few of MacArthur's rules and procedures issued to Styer in late September were original. Nevertheless, they were binding on all his subordinates and would provide the basis for the trial of the Japanese. Unfortunately for General Yamashita he would become the first Japanese leader to face trial under those regulations.

---

[59]"Regulations Governing the Trial of War Criminals," 24 September 1945, Transcript, pp. 6–16.

CHAPTER FOUR
TOMOYUKI YAMASHITA AND
COMMAND RESPONSIBILITY

It should have surprised no one that Tomoyuki Yamashita would be tried by an American military commission in Manila, capital of the Philippines. According to both the Moscow Declaration and the London Charter, lesser criminals would be returned to the nations "in which their abominable deeds were done in order that they may be judged and punished according to the laws of [those] liberated countries. . . ."[1] As a prisoner incarcerated on Luzon, Yamashita logically faced trial for the crimes committed by his forces in the Philippines rather than for similar crimes committed against British subjects in Malaya in 1942. The archipelago remained, after all, American territory. The ultimate sovereignty rested not in the Philippine legislature or in its people but in the United States. Washington supervised the islands' foreign affairs and exercised a veto over all Filipino congressional acts involving immigration, international trade, and currency matters. In judicial matters, even those involving the Philippine constitution, the U.S. Supreme Court and not its Philippine counterpart exercised the highest authority.[2] Therefore, trial by an American military commission in U.S. territory for crimes committed against America's Filipino wards had seemed appropriate.

That Lieutenant General Styer chose the ballroom of the U.S. High Commissioner's residence in Manila as the site of criminal proceedings against Yamashita also seemed appropriate. The residence itself not only symbolized U.S. authority in the Philippines but also symbolized the commitment of Washington to guide the archipelago to independence.[3] Its shell-scarred exterior and its location amidst the ruins of downtown

---

[1] See Chapter Two.

[2] For the Tydings-McDuffie legislation, which regulated U.S.-Philippine relations, see U.S., *Statutes at Large* 48:456–62. For a fuller examination of the degree of control during the Commonwealth period, see Theodore Friend's *Between Two Empires: The Ordeal of the Philippines, 1929–1946* (New Haven: Yale University Press, 1965); Garel A. Grunder and William E. Livezey's *The Philippines and the United States* (Norman: University of Oklahoma Press, 1951); and Gregorio F. Zaide's *Philippine Constitutional History and Constitutions of Modern Nations* (Manila: Modern Book Co., 1970). Also see 30 *Stat.* 1754–62.

[3] The High Commissioner was the most powerful civilian representative of the United States in the Philippines after 1934.

Manila further served as stark reminders to Japanese, Filipinos, and
Americans of the devastation and death that Tokyo's expansionism had
precipitated. Trial in that residence also dramatically reaffirmed U.S.
sovereignty, lost in 1942. Perhaps it even soothed the memories of that
dramatic collapse, with its loss of American lives and surrender of an
American army. Finally, trial in that residence reminded Filipinos of
Franklin Roosevelt's words to President Sergio Osmena in 1944 that the
Japanese invasion and occupation of the Philippines had aroused in the
American people "a righteous anger [and] a stern determination to punish
the guilty."[4]

On 8 October 1945 in the ballroom of the U.S. High Commissioner's residence amidst rows of anxious Filipino war correspondents
and distinguished guests, among whom were Lieutenant General Styer
and Mrs. Osmena, five U.S. generals arraigned the 14th Area Army
commander.[5] The charge, formulated by Colonel Carpenter in compliance
with the wishes of MacArthur and Marshall as expressed at the 14
September conference, included both general and specific allegations
involving the concept of command responsibility. Neither the comprehensive overriding charge nor the sixty-four individual charges specifically
accused the Japanese commander of personally committing, or of personally ordering the commission of, atrocities and other war crimes. The
general comprehensive charge simply argued:

> [that] between 9 October 1944 and 2 September 1945, at Manila and
> at other places in the Philippine Islands, while commander of armed
> forces of Japan at war with the United States of America and its allies,
> [General Tomoyuki Yamashita] unlawfully disregarded and failed to
> discharge his duty as commander to control the operations of the
> members of his command, permitting them to commit brutal atrocities
> and other high crimes against people of the United States and of its
> allies and dependencies, particularly the Philippines; and he, General
> Tomoyuki Yamashita, thereby violated the law of war.[6]

While the additional specific charges involved the murder and mistreatment of over thirty-two thousand Filipino civilians and captured Americans,
the rape of hundreds of Filipino women, and the arbitrary destruction of
private property, they established no direct link between Yamashita and

---

[4]Roosevelt to Osmena, 20 October 1944, contained in "Landing of American
Forces in the Philippines," U.S. Department of State *Bulletin* 11 (July–December 1944):
455.

[5]The five generals appointed by Styer were Major General Russell B. Reynolds,
Major General Clarence Sturdevant, Major General James Lester, Brigadier General
William Walker, and Brigadier General Egbert Bullene.

[6]The charge may be found in AG 000.5 (9-24-45) JA, "Before the Military
Commission Convened by the Commanding General United States Army Forces, Western
Pacific: Yamashita, Tomoyuki," p. 31 (hereafter cited as Transcript).

the commission of those criminal acts.[7] For that Japanese officer the reason the prosecution had failed to discover such a connection seemed obvious. He was, he informed the court, "not guilty" of any of the charges.

During the two- and one-half-hour arraignment proceedings on 8 October, the court, in addition to reading the charges and eliciting Yamashita's plea, firmly laid the groundwork for the upcoming full-fledged trial. It inquired of Yamashita whether he found acceptable the six U.S. Army officers assigned as his defense counsel. He did. It announced, as its basic rules of procedure, MacArthur's 24 September communiqué to Styer. It also reminded prosecution and defense that that order clearly permitted the commission to conduct the proceedings as it deemed necessary and to admit into evidence anything that it deemed to have probative value. The commission then affirmed that the trial would "be conducted in a fair and impartial manner, which is," the court noted, "traditional American justice." Referring to that concept of fairness, the commission ruled, over the objections of Major Kerr, that Yamashita would be allowed two associate defense counsel, Chief of Staff Muto and Assistant Chief of Staff Naokata Utsunomiya, even though they themselves would be witnesses at the trial.[8]

Having overruled one prosecution motion, the court then dealt the defense several blows. First, it rejected a motion to drop the general charge, which, Yamashita's counsel argued, failed to accuse their client of any specific violation of the law of war. Second, it accepted a prosecution request that, in addition to the sixty-four charges already levied against the Japanese general, a supplemental bill of particulars could be introduced at a later time. Finally, in setting the trial date, the commission disregarded Colonel Harry Clarke's request for two weeks in which to prepare the case for the defense. Rather, agreeing with Major Kerr that three weeks would be more appropriate, the court scheduled the trial of the "Tiger of Malaya" for 0800 hours on 29 October 1945.[9]

Three days before that trial date Kerr presented to the defense counsel his supplemental bill of particulars, an additional fifty-nine charges against Yamashita involving the murder of over forty-five hundred

---

[7]Transcript, pp. 38–57.

[8]This paragraph and the following is based on Transcript, pp. 1–61. Yamashita could have chosen his own defense counsel but expressed satisfaction with the U.S. Army officers that the court had appointed to conduct his defense. Those officers were Colonel Harry Clarke, Lieutenant Colonel Walter Hendrix, Lieutenant Colonel James Feldhaus, Major George Guy, Captain A. Frank Reel, and Captain Milton Sandberg.

[9]Kerr had been surprised by the short period of time that the defense requested. Hoping to arrange for the transport of certain witnesses from the United States to the Philippines, he believed that the prosecution needed the additional week, even if defense did not. On 1 October 1945, MacArthur's Manila headquarters requested the War Department's assistance in locating potential witnesses living in the United States. See CinCAFPAC to WARTAG, 000.5 Yamashita, box 763, RG 331.

civilians, the mistreatment of Filipinos and American prisoners of war, and the arbitrary destruction of private property. Despite the court's ruling on 8 October that such a supplemental bill could be submitted by Kerr, the defense counsel objected on the twenty-ninth to the admission of the fifty-nine new charges. For one thing, Captain A. Frank Reel argued, the new charges failed to accuse Yamashita directly of commission, or ordering the commission, of the war crimes covered in the new bill. Such reasoning failed to impress Major General Russell B. Reynolds, presiding officer of the commission, who overruled Reel's objection. Reynolds then proceeded to reject a second defense request that the court order Kerr to indicate which of the 123 specific charges personally involved Yamashita or occurred as a direct result of his orders or permission.[10]

Having lost on both motions, the defense then moved for a two-week recess during which it could research the fifty-nine new charges. The court, after a conference behind closed doors, rejected such a continuance, although Reynolds indicated that initially only evidence would be admitted relating to the first sixty-four charges originally submitted to the defense on 8 October.

Quickly following that ruling, Colonel Clarke, as senior defense counsel, made an impassioned plea to dismiss all charges against Yamashita. His arguments would provide the framework around which the defense would structure its case:

> The charge alleges that the Accused failed in his duty to control his troops, permitting them to commit certain alleged crimes. The Bill of Particulars, however, sets forth no instance of neglect of duty by the Accused. Nor does it set forth any acts of commission or omission by the Accused as amounting to a 'permitting' of the crimes in question.
>
> The Accused is not charged with having done something or having failed to do something, but solely with having been something. For the gravamen of the charge is that the Accused was the commander of the Japanese forces, and by virtue of that fact alone, is guilty of every crime committed by every soldier assigned to his command.
>
> American jurisprudence recognizes no such principle so far as its own military personnel is concerned. The Articles of War denounce and punish improper conduct by military personnel, but they do not hold a commanding officer for the crimes committed by his subordinates. No one would even suggest that the Commanding General of an American occupational force becomes a criminal every time an American soldier violates the law. It is the basic premise of all

---

[10]Transcript, pp. 70–82. When the commission reconvened on 29 October, Generals Sturdevant and Walker had been replaced by Major General Leo Donovan and Brigadier General Morris Handwerk. For a biting critique of the commission and the trial, see A. Frank Reel, *The Case of General Yamashita* (1949; reprint ed., New York: Octagon Books, 1971).

civilized criminal justice that it punishes not according to status but according to fault, and that one man is not held to answer for the crime of another.[11]

Convinced that the defense logic was in error, Major Kerr countered by explaining that the atrocities

were so notorious and so flagrant and so enormous, both as to the scope of their operation and as to the inhumanity, the bestiality involved, that they must have been known to the Accused if he were making any effort whatever to meet the responsibilities of his command or his position; and that if he did not know of those acts, notorious, widespread, repeated, constant as they were, it was simply because he took affirmative action not to know.[12]

As the arguments of the senior prosecution and defense counsel clearly emphasized on that first day, the crucial issue in the proceedings was the question of command responsibility: Should an officer be held responsible for the conduct of his subordinates?[13] That question, as Clarke had so appropriately argued, could have dramatic future ramifications for all armies, including that of the United States.

For nineteen days, from 29 October to 20 November, the court listened to prosecution evidence that sought to demonstrate the bestiality, enormity, and widespread nature of Japanese war crimes in the Philippines, and that sought to convict Yamashita of dereliction of duty.[14] In whispers and in screams, it heard how over thirty-two thousand Filipino civilians had died. It learned how Japanese soldiers executed priests in their churches, slaughtered patients in their hospitals, machine-gunned residents in their neighborhoods, and beheaded or burned alive American prisoners of war. It learned of Japanese torture, including the water cure, the burning of feet, and the removal of fingers. It learned how one

---

[11]Transcript, pp. 86–87.

[12]Ibid., p. 100.

[13]Despite the 14 September conference and Colonel Carpenter's overriding charge formulated in September, MacArthur's staff was obviously concerned over the idea of command responsibility. On 18 October 1945, MacArthur's Manila headquarters posed a crucial question to the War Department: "Is the commanding officer of a military force responsible for war crimes committed by his subordinates by virtue of his command function, and without regard to any order by him directing the commission of the acts, or to any authorization thereof, or to his knowledge thereof?" While a copy of the War Department's response is unavailable, SCAP legal records reveal three files that substantiate such a charge. See the documents entitled "Responsibility of Commanding General for Atrocities Committed by Subordinates," "Commanding Officer," and "Criminal Liability for Negligence," files 6A, 6F, and 6H, box 1853, RG 331.

[14]For the testimony from 29 October to 20 November, see Transcript, pp. 62–2957. The court did not meet on four of the twenty-three days between 29 October and 20 November.

Japanese soldier tossed a baby in the air and impaled it on the ceiling with his bayonet, and how others bayoneted an eleven-year-old girl thirty-eight times. It learned of rape and necrophilia; of how 476 women in Manila were imprisoned in two hotels and repeatedly raped over an eight-day period by officers and enlisted men alike; of how twenty Japanese soldiers raped one girl and then, as a grand finale, cut off her breasts; and of how drunken soldiers, after killing women civilians, then raped the corpses. For nineteen days the court and the Philippine nation listened.

Only twice during that lengthy, grisly testimony did prosecution witnesses link Yamashita directly to the atrocities. On the sixth day of the trial, Narciso Lapus, imprisoned by the United States as a collaborator, attempted to connect Yamashita directly to the commission of atrocities on the islands. As private secretary to General Artemio Ricarte, an elderly compatriot of the legendary Emilio Aguinaldo, around whom the Japanese had hoped to rally the Filipino people, Lapus insisted he had gained information that would incriminate Yamashita. That ruthless, cruel officer, he swore, had notified Ricarte twice in October 1944 that he had ordered his officers "in the Philippine Islands to wipe out the whole Philippines if possible." He also testified that Ricarte had informed him that Yamashita had refused to modify that order. The old general, according to Lapus, also claimed that Yamashita had rejected one appeal by arguing that "war is war and the enemy should not be given quarters [sic]." He further claimed, Lapus testified, that Yamashita planned to destroy Manila and kill its inhabitants.[15]

To substantiate these first dramatic accusations against Yamashita personally, Major Kerr produced a second witness, Lapus's brother-in-law Joaquin Galang. Galang, also imprisoned as a Japanese collaborator, testified that he had personally witnessed a conversation between Yamashita and Ricarte in late December, during which the 14th Area Army commander reaffirmed his intention of killing all Filipinos and destroying Manila. He had understood that conversation, he explained to the court, because Ricarte's grandson, Bislumino Romero, had translated Yamashita's comments to his grandfather.[16]

The Lapus testimony seemed shaky. Under cross-examination a stumbling, nervous Lapus seemed unable to remember his earlier statements. The result was a contradictory testimony. Furthermore, he had to admit that this evidence was hearsay and that he had not attended the supposed Ricarte-Yamashita conferences but was only recounting the conversation based on his later discussions with Ricarte. Nor was he able to answer satisfactorily two nagging issues. He was unable to explain why Ricarte would leave his family in Manila when he journeyed to Baguio in

---

15Ibid., pp. 912–1052.
16Ibid., p. 1069.

December 1944, when Ricarte, according to Lapus's own testimony, already knew of Yamashita's orders to destroy that city and massacre its inhabitants. Nor could he explain why the orders theoretically issued by Yamashita in October and November to kill Filipinos and to destroy barrios and cities—orders which he testified Yamashita had refused to rescind—were not carried out in 1944 when they were issued.[17]

The defense counsel further undermined Lapus's testimony by arguing that he simply wanted to use his cooperation during the Yamashita trial as a means for negotiating his release from prison, where he had been incarcerated by the Americans as a collaborator. To prove that point the defense presented as evidence a letter that Lapus had written to the chief of MacArthur's Counter Intelligence Corps in Manila.[18] In that document he had promised to reveal all he knew about the Japanese if he, his son, and houseboy were freed from prison and received immunity from all future arrest and prosecution; if all his son's holdings, including land, were returned; if he were paid personal expenses during the time he helped the Americans; if he, his wife, his three children, his mother-in-law, his sister-in-law, and houseboy were sent by the United States, free of charge, to either New York City or to a Latin American country; if the United States gave him the equivalent of one year's salary; and if the United States helped him find an adequate job after his transfer out of the Philippines. While he had finally agreed to testify without assurances that any of those provisions would be met by the United States, the defense argued that his testimony was still predicated on cultivating the good will of his captors for his own personal ends.

That same reason, the defense argued, motivated Galang as well. Since Galang was an eyewitness to the Ricarte-Yamashita conversation, his testimony, unlike that of Lapus, was potentially quite damaging to the defense. The defense counsel, however, undermined his credibility by producing Romero, whose testimony totally refuted Galang's earlier account. The defense reminded the court that Galang came forward with his "evidence" only after he had read Lapus's testimony before the court and no doubt realized that he too could profit by presenting damaging information against Yamashita.[19] As Major George Guy, one of the defense counsel, later observed of Lapus and Galang, "so worthless did their testimony become ... that Major Robert Kerr ... in his final argument to the commission, did not even mention [them]."[20]

---

[17]Based on the charges against Yamashita, the vast majority of the atrocities occurred after 1 February 1945, during the military struggle for Luzon, and not in October, November, and December 1944.

[18]Lapus to CIC, 8 June 1945, Defense Exhibit 11; Transcript, p. 2985.

[19]Transcript, pp. 1073–76, 2017–18.

[20]"The Defense of Yamashita," *Wyoming Law Journal* 4 (Spring 1950): 163.

Neither the Lapus nor the Galang testimony was essential to finding Yamashita guilty. That thousands of Filipinos had been ruthlessly slaughtered by Yamashita's soldiers was indisputable. As the original charge had succinctly argued, by failing to restrain his officers and men, the 14th Area Army commander had "unlawfully disregarded and failed to discharge his duty as commander." For that, the prosecution believed, he should be severely punished, even if no direct incriminating evidence linking him specifically to one or more of the atrocities existed.

Since the prosecution had not clearly proven that Yamashita had ordered atrocities, nor that he had even known of them, its case hinged on the argument that Yamashita "should have known" or "must have known" of such widespread atrocities involving so many individuals. Of the hundreds of witnesses produced by Kerr and his colleagues, almost all emphasized the actual commission of atrocities and war crimes rather than any evidence linking them to high-ranking Japanese officers. By proving the commission of the numerous murders and rapes, the prosecution hoped to convince the court that there was no way for Yamashita not to have known, unless he had made a determined effort not to know. In either case, he was guilty of failure to control his men, guilty of failing to exercise his command responsibility.

The defense countered with a long series of arguments meant to demonstrate that not only was Yamashita ignorant of the violations of the law of war but that, due to battle conditions, he also had no way of knowing that they had occurred. By especially examining Yamashita's relation to the more than thirty-two thousand atrocities committed in Manila and Batangas Province, the defense hoped to drive home its argument.

Defense witnesses Yamashita, Muto, Yokoyama, and other staff officers testified that the 14th Area Army had planned neither to defend Manila nor to destroy it. To defend Manila, Yamashita had explained, would have been folly. First, American air and naval power would have given MacArthur the advantage in any fight for Manila. Second, the capital's approximately one million civilians would have overtaxed Japanese defenders since they would have required potentially scarce food and water. Finally, the flammable construction of Manila's buildings further made defense undesirable.[21]

As for the atrocities that occurred in early 1945 in Manila, Yamashita denied all knowledge. He informed the court that he had turned over evacuation of that city to Lieutenant General Yokoyama and already

---

[21]See Transcript for the full record of defense witnesses' testimony. Also see Chapter One. No doubt Yamashita still clearly remembered his classic siege of Singapore in 1942, where civilians had become a great liability for General Percival and had been a major factor in his decision to surrender.

had led his Shobu Army into the mountains southwest of San José by the time most of the atrocities had occurred. Yokoyama supported that testimony and informed the court that his superior had at no time ordered him to massacre the residents of Manila. Instead, Yamashita had cautioned him "to be fair in all my dealings with the Filipino people." Nor had he informed Yamashita of atrocities in Manila since not even he, at his headquarters just east of Manila, had learned of their commission.[22]

If one accepts the testimony of Colonel Masatoshi Fujishige, then Yamashita had not been informed of the 25,000 murders in Batangas Province. Fujishige, who had been granted virtual military autonomy by Yokoyama for many of the same reasons Yamashita had given Yokoyama his virtually autonomous command, admitted that he had ordered the suppression of guerrillas, an order that had led to civilian deaths. As his testimony revealed, he perceived that women and children in Batangas were as potentially dangerous as the men, since they had destroyed Japanese property and had killed Japanese soldiers. Civilians had been killed, he noted, as guerrilla combatants and not as innocent noncombatants. Furthermore, he had given those orders on his own initiative. He had never been instructed by General Yokoyama or by Yokoyama's superior, General Yamashita, to adopt a policy of killing noncombatants. Nor, he testified, had he reported the killings of any Filipinos in his province to either of his superiors.[23]

Reflecting upon the testimony of the defense witnesses, those sitting in the spacious ballroom could visualize the chaotic battle conditions on Luzon between October 1944 and August 1945. They could envision the poor communications among units within, as well as among, the three Japanese defense sectors. They could understand the difficulties confronting Yamashita: assumption of a new command with little time for careful reflection upon its problems, its dispositions, or its personnel; the concentration required of a hastily assembled staff on the American invasions at Leyte and Lingayen; an increasingly damaging guerrilla movement; a loss of air and naval power; a shortage of vital spare parts, fuel, and food; and a vague, tenuous coordination between traditionally estranged army and naval units. And they could, if they found the defense logic convincing, clearly understand why Yamashita should not have known of the heinous crimes committed on Luzon and its surrounding islands.[24]

Colonel Clarke and his defense colleagues avowedly hoped that

---

[22]The interrogation of Lieutenant Colonel Tsuginori Kuriya, assistant operations officer, 14th Area Army, supports Yokoyama's statement. 201 Yamashita File, box 1217, RG 331. Also see testimony of Colonel Hiroshi Hashimoto, Transcript, pp. 3123–26.

[23]Transcript, pp. 2810–28.

[24]See Chapter One.

the five army generals, aware of the pitfalls of command, might understand Yamashita's predicament and find him innocent of the charges. Of those five officers, however, only one apparently had recent combat experience, a fact that the defense team lamented.[25] Perhaps had the court members recently experienced their own problems of control during combat situations, the defense reasoned, they would be more sympathetic to Yamashita's position. The presiding officer, Major General Reynolds, who also served as the law member, had been attached to the Military Personnel Division of the War Department General Staff before his arrival in the Philippines in June 1945. Likewise, Major General Leo Donovan and Brigadier General Egbert Bullene had joined MacArthur's army in the summer of 1945 following stateside tours. Of the four generals on whom information is available, only Major General James Lester had served in combat during World War II. Lester from 1942 to 1944 had commanded the 24th Infantry Division's artillery and had participated in the Hollandia campaign. From 1944 to May 1945 he also had commanded the XIV Corps' artillery, which had participated in the capture of Clark Field and Manila.[26] But although Lester had combat experience, he, just as his four brethren on the bench, lacked formal legal training. And that bothered the defense counsel even more than the absence of combat officers on the bench.[27]

Captain Reel, in his postwar reflections on the trial, catalogued Bullene, Reynolds, and Donovan as at least interested participants in the proceedings. Brigadier General Morris Handwerk, on the other hand, "just gazed out into space." General Lester, Reel added, "from the moment the trial began made it clear that he was antagonistic to the accused and impatient with what he considered delays caused by accused's counsel."[28] In Lester's case perhaps his combat experience hurt rather than helped the defense. As an officer of the XIV Corps he had participated in the capture of Manila and most probably toured the devastated city immediately upon its fall, seeing firsthand the barbarity of the Japanese excesses committed there in February. All things considered, Generals Styer and MacArthur might have aided the defense by staffing the court with their recently acquired stateside-duty officers.

---

[25]Reel believed at the time that none of the officers had had recent combat experience. *The Case*, p. 40.

[26]Information on Generals Reynolds, Bullene, and Lester may be found in OPD Biographical File, 1944–49, RG 319, Records of the Army Staff, National Archives. Information on Donovan may be found in the Biographical File, Center for Military History. Neither biographical file contains information on Handwerk. A summary of his military service up to 1942 may be found in *Who's Who in America* (Chicago: A. N. Marquis Co., 1944), p. 874.

[27]Reel, *The Case*, p. 40; Guy, "The Defense of Yamashita," p. 161; J. Gordon Feldhaus, "The Trial of Yamashita," *South Dakota Bar Journal* 15 (October 1946): 185.

[28]Reel, *The Case*, pp. 43–44.

Newsweek correspondent Robert Shaplen, in one of his December 1945 dispatches, painted an even gloomier picture of the court than Reel. "In the opinion of probably every correspondent covering the trial," he wrote, "the military commission came into the courtroom the first day with the decision already in its collective pocket."[29] Shaplen based that observation, however, on opinion and not fact. The court's permission to allow Muto and Utsunomiya to serve as associate defense counsel, its early ruling requiring that affidavits must not be the only basis for a charge, and its apparent willingness as late as 8 November to consider a defense motion for additional time to prepare the case for certain charges contained in the supplemental bill of particulars indicated that the court had not attempted initially to erect artificial obstacles for the defense.[30]

But even during the first week of the trial, the court seemed overly sensitive to the slow pace of the proceedings. Perhaps that concern merely reflected the emphasis on speed contained in Truman's instructions to MacArthur on 12 September, or Marshall's remarks to the 14 September conferees, or MacArthur's instructions to Styer on 24 September. Or the court may have been aware of General Styer's concern in October that, due to a "shortage of personnel of right rank and qualifications," he might need to delay other war-crimes prosecutions until the Yamashita court members were available for reassignment to other tribunals.[31]

Whatever the motivation, on 5 November the court reversed its 1 November ruling that required prosecution affidavits relating to a particular charge to be submitted in conjunction with oral testimony.[32] After the fifth, the court announced, it would receive any affidavit or deposition without accompanying oral testimony, and it would determine its probative value. That same day the court cautioned the defense counsel on three separate occasions during its cross-examination of Lapus that they needed

---

[29]"Yamashita: Too Busy," *Newsweek*, 10 December 1945, p. 44.

[30]MacArthur's headquarters also aided defense by requesting, on at least two occasions, books and materials from the War Department. According to defense counsel Guy, it also courteously and promptly aided MacArthur in his efforts to secure defense witnesses in Japan. See CinCAFPAC to WARJAG, 13 and 18 October 1945, 000.5 Yamashita, box 763, RG 331; and Guy, "Defense of Yamashita," p. 159.

[31]Styer to DC/S for Administration, 9 October 1945, Radiograms, box 1945, RG 331.

[32]For the two rulings, see Transcript, pp. 642, 1124. Lack of documentation prevents a definitive explanation of the court's action. However, the court may well have adopted this decision as a result of information received from Tokyo on 2 and 5 November, which indicated that Yamashita's control of the army and naval forces could not be proven by oral testimony "but only through documentary evidence" including newspaper accounts of military orders. See CinCAFPAC Advance to CinCAFPAC, 2 November 1945, 201 Yamashita File, box 1217, RG 331; and 5 November 1945, 000.5 Yamashita, box 763, RG 331.

to shorten the cross-examination so as not to prolong the proceedings. Five days later on the tenth the court informed both the prosecution and the defense that their wrangling over the accuracy of translations of witnesses' testimony wasted time and reflected badly on the "dignity of the trial." As a result, the court ordered that neither side should directly or indirectly criticize any interpreter in open court. Should either counsel be dissatisfied with a translation, they should await the next recess and then lodge their complaints with the chief interpreter. Should the chief interpreter fail to resolve their concerns satisfactorily, the complaining counsel should, as a last resort, request an "off-the-record conference" with the court. Furthermore, the court ruled, neither counsel should ask long, complicated questions or conditional, sarcastic, negative queries. They were to use "short, simple questions as free from artifice as if examining a small child."[33] Such restrictions, the defense believed, impaired the effectiveness of their cross-examination and therefore harmed Yamashita's chances for acquittal.

The court's sensitivity to the length of the trial intensified dramatically on 12 November. MacArthur, concerned lest the court recess in order to allow the defense more time to complete its research on the 26 October supplemental bill of particulars, cautioned Colonel Carpenter in Manila against such a decision. Deputy Chief of Staff Marshall, speaking for his superior, wrote that MacArthur was "disturbed by reports of possible recess" and "doubts need of Defense for more time." Furthermore, he continued, MacArthur "desires proceedings completed [at] earliest practicable date." Marshall's next comment, however, indicated that the general wanted all war-crimes trials promptly concluded, not just Yamashita's.[34] What motivated MacArthur to place renewed emphasis on speed is unclear. Neither the records of Truman, the Joint Chiefs of Staff, nor MacArthur's own headquarters indicate that he was receiving pressure from superiors in Washington. Perhaps he merely wanted to dispose of the proceedings as quickly as possible so he and his staff could focus their attention more fully on postwar reconstruction in the Far East. Or perhaps he thought Truman's 12 September comments not only required him to initiate the trials quickly but also required him to ensure that they dispensed justice swiftly.

Whatever MacArthur's motivation, the military judges in Manila

---

[33]For the court's explanation of its position, see "Memorandum for Members of the Prosecution and Defense Counsel" [n.d.], 201 Yamashita File, box 1217, RG 331. That memorandum had been based upon a proposal to the court by Lieutenant Commander S. C. Bartlett, Jr., chief interpreter for the trial. See memorandum to commission, 10 November 1945, ibid.

[34]Marshall to Major General Whitlock, DC/S for Administration, CinCAFPAC, 12 November 1945, Radiograms, box 1945, RG 331.

responded immediately to his warning. They quickly dispelled the impression they had left with the defense counsel that the court might well grant a temporary delay. "The Commission," Reynolds explained on 12 November, "will grant a continuance only for the most urgent and unavoidable reasons." Since the defense had earlier refused additional counsel and since they believed some of the defense counsel present in the courtroom could be better utilized in preparing a response to the items on the supplemental bill, the five judges, through Reynolds, clearly hinted that they would not look favorably upon any defense request for continuance that cited insufficient time as its justification. Reynolds continued:

> The Court directs both Prosecution and Defense to so organize and direct the preparation of their cases, including the use of assistants, to the end that need to request a continuance may not arise.
>
> As a further means of saving time both Prosecution and Defense are directed to institute procedures by which the Commission is provided essential facts without a mass of non-essentials and immaterial details. We want to know (1) what was done, (2) where it was done, (3) when it was done, [and] (4) who was involved. Go swiftly and directly to the target so the Commission can obtain a clear-cut and accurate understanding of essential facts. Cross-examination must be limited to essentials and avoid useless repetition of questions and answers already before the Commission. We are not interested in trivialities or minutia of events or opinions. Except in unusual or extremely important matters the Commission will itself determine the credibility of witnesses. Extended cross-examinations which savor of fishing expeditions to determine possible attacks upon the credibility of witnesses serve no useful purpose and will be avoided.[35]

Speed had obviously become the key word for the Yamashita court.

Six days following Reynolds's dramatic announcement, Colonel Carpenter, now in Tokyo, informed Major Kerr in a telephone conference call that defense witnesses in Japan would be sent immediately to the

---

[35]Transcript, pp. 1836–37. Reel argues in his book that the defense team simply had no time to train new colleagues in the Yamashita case. *The Case*, pp. 80–81. He also points out that the court "again called senior defense counsel into chambers" on 12 November to indicate its displeasure over a possible request for a recess. Ibid., pp. 80–81; also see p. 39. Both Reel and Guy imply that the departmentalized nature of the defense chores required most of the defense counsel in the courtroom during the trial since no one officer had had time to familiarize himself with all aspects of the case and its 123 charges. See Reel, *The Case*; and Guy, "Defense of Yamashita."

Major Kerr, writing to L. H. Redford on 23 August 1975, claimed that when the trial began Reynolds had informed him that it must be completed within ten days. See Redford, "The Trial of General Tomoyuki Yamashita: A Case in Command Responsibility" (M.A. thesis, Old Dominion University, 1975). Also see Kerr's reference to the commission's haste in his opening address to the court. Transcript, p. 103.

Philippines. But, the Colonel added, "if the defense has more witnesses to call they must do so immediately because the trial will not, repeat, not, be delayed awaiting more witnesses. . . ."[36]

While the court pressed for an early conclusion to the trial, Yamashita's army defense counsel prepared an appeal to the Philippine Supreme Court. Realizing that the Philippine court would require fifteen copies of the trial transcript before it would hear the appeal, defense counsel requested the assistance of the military commission in producing those copies. The commission refused. So, too, did Lieutenant General Styer when the defense counsel appealed for his assistance.[37] Despite such lack of cooperation, however, the defense prepared its own copies by working at night following their daily labors in court.[38]

By the second week of November the defense had submitted the appeal and the necessary transcripts to the Philippine court. That court then routinely instructed its assistant bailiff to serve a summons on General Styer who had established the commission and who held Yamashita in confinement. The summons simply required Styer to respond to the appeal in person or in writing within five days. Julio S. Arzadon, assistant bailiff, arrived at Styer's office on 13 November and explained to an American major his mission and his need to see the general. The major carried the summons to Styer, who discussed it with a member of his staff for ten to fifteen minutes. Rather than formally accept the document, Styer returned the summons to the major who returned it to Arzadon, instructing the assistant bailiff to return the next morning after the general had had more time to secure additional counsel in the matter. When Arzadon returned the following morning, he discovered that "General Styer was out the whole day on an airplane trip" and had left no instructions relating to the papers. Citing the absence of instructions, Styer's staff refused to accept the summons and once again notified Arzadon that he should return the next morning.[39]

MacArthur wholeheartedly approved his subordinate's decision to avoid the bailiff. Within twenty-four hours of Arzadon's first appearance, Marshall ordered that Styer's headquarters be informed that "under no circumstances" should it recognize the jurisdiction of the Philippine

---

[36]Telephone conference call between Colonel Carpenter and Colonel Fulcher in Tokyo and Lieutenant Colonel Meek, Lieutenant Colonel Morgan, Major Kerr, and Captain Hill in Manila, 18 November 1945, Radiograms, box 1945, RG 331.

[37]Reel, *The Case*, pp. 185–86. Also see Clarke to Styer [n.d.], 000.5 Yamashita, box 763, RG 331. Although MacArthur's headquarters also saw that request, it refused to comment on the matter since Styer on 10 November already had rejected Clarke's request.

[38]Reel, *The Case*, pp. 186–87.

[39]Memorandum to chief justice from Arzadon, 14 November 1945, 000.5 Yamashita, box 763, RG 331.

Supreme Court.[40] MacArthur's staff repeated those same instructions on the fifteenth and again on the eighteenth.[41] On the latter date, for example, Colonel Carpenter notified Major Kerr that the supreme commander not only opposed the appearance of representatives of the prosecution or of Styer's staff before the Supreme Court of the Philippines, but that he also opposed—indeed as commander in chief forbade—any member of the Philippine army from appearing.[42] The judgment of Yamashita, Carpenter exclaimed, must remain in the hands of the military commission. "No outside interference will be countenanced," he concluded, "and any order issued by the Philippine Supreme Court will be ignored."

While Styer studiously avoided the formal serving of the summons, Major Kerr completed the prosecution's case on 20 November. As soon as he had done so, Colonel Clarke urged the court to acquit Yamashita. The prosecution, he emphasized, had failed to present direct evidence that Yamashita had ordered or permitted the commission of the atrocities. Then, when the court failed to follow his suggestion, Carpenter quickly moved for a continuance to allow his defense team more time to prepare its position on charges contained in the supplemental bill. Citing its 12 November declaration, the court refused to grant that requested continuance. It would, however, allow the defense to delay the presentation of its case until 0830 hours on 21 November. That reprieve gave the defense counsel an extra twenty-two and one-half hours to develop their case, provided they went without sleep.[43]

Almost simultaneously with the beginning of their presentation of evidence to the military commission, the defense attorneys presented their oral arguments to the Philippine Supreme Court.[44] Not only did MacArthur and Styer's military commission lack authority to try Yamashita, they argued, but it also had failed to charge Yamashita with any traditional violation of the law of war. Any remote hope that the defense may have harbored that the Philippine justices would actually intervene on Yamashita's behalf collapsed on 27 November. On that date the justices denied the defense petition. They argued that their tribunal lacked jurisdiction over the U.S. Army, and that the military commission trying

---

[40]See Major General Whitlock to CinCAFPAC Advance, 13 November 1945, and Marshall to Whitlock, 14 November 1945, 000.5 Yamashita, box 763, RG 331.

[41]Marshall to Whitlock, 15 November 1945, Yamashita File, Radios, box 1945, RG 331; telephone conference call between Tokyo and Manila, 18 November 1945, Radiograms, 1945–49, box 1945, RG 331.

[42]Since the Philippines legally remained American territory, MacArthur, even disregarding his role as field marshal of the Philippines, controlled the Filipino forces.

[43]Transcript, pp. 2946–55.

[44]Major George Guy and Lieutenant Colonel Walter Hendrix presented the defense case. See Guy, "The Defense of Yamashita," pp. 168–71.

Yamashita, in their opinion and contrary to defense arguments, had been "validly constituted" by General Styer.[45]

Anticipating that negative vote, defense counsel already had dispatched an appeal to the U.S. Supreme Court. Had the defense not taken that rather unorthodox step and had the Philippine court delayed judgment until the regular trial had ended, as defense feared, Yamashita might have been executed before the justices in Washington could act.[46] Since it would take a minimum of seven days to get the necessary briefs and papers to the American judges following the conclusion of the military trial, MacArthur could have legally executed Yamashita before the Supreme Court had even received the appeal.[47] The defense counsel planned to deny MacArthur that opportunity.

Colonel Abe Goff, acting director of the U.S. War Crimes Office, who had opposed MacArthur's decision to boycott the Philippine Supreme Court proceedings, informed the judge advocate general in Washington that Styer would fly to Tokyo to discuss this latest defense appeal with MacArthur personally.[48] MacArthur met Styer for one and one-half hours on 30 November and then lunched with him immediately thereafter.[49] While the files of neither MacArthur nor Styer reveal the nature of those discussions, the supreme commander probably continued to reject the right of civil courts, whether Philippine or American, to hear the case. That at least was his position when he cabled the War Department on 8 December: "It is believed that the Supreme Court has no jurisdiction and the military authorities propose to proceed in normal military jurisprudence with the case."[50] According to the 24 September charter, that normal procedure would entail, if Yamashita were sentenced to death, a review by Styer's headquarters and then by MacArthur himself. Once approved, execution would follow. Those findings were, as the 24 September charter so concisely noted, "not subject to review."[51]

While MacArthur and Styer considered reaction to the defense's appellate maneuverings, the trial of Yamashita finallly ground to a close. In his summation on 5 December, Major Kerr reaffirmed his conviction that Yamashita should be found guilty for failing to exercise control over personnel under his command. Following Kerr's closing remarks, General

---

[45]The Philippine Supreme Court to Styer, 28 November 1945, box 2002, RG 331.

[46]Normal procedure would have entailed waiting until the Philippine court had delivered its verdict.

[47]Naturally, Yamashita could have been executed only if found guilty and sentenced to death by the court.

[48]Goff memorandum to Cramer, 28 November 1945, Y119-3-4, RG 153.

[49]Daily appointments, 30 November 1945, box 2, RG 5.

[50]CinCAFPAC Advance to WARTAG, 000.5 Yamashita, box 763, RG 331.

[51]Transcript, p. 16.

Reynolds made one final surprise announcement—the court would deliver its verdict within forty-six hours.

When the court reconvened, the session was short. Within fifteen minutes Yamashita knew his fate:

> It is absurd [General Reynolds explained] to consider a commander a murderer or rapist because one of his soldiers commits a murder or rape. Nevertheless, where murder and rape and vicious, revengeful actions are widespread offenses, and there is no effective attempt by a commander to discover and control the criminal acts, such a commander may be held responsible, even criminally liable, for the lawless acts of his troops, depending upon their nature and the circumstances surrounding them.

The violations of the law of war that occurred in the Philippines while Yamashita commanded the 14th Area Army, Reynolds continued, "were not sporadic in nature." As a result, the court believes that "you failed to provide effective control of your troops as was required by the circumstances. . . . Accordingly, the Commission finds you guilty as charged and sentences you to death by hanging."[52] The date upon which the court had chosen to render its verdict was 7 December 1945, the fourth anniversary of the devastating Japanese attack on Pearl Harbor that had catapulted the United States into the Pacific conflict.

---

[52]Ibid., pp. 4061–63.

CHAPTER FIVE
IN RE YAMASHITA

In the waning days of 1945 ten men stood between General Tomoyuki Yamashita and death. He could escape hanging only if either Lieutenant General Wilhelm Styer or General Douglas MacArthur, in their mandatory reviews, decided to commute or reduce the commission's verdict, or if the eight justices of the U.S. Supreme Court, acting on the 25 November appeal, overturned that verdict on constitutional grounds.[1] Having already dispatched their appeal to the Court, the defense attorneys at the end of the trial focused their attention on the clemency option. In messages to both Styer and MacArthur, which emphasized the novelty of the charges, they urged them, at the very least, to reduce the sentence:

> This is the first time in modern history that a commanding officer has been held criminally liable for acts committed by his troops. It is the first time in modern history that any man has been held criminally liable for acts which according to the conclusion of the Commission do not involve criminal intent or even gross negligence. The Commission therefore by its findings created a new crime. The accused could not have known, nor could a sage have predicted, that at some time in the future a Military Commission would decree acts which involved no criminal intent or gross negligence to be a crime, and it is unjust, therefore, that the punishment for that crime should be the supreme penalty.[2]

Surely, they reasoned, both generals could see that the retroactive application of the new concept of command responsibility was inherently unfair and warranted clemency.

Colonel Chas Young, Styer's staff judge advocate, could not accept the defense arguments.[3] Reviewing the trial records in light of the defense appeal, he recommended on 9 December that Styer approve Yamashita's execution. Not only did he accept the Lapus and Galang

---

[1]Associate Justice Robert Jackson, chief prosecutor at Nuremberg, did not participate in the Yamashita decision.

[2]The defense clemency petition to Styer and MacArthur is located in Y119-3, book 34, p. 2, Washington National Records Center, Suitland, MD.

[3]For Young's review, see Y119-3A: Reviews.

testimony without reservation, but he also concluded that the enormity
and widespread nature of the offenses must have been deliberately
planned. "It is impossible to escape the conclusion," he wrote, "that
[Yamashita] knew or had the means to know of the widespread commission of atrocities. . . . His failure to inform himself . . . of what was
common knowledge throughout his command and throughout the civilian
population can only be considered as criminal dereliction of duty on his
part." Young's observations hinged on major assumptions that had not
been proven by the prosecution. He assumed that Yamashita must have
known of the crimes, although the prosecution had been unable to prove
that he had indeed known. He assumed that Yamashita had the means to
know, even though the testimony indicated that that was simply not the
case. He assumed that the atrocities were common knowledge throughout
the Japanese command, an assumption not borne out by trial testimony.
And he assumed that the atrocities were common knowledge throughout the
civilian population, a fact not clearly proven in the trial transcript. Given
such suppositions, however, his final recommendation that Styer uphold
the court's verdict logically followed.

It was a recommendation Lieutenant General Styer decided to
accept. On 12 December, following receipt of Young's analysis of the
case, Styer officially declined to commute or reduce the commission's
sentence.[4] Yamashita's fate now rested in the hands of MacArthur and the
justices of the Supreme Court.

Colonel C. M. Ollivetti, MacArthur's theater judge advocate,
discussed both Styer's ruling and the commission's findings with four
members of his staff before submitting his own observations on the case to
his supreme commander.[5] Reluctant to base his reasoning and recommendations as directly and as heavily upon unproven assumptions as had
Young, Ollivetti simply recounted prosecution and defense testimony,
emphasizing in the process the responsibility of individual officers to
control their men. "Since the duty rests on a commander to protect by
every means in his power both the civilian population and prisoners of war
from wrongful acts of his command," he argued in his formal memorandum to MacArthur, "and since the failure to discharge that duty is a
violation of the Laws of War, there is no reason, either in law or morality,
why he should not be held criminally responsible for permitting such
violations by his subordinates, even though that action has heretofore
seldom or never been taken." That Yamashita expected the Americans to
believe that he knew nothing of the war crimes seemed incredible to
Ollivetti. "Surely, a matter so important as the massacre of 8,000 people

---

[4]Ibid.
[5]Ibid.

by the Japanese troops [in Manila, for example] must necessarily have been reported," he wrote. His astonishment and skepticism that combat circumstances could precipitate such a complete collapse of communication simply echoed that of Major Kerr and the prosecution, the five-man military commission, Colonel Young, and Lieutenant General Styer. Troubled by the enormity and the widespread nature of the offenses, Ollivetti could not justify a recommendation to MacArthur favoring clemency. Instead, he concluded that MacArthur should deny the defense appeal for leniency and approve Yamashita's sentence.

Had the review process unfolded according to the plan outlined in the 24 September regulations, MacArthur would have studied the commission's findings, Styer's review, Ollivetti's opinion, the defense petition, and perhaps even the trial transcript, and would have issued the final ruling sealing Yamashita's fate.[6] The defense appeal of 25 November to the nation's highest judicial tribunal, however, scuttled that process.

Angered that the defense hoped to circumvent his 24 September regulations, which limited review to Styer and himself, MacArthur notified the War Department on 8 December that he believed the U.S. Supreme Court lacked jurisdiction.[7] Therefore, he planned to dispose of the Yamashita case according to the procedures outlined in his earlier regulations. That surprising declaration prompted an immediate response from Secretary of War Robert Patterson. Reading Patterson's communiqué, MacArthur angrily realized that the defense counsel had temporarily blocked his ability to determine Yamashita's fate. Anxious to curb his sometimes impetuous subordinate, Patterson had simply ordered MacArthur to suspend implementation of the commission's verdict until the Supreme Court evaluated the defense petition.[8]

Eight days later on 17 December the Supreme Court stayed all further proceedings in the Yamashita case.[9] Even if Secretary Patterson had changed his mind, after that date neither he nor MacArthur could legally authorize the execution of Yamashita. A stay of execution issued by the Court could only be lifted by the Court. Nevertheless, as the defense counsel acutely realized, that court order offered only a momentary reprieve. Should the justices vote not to hear oral arguments on the case, they would quickly lift their stay, permitting Yamashita's execution, perhaps before Christmas. The order of the seventeenth had simply

---

[6]For a copy of the 24 September 1945 regulations, see Transcript, pp. 6–16.
[7]000.5 Yamashita, box 763, RG 331.
[8]ServJag to MacArthur and Styer, 9 December 1945, ibid.
[9]File 000.5 (10-4-45), box 311, RG 165, Records of War Department General Staff, Washington National Records Center, Suitland, MD.

assured the justices that Yamashita would not hang until they could debate the merits of the defense appeal.

Although the justices completed some of their preliminary preparations for a debate on 18 December, the defense petition on Yamashita's behalf did not come up for formal discussion until late afternoon on the nineteenth. Had any justice anticipated a quick resolution of the issues he was disillusioned. The initial two-hour debate revealed only that the justices could reach no agreement on whether to hear oral arguments. Nor did a three-hour session the next morning resolve that issue. Not until the conclusion of a one- and one-quarter-hour afternoon session did a badly divided Court finally reach a decision. The justices, the defense and prosecution learned, would hear oral arguments on 7 January 1946, following the Court's regular Christmas recess.[10]

On 10 December, ten days before the Court had even agreed to hear oral presentations, Colonel Clarke requested military authorization for the defense to fly to Washington where it could "expedite proceedings." Styer rejected that request, notifying MacArthur's headquarters of his action.[11] But the Court's subsequent announcement dramatically altered the circumstances. The defense's journey to Washington would no longer be a fishing expedition but would have a definite purpose: to prepare its brief and its oral arguments in anticipation of the 7 January confrontation. Whether Styer, on his own initiative, would have reversed his earlier decision is unknown. He received no such opportunity. Secretary of War Patterson, acting upon a suggestion by the Supreme Court, ordered MacArthur to permit three members of the defense team to fly to Washington. MacArthur, in turn, ordered Styer to comply.[12]

On 7 December, Yamashita's fate had rested in the hands of five U.S. Army generals; on 7 January 1946 it lay in the hands of eight U.S Supreme Court justices. Those justices, however, would render judgment on constitutional issues and not on the military commission's findings of fact. The nature of the defense arguments, therefore, would have to differ

---

[10]Diary of Harold Burton, 18, 19, and 20 December 1945, box 1, Papers of Harold Burton, Library of Congress Manuscript Division (hereafter cited as Burton Papers). For the Court's ruling, see clerk of the Supreme Court to secretary of war, 20 December 1945, 000.5 (10-4-45), box 311, RG 165.

[11]AFWESPAC to CinCAFPAC Advance, 000.5 Yamashita, box 763, RG 331. MacArthur's headquarters merely acknowledged receipt of the message; the decision was Styer's alone.

[12]ServJag to CinCAFPAC Advance, 22 December 1945, ibid. MacArthur's headquarters notified Colonel Clarke by telephone on 23 December. See Yamashita files, Radios, box 1945, RG 331. The cost of dispatching the three officers to Washington was $3,256.96. When defense counsel arrived in Washington, the judge advocate general appointed a specialist in international law to assist them in the preparation of their case. See A. Frank Reel, *The Case of General Yamashita* (1949; reprint ed., New York: Octagon Books, 1971), p. 210.

dramatically from those elaborated in the High Commissioner's ballroom in Manila.

Rather than discuss battle conditions in the Philippines, or diversity of command, or interservice coordination, the defense chose three issues that they hoped would convince a majority of the justices to reverse the 7 December verdict.[13] Reflecting arguments used earlier by Lieutenant Colonel Walter Hendrix in his appearance before the Philippine Supreme Court, Captain Reel questioned the legality of the military commission that had tried his client. Although Japan and the United States had not as yet formally agreed to a peace treaty, Reel argued that the cessation of hostilities, coupled with the normal operation of government in the Philippines in late 1945, voided the right of MacArthur to appoint a military commission. Reel conceded that the use of military commissions in active battle zones seemed justifiable, but their use on Luzon in October 1945, weeks after active resistance had ceased, appeared both ill-advised and illegal. Once the disrupting effect of combat ceased, normal judicial procedures should have been reinstated. MacArthur's failure to make that vital adjustment, in Reel's opinion, justified an invalidation of the military commission's verdict.

Colonel Clarke, offering the Court a second legal reason for overturning the Yamashita verdict, also questioned the commission's authority. Since the U.S. Army had failed to charge the 14th Area Army commander with a traditional violation of the law of war, he argued that Yamashita's trial was illegal and his sentence without validity. The charges levied by the military authorities, Clarke continued, involved the "novel concept" of command responsibility, a concept not supported by legal precedent. "It is a basic premise of all civilized criminal justice," he had written in the defense brief, "that punishment is adjudged not according to status, but according to fault, and that one man is not held to answer for the crime of another." Restating that basic premise, the colonel reasoned that the Supreme Court should overturn the verdict of the Manila commission.[14]

Captain Milton Sandberg, the third member of the defense team, offered the Court yet another legal reason that justified invalidation of the Yamashita verdict. He emphasized that section of the defense brief that

---

[13]The following paragraphs examining the defense position are based on the defense's initial petition and its brief to the Court. Both are found in Y119-3A. Also see Yamashita file, box 283, Papers of Hugo Black, Library of Congress Manuscript Division (hereafter cited as Black Papers). Reel outlines the topics he, Clarke, and Sandberg presented to the Court in *The Case*, pp. 210–12. Also see Yamashita vs. Patterson, box 149, Burton Papers; and Stone's synopsis of the arguments in Yamashita vs. Styer, *U.S. Supreme Court Reports*, 90 L. Ed. 499.

[14]90 L. Ed. 499.

argued "that the directive governing the Commission and its operations . . . constituted such extreme departures from basic standards of fairness that [Yamashita] did not have a fair trial."[15] He specifically attacked the admission into evidence of hearsay testimony, depositions, and affidavits received over defense objections. As the defense had noted earlier in its brief, Article of War 38, passed by the U.S. Congress, clearly stated that evidence before military commissions should reflect standard rules of evidence insofar as possible and unless altered by the president. Since Article of War 25 clearly prohibited depositions as evidence in capital cases, and since traditional military justice absolutely prohibited the use of hearsay testimony and permitted the use of affidavits only with defense approval, the 24 September regulations unquestionably violated Article 38.[16] The admission of such "highly unorthodox and prejudicial evidence," contrary to the wishes of Congress, Sandberg observed, alone should convince the Court that Yamashita had been illegally tried and sentenced.

Solicitor General J. Howard McGrath quickly attacked each of the three major issues raised by Reel, Clarke, and Sandberg.[17] First, he reminded the Court, President Roosevelt had specifically ordered that the trial of the German saboteurs in 1942 be before a military commission. Even though that commission had convened in Washington, DC, which lay well outside the actual combat zones, it had not been declared illegal. Indeed, the Supreme Court had upheld the president's power to appoint such a commission. Furthermore, McGrath noted that military commissions, contrary to Reel's argument, traditionally ceased functioning only after the signing of a formal treaty of peace rather than after the actual cessation of hostilities.

Turning to Clarke's charge that Yamashita had not been accused of a violation of the law of war, McGrath faulted the colonel for ignoring three crucial international agreements: Articles 1 and 43 of the annex to the Fourth Hague Convention, Article 19 of the Tenth Hague Convention, and Article 26 of the Geneva Red Cross Convention of 1929. All imposed grave responsibilities on military commanders, responsibilities that Yamashita had ignored.[18] And Sandberg's assertions that the safeguards provided ordinary defendants under the articles of war should apply to Yamashita were equally erroneous. The U.S. Congress, McGrath noted, never intended the articles to apply to an enemy officer charged with war-crimes violations.

---

[15]Ibid.

[16]For the text of Articles 25 and 38, see Appendix in this volume, p. 143.

[17]The following paragraphs examining the solicitor general's position are based on his brief and arguments found in Y119-3A, and in box 283, Black Papers. Also see Stone's synopsis in 90 L. Ed. 499.

[18]For the text of these articles, see Appendix in this volume, pp. 143–44. Defense believed none of these articles applied to Yamashita.

In his brief, and again in his oral arguments, the solicitor general moved beyond the mere demolition of the defense case. He pointedly reminded the justices that they should not interfere in the war-crimes process. Intervention would place the Court in a policymaking position. "Are the civil courts to assume the burden of deciding in what manner the policy of the United States with respect to war criminals is to be carried out?" "Is the pledge of the swift punishment of war criminals given by two Chief Executives of the United States, Presidents Roosevelt and Truman, and supported by a Joint Resolution of the Congress, to be thwarted by lengthy appeals to the civil courts?"[19] By raising those two pivotal questions, McGrath knowingly touched a notable sensitivity, made tender in the bitter debate over Roosevelt's court-packing plan of 1937. While Roosevelt's political maneuver to undermine a conservative majority, which he believed had unacceptably hindered his recovery measures, had failed, the reverberations of that failure still could be felt in 1946. Lest any justice had forgotten that political battle nine years earlier, the solicitor general's pointed questions starkly reminded him that the Court should seriously consider the political as well as legal ramifications of any decision, especially one that placed it at loggerheads with the two popularly elected branches of government.

Not until Saturday, 12 January, during the Court's regular conference on pending cases, did the eight Supreme Court justices debate the merits of the government and defense arguments.[20] Chief Justice Harlan Fiske Stone and Associate Justices Felix Frankfurter, William O. Douglas, and Stanley Reed found McGrath's arguments more convincing. Associate Justice Hugo Black, although disagreeing with McGrath's legal reasoning, reached the same conclusion as the solicitor general: Yamashita's conviction should not be overturned. Of the remaining justices, Wiley B. Rutledge and Frank Murphy definitely harbored serious reservations about the government's position, while Harold Burton probably expressed similar, although much less strident, misgivings.

Emerging from that Saturday conference, the justices agreed that Chief Justice Stone, who had written the Quirin decision, also would write the majority opinion of this war-crimes case. An advocate of judicial restraint, Stone was a twenty-year veteran of the Court and the only current member who had served during the Roosevelt court-packing

---

[19]McGrath brief in Y119-3A and in box 283, Black Papers. For the presidential and congressional pledges, see Chapter Two.

[20]See Burton Diary, 12 January 1946, box 1. Also see Burton's conference notes in box 149, Burton Papers; and Rutledge's conference notes in box 137, Papers of Wiley B. Rutledge, Library of Congress Manuscript Division (hereafter cited as Rutledge Papers). Both men comment on the positions of their fellow justices.

battle.[21] Stone's judicial restraint, however, antedated the 1937 fight. His sharp dissent, written in 1936 in response to the Court's invalidation of certain sections of Roosevelt's Agricultural Adjustment Act, for example, reflected his concern over unwise judicial meddling with measures supported by the two popularly elected branches of government. Troubled that his conservative brethren invalidated New Deal measures because of personal philosophies rather than firm legal reasons, he pointedly emphasized "that courts are concerned only with the power [of Congress] to enact statutes, not with their wisdom." The ballot offered adequate relief from foolish, but legal, legislation. Given the nature of American government, Stone concluded, "the only check upon [the Court's] exercise of power is our own sense of self-restraint." Therefore, when considering overturning actions of either Congress or the president, justices should remember that "courts are not the only agency of government that must be assumed to have a capacity to govern."[22]

Although Roosevelt's blatant attempts to curb the Court's interference in 1937 had failed, that event only strengthened Stone's belief that the Court must tread carefully. Upon assuming the mantle of chief justice in 1941, Stone believed that it was his responsibility to steer his sometimes obstinate brethren along responsible legal paths, which avoided unnecessary and legally questionable challenges to the powers of Congress and/or the president.[23] According to C. Herman Pritchett, noted scholar of the Roosevelt court, the justices under Stone's guidance more frequently issued decisions that reflected "a marked judicial deference toward Congress, a change which signalled the Court's acceptance of its limitations as a policy-forming agency."[24]

Stone also practiced what he preached. During the Nuremberg trials, for example, he refrained from publicly attacking the proceedings although he found them deeply disturbing. While the concept that the victor had the authority to punish the vanquished did not greatly distress him, Washington's assertions that legal, common-law safeguards protected the defendants did. Writing to a friend in December 1945, Stone admitted his displeasure with Associate Justice Robert Jackson, who, against his wishes, had become chief prosecutor at Nuremberg, and with

---

[21]For a fuller discussion of Stone's judicial philosophy, see Alpheus T. Mason, *Harlan Fiske Stone: Pillar of the Law* (New York: Viking Press, 1956). Also see C. Herman Pritchett, *The Roosevelt Court: A Study in Judicial Politics and Values, 1937–1947* (New York: Macmillan Co., 1948).

[22]297 U.S. 78–88.

[23]For Stone's sometimes humorous characterizations of his obstinate brethren, see Stone to Sterling Carr, 22 March 1943, 13 June 1943, 17 February 1944, 16 June 1944, and 26 February 1945, box 9, Papers of Harlan Fiske Stone, Library of Congress Manuscript Division (hereafter cited as Stone Papers).

[24]Pritchett, *Study in Judicial Politics*, p. 72.

the European proceedings in general. He wrote: "Jackson is over conducting his high-grade lynching party in Nuremberg. . . . I don't mind what
he does to the Nazis, but I hate to see the pretense that he is running a
court or proceeding according to common law. That is a little too sancti-
monious a fraud to meet my old-fashioned ideas."[25] But that was the
private Stone. Officially he kept his reservations to himself.

Despite his criticism of Jackson and Nuremberg, and despite the
similarities of procedure between the European trial and the proceedings
in Manila, Stone planned in January 1946 to uphold the government's
power to try to execute Yamashita. All that remained was the drafting of
an opinion that satisfied a majority of his brethren. Based on the
12 January conference and on a letter he had received three days later, Stone
realized that his strongest supporter on the bench would be Frankfurter.[26]
An avid advocate of judicial restraint, Frankfurter shared Stone's fear of
unnecessary and unwise judicial interference with the other branches of
government. Should either or both of those branches decide to retaliate
against the Court, as Roosevelt had done in 1937, Frankfurter feared for
the Court's prestige, power, and effectiveness. To prevent just such a
confrontation in 1946, he favored basing the Yamashita decision on the
narrowest possible constitutional grounds. Having done so, the Court
could easily defend its judgment and undercut its critics. Frankfurter
fervently believed that war-crimes policy formulation must remain in the
hands of the two popularly elected branches and not in those of the judicial
organ.[27]

Stone also realized that he could probably count on the support of
Douglas and Reed, judging from their positions at the 12 January conference.[28] Any doubts he may have entertained of their approval vanished
on 22 January when he circulated his first Yamashita draft. "You have
done a grand job," Douglas informed him. Reed also labeled his decision

---

[25]Stone to Carr, 4 December 1945, box 9, Stone Papers. Also see Stone to Carr,
13 April 1946, box 9: Stone to Louis Lusky, 13 November 1945, box 19; and Stone to
Luther Smith, 2 January 1946, box 27.

[26]Conference notes, box 149, Burton Papers; conference notes, box 137, Rut-
ledge Papers; Frankfurter to Stone, 15 January 1946, box 106, Papers of Felix Frankfurter,
Library of Congress Manuscript Division. For Frankfurter's letter, also see box 73, Stone
Papers.

[27]For a sample of Frankfurter's logic, see 335 U.S. 538ff.; and 323 U.S. 224. For
a fuller discussion of Frankfurter's views on judicial restraint, the separation of powers, and
due process of law, see Philip B. Kurland's *Mr. Justice Frankfurter and the Constitution*
(Chicago: University of Chicago Press, 1971), chapts. 2, 5, 11; and Helen S. Thomas's *Felix
Frankfurter: Scholar on the Bench* (Baltimore: Johns Hopkins Press, 1960).

[28]Conference notes, box 149, Burton Papers; and conference notes, box 137, Rutledge Papers. Douglas had not even wanted the Court to hear oral arguments on the
Yamashita case. See William O. Douglas, "Memorandum for Conference," 20 December
1945, box 137, Rutledge Papers.

as "a fine piece of work," although he suggested certain problems with a few of the legal arguments. Nevertheless, Reed indicated his willingness to support the decision.[29]

The favorable responses of Frankfurter, Douglas, and Reed probably convinced Stone that obtaining a majority would be easier than perhaps originally expected. Whatever his motivation, the chief justice urged his brethren on the twenty-second to be prepared to issue its Yamashita ruling on 28 January rather than on 4 February, the date chosen during the conference on the twelfth.[30] That change of plan left the chief justice six days to secure the support of at least one additional justice so that his opinion would achieve majority support. In fact, Stone knew on the twenty-second that Black would support the conclusion of the majority but not its reasoning.[31]

Although Black had been one of the four justices in December who was desirous of hearing Yamashita's appeal, by mid-January he had decided that the case lay outside the Court's jurisdiction.[32] Therefore, he could easily accept Stone's rejection of the defense petition. It was Stone's implication in his first draft that Yamashita had been tried according to constitutional due process that prevented Black from agreeing whole-heartedly with the majority opinion. In Black's estimation, Yamashita had not been tried in conformity with the constitutional standards of due process of law. But then, as far as the Supreme Court was concerned, it made no difference whether he had been tried by those standards or not. The reasoning that justified such a conclusion, Black argued, was simple. The Court lacked authority "to regulate military proceedings intended to punish enemy combatants." The military, Black asserted, "has final power

---

[29]Douglas to Stone, 22 January 1946; two letters from Reed to Stone, 22 January 1946, box 73, Stone Papers. For a copy of Stone's first draft, which contains marginal comments by Frankfurter, see "Yamashita v. Styer," ibid. For Stone's second draft, which incorporated the Reed and Frankfurter criticisms, see the document in box 73 labeled "With additions of Jan. 22, 1946." Also see Stone's "Memorandum for the Court," 22 January 1946, box 283, and 23 January 1945, box 73. The labeled document is somewhat misleading. That draft did not circulate on the twenty-second, although Stone had decided to make the revisions on that date. Circulation probably came either late on the twenty-third or the twenty-fourth.

[30]Stone's memorandum to Court, 22 January 1946, box 71, Papers of Frank Murphy, Michigan Historical Collections, Bentley Historical Library, University of Michigan, Ann Arbor (hereafter cited as Murphy Papers). Also see Rutledge to John Frank, 13 and 22 February 1946, box 137, Rutledge Papers; Fowler Harper, *Justice Rutledge and the Bright Constellation* (New York: Bobbs-Merrill, 1965), pp. 185–89; and John P. Frank, *Marble Palace: The Supreme Court in American Life* (New York: Alfred A. Knopf, 1961), pp. 136–37.

[31]Black to Stone, 22 January 1946, box 283, Black Papers.

[32]Black's conference memorandum, 19 December 1945, box 283, Black Papers. Murphy, Rutledge, and Burton were probably the other justices who voted to accept the case. See Rutledge to Frank, 13 and 22 February 1946, box 137, Rutledge Papers.

to establish rules of war and to enforce them against the enemy." Since he believed that Yamashita's trial fell within the realm of legitimate military power, the Court could not intervene by citing violations of due process.[33]

If Black carried through with his intention of writing a concurring opinion, Stone needed additional support from the three remaining justices so as to give greater strength to his formal opinion. The chief justice realized that he would receive no such support from Murphy. Following the conclusion of the 12 January conference, Murphy had begun the preparation of his dissent, even before Stone had completed his own opinion. Murphy's action was not surprising. In his role as the U.S. attorney general and as associate justice of the Supreme Court, he already had gained a reputation for his devotion to civil liberties. In 1939, in his remarks to the U.S. Conference of Mayors in New York City, he had argued: "You begin to undermine democracy the moment you begin to draw the line and say that this or that person or group shall not have civil liberty. Draw the line against one group and it is an easy step to draw it against another and then another."[34] So devoted to this concept was he that his biographer notes that after 1943 "his votes were virtually predictable in favor of individual claimants in civil liberties cases. . . . Lawyers soon learned that Murphy . . . could be expected to lend sympathetic ears to any plausible plea of infringed personal freedom."[35] In addition, Murphy had not developed a reputation of being a team player. He often dissented vigorously. Those dissents, he revealed to an acquaintance in 1943, when on behalf of just causes, ensured him of "inward peace" in the future.[36] Murphy's past performance, therefore, indicated that Stone had little chance of securing his support for the majority opinion.

The chief justice, however, had hopes of securing the support of

[33]Ibid. For further elaboration of Black's criticisms, see his various drafts of his anticipated *Yamashita* concurring opinion in box 283. For a fuller discussion of Black's general judicial philosophy, see Hugo Black, *A Constitutional Faith* (New York: Alfred A. Knopf, 1969); and John P. Frank, *Mr. Justice Black: The Man and His Opinions* (New York: Alfred A. Knopf, 1949). Also see Black's comments on the powers of the Supreme Court, delivered while he was a member of the U.S. Senate. U.S., Congress, Senate, *Congressional Record*, 75th Cong., 1st sess., 81, pt. 9: app., pp. 224, 306–7.

[34]A copy of that address is found in "Frank Murphy: Civil Liberties and the Cities," *Vital Speeches* 5 (15 June 1939): 542–44.

[35]J. Woodford Howard, Jr., *Mr. Justice Murphy: A Political Biography* (Princeton: Princeton University Press, 1968), p. 341. Also see Murphy's commencement address to John Marshall College, 21 June 1939, in U.S., Senate, Congress, *Congressional Record*, 76th Congress., 1st sess., 84, pt. 13: app., p. 2922; his letters to Black in "Special Correspondence: Frank Murphy, 1939–1969," box 61, Black Papers; and Black's eulogy for Murphy, ibid.

[36]Quoted in Howard, *Murphy*, p. 322. Also see Murphy to Fred Nolan, 8 February 1945, box 44, Murphy Papers.

Burton and Rutledge. Burton obviously had reservations about Stone's draft. As his desk calendar indicates, the Yamashita case and Stone's opinion consumed a considerable portion of his time during the week of 21 January.[37] But while he had not joined the majority, he also had not come out in opposition. Stone's argument relating to judicial self-restraint may well have reminded Burton of Truman's words in September 1945 when the president had asked him to become an associate justice: "I want someone who will do a thoroughly judicial job and not legislate."[38] Mary Berry, Burton's biographer, argues that the justice believed in "judicial restraint, executive discretion, and legislative supremacy under the war powers."[39] As a newcomer to the bench and as a justice who, as of 22 January, had not yet delivered a formal opinion for the Court, Burton was perhaps viewed by Stone as a likely convert to his reasoning.

Convincing Rutledge would be more taxing. Unlike Burton, Rutledge had decided to dissent. But Stone, who had not lamented Murphy's loss, was unwilling to accept this defection without a fight. However, his reasoned arguments and his vigorous efforts to swing his colleague into line failed to convert Rutledge. His unsuccessful maneuvering merely resulted in the postponement of the Yamashita decision from the twenty-eighth to the original date of 4 February.[40]

When Stone formally announced the Court's decision on the first Monday in February, he did so with the support of Frankfurter, Reed, Douglas, Black, and Burton.[41] He began with reference to the Quirin decision, which demonstrated that Congress, by passing the articles of war, had recognized and sanctioned the use of military tribunals to try war criminals. The 1942 decision also had acknowledged that the only judicial review granted by Congress concerning military tribunals came under the habeas corpus power of the Court.[42] The logic of that decision, Stone continued, prompted the present Court to rule that military commissions "are not courts whose rulings and judgments are made subject to review by this court." Applying the habeas corpus power to the Yamashita case limited the Court's review to two crucial questions: Did the government have the right to detain Yamashita for trial? Did the military tribunals have

---

[37]Burton Diary (1946), box 1.

[38]Burton Diary (1945), 17 September, box 1.

[39]Mary F. Berry, *Stability, Security and Continuity: Mr. Justice Burton and Decision-Making in the Supreme Court, 1945–1958* (Westport, CT: Greenwood Press, 1978), p. 40.

[40]Mason, *Stone*, p. 671n; Harper, *Rutledge*, pp. 185–89.

[41]The following discussion of the judicial opinions of Stone, Murphy, and Rutledge, unless otherwise noted, is based on the formal opinions delivered in the case. See 90 L. Ed. 499.

[42]Stone's opinion, while narrowly defining the Supreme Court's power of review, rejected Roosevelt's statement denying the saboteurs any access to civil courts. See Stone to Carr, 17 November 1942, box 9, Stone Papers.

lawful authority in this instance to try and condemn him? If the government had detained Yamashita legally, and if the tribunal had exercised legal authority, then any decision by that tribunal "is not subject to judicial review merely because they have made a wrong decision on disputed facts. Correction of their errors of decision is not for the courts but for the military authorities which are alone authorized to review their decisions." If, on the other hand, the government or the military tribunal had acted illegally in either detaining or trying the accused, then the verdict and sentence imposed on Yamashita could be clearly overthrown by the Supreme Court.

In order to determine the answers to these two key questions, Stone's opinion addressed five major issues: Was the military commission that tried Yamashita lawfully created? Could Yamashita be legally tried before a military commission after hostilities had ended? Was Yamashita charged with a violation of the law of war? Was the admission of evidence used to convict Yamashita in violation of Articles of War 25 and 38 and in violation of Article 63 of the Geneva Convention of 1929? And finally, did the Fifth Amendment of the U.S. Constitution, with its guarantee of due process of law, apply to a defeated Japanese general?[43]

In disposing of the first question as to whether the commission had been lawfully created, Stone had the unanimous support of all seven of his brethren. Even the dissenting justices acknowledged that the creation of the tribunal, although not its rules of evidence, had conformed with the guidelines established by the U.S. Congress under the articles of war. They realized that Styer had acted on MacArthur's orders, that MacArthur had acted on the orders of the Joint Chiefs of Staff, and that the Joint Chiefs had acted on orders of the president.

The chief justice's handling of question two, however, failed to generate the same degree of support. Rejecting defense counsel Reel's contention that the cessation of hostilities automatically voided the authority of a military commission to try Yamashita, Stone demonstrated that Congress had sanctioned trial of war criminals by military commission so long as a formal state of war existed. Furthermore, he pointed out, a review of the nation's military history revealed "numerous instances" where trials by military commissions had occurred after a cessation of hostilities but before a formal declaration of peace. "The extent to which the power to prosecute violations of the law of war shall be exercised before peace is declared rests," he concluded, "not with the courts, but with the political branch of the Government. . . ." Since the United States had not yet formally concluded its war with Japan—and, indeed, would

---

[43]For the text of Article 63 and the Fifth Amendment, see Appendix in this volume, pp. 144–45.

not do so until 1952—the trial of Yamashita before a military commission was quite proper.

Neither Justices Murphy nor Rutledge, the two court dissenters, viewed this particular question as the crucial one. Murphy ignored it altogether, while Rutledge devoted only a single paragraph to a refutation of Stone's logic. Since enemy belligerents were at the complete mercy of their conquerors in that interim period, Rutledge briefly noted, they needed greater protection, not less. He remained unconvinced that military necessity during that interim period required prosecution of enemy belligerents by the same rules utilized during actual combat. While legally such actions could be justified, from a moral point of view the United States should abandon that technical interpretation of its powers that allowed it to avoid traditional constitutional protections. But since he based his arguments on moral/humanitarian grounds, rather than legal ones, Rutledge realized the futility of further discussion. For him, as for Murphy, the answers to the remaining three questions offered more than ample justification for overturning the military commission's December judgment.

Just as Rutledge and Murphy realized the importance of questions three, four, and five, so, too, did Stone. The defense counsel erred, Stone explained, when it alleged that Yamashita bore no guilt because he had neither committed nor ordered the commission of war crimes. While the law of war may have failed to define specifically the concept of command responsibility so as to hold a commander personally responsible for the actions of his men, Stone argued that the intent of the law clearly embraced such a definition. Articles 1 and 43 of the annex to the Fourth Hague Convention, Article 19 of the Tenth Hague Convention relating to naval bombardment, and Article 26 of the Geneva Red Cross Convention of 1929, Stone wrote, presumed that in order to protect civilians and prisoners of war a commander must take reasonable measures for their protection. In addition, "these provisions plainly imposed on [Yamashita] . . . an affirmative duty to take such measures as were within his power and appropriate in the circumstances to protect prisoners of war and the civilian population." Question three, therefore, could be answered only in the affirmative. For Stone, there was no doubt that Yamashita had been charged with a legitimate violation of the law of war.

Even Clark, Reel, and Sandberg could have accepted that analysis had Stone then considered those extenuating circumstances surrounding the commission of atrocities in the Philippines that they believed lifted the responsibility from Yamashita's shoulders. After all, they had argued during the trial in Manila that Yamashita had indeed taken all such measures "as were within his power and appropriate in the circumstances." He should not, therefore, be executed for crimes beyond his control.

Stone, however, did not consider extenuating circumstances. It simply was not the responsibility of the U.S. Supreme Court to reexamine or reconsider the facts presented to the five officers in Manila:

> We do not here appraise the evidence on which petitioner was convicted. We do not consider what measures, if any, petitioner took to prevent the commission, by troops under his command, of the plain violations of the law of war detailed in the bill of particulars, or whether such measures as he may have taken were appropriate and sufficient to discharge the duty imposed upon him. These are questions within the peculiar competence of the military officers composing the commission and were for it to decide.

Upon consideration of the extenuating circumstances, those military justices, Stone continued in a footnote, had found Yamashita guilty. That was sufficient. "We do not weigh the evidence," he emphasized once again. "We merely hold that the charge sufficiently states a violation against the law of war, and that the commission . . . could properly find [Yamashita] guilty of such a violation." Having thus resolved the issue, the chief justice refused to address the question of whether a military commander still could be tried and punished even if he had no knowledge of violations of the law of war. To comment on that facet of the defense's case, according to Stone's logic, would be unwise and unnecessary. With the decision that Yamashita had been properly charged with a violation of the law of war, it was undesirable to introduce additional extraneous factors. Such a conclusion merely reflected Stone's belief that in his judicial utterances he should limit himself precisely to the issue at hand.

Stone's narrow construction angered Rutledge and Murphy. Both men reminded their brethren that in its findings the military commission had failed to demonstrate that Yamashita had either committed or ordered the commission of war crimes. Rutledge also quickly pointed out that the military commission had failed to express its opinion on whether Yamashita actually had knowledge of the crimes:

> It is not in our tradition for anyone to be charged with crime which is defined after his conduct . . . has taken place. . . . Mass guilt we do not impute to individuals, perhaps in any case but certainly in none where the person is not charged or shown actively to have participated in or knowingly to have failed in taking action to prevent the wrongs done by others, having both the duty and the power to do so.

The charges against Yamashita, he concluded, were invalid and the judgment of the military court therefore void.[44]

Rutledge's negative comments, however, were dispassionate when compared to Murphy's. The charges, the former attorney general emphasized, amount to this:

---

[44]For earlier drafts of Rutledge's decision, see box 137, Rutledge Papers.

We, the victorious American forces, have done everything possible to destroy and disorganize your lines of communication, your effective control of your personnel, your ability to wage war. In those respects we have succeeded. We have defeated and crushed your forces. And now we charge and condemn you for having been inefficient in maintaining control of your troops during the period when we were so effectively besieging and eliminating your forces and blocking your ability to maintain effective control. Many terrible atrocities were committed by your disorganized troops. Because these atrocities were so widespread we will not bother to charge or prove that you committed, ordered or condoned any of them. We will assume that they must have resulted from your inefficiency and negligence as a commander. In short, we charge you with the crime of inefficiency in controlling your troops. We will judge the discharge of your duties by the disorganization which we ourselves created in large part. Our standards of judgment are whatever we wish to make them.

Nothing in all history or in international law, at least as far as I am aware, justifies such a charge against a fallen commander of a defeated force. To use the very inefficiency and disorganization created by the victorious forces as the primary basis for condemning officers of the defeated armies bears no resemblance to justice or to military reality.

As he had noted earlier in his dissent, the decision by the government, through its military arm, to adopt such a policy seemed "a practice reminiscent of that pursued in certain less respected nations in recent years."[45] It was a practice unsupported, despite Stone's assertions, by either of the two Hague Conventions or of the Red Cross Convention. Those conventions not only had failed to define precisely a commander's general responsibility but also had failed to address or anticipate the special circumstances that faced Yamashita and his forces on Luzon in 1944 and 1945.[46]

Murphy's vehemence, Rutledge acknowledged in late February, diverted attention from his arguments, diminishing their effectiveness.[47] Given their judicial philosophies, no doubt Stone, Frankfurter, and Black would have agreed with Rutledge. Murphy had seemingly allowed his emotions and personal bias to govern his vigorous dissent. For all three that was unacceptable. Frankfurter had earlier addressed that issue most

---

[45]Murphy's jabs at the military may have been influenced to some small degree by his dislike for MacArthur. When Murphy had been high commissioner in the Philippines in the 1930s, he and MacArthur had frequently clashed. See Howard, *Murphy*, pp. 93–108.

[46]90 L. Ed. 499. For an earlier draft of Murphy's opinion, see draft of 28 January 1946, box 71, Murphy Papers.

[47]Rutledge to Frank, 13 and 22 February 1946, box 137, Rutledge Papers. Also see Harper, *Rutledge*, p. 188.

concisely. If a judge's personal feelings dominate in his decisions, he had observed, "the judicial process becomes a dangerous sham."[48]

Although Rutledge was no less concerned over Yamashita's case than was Murphy, his response to Stone's handling of question four revealed the more commonly accepted method of preparing dissents.[49] In a calm, rational, legal refutation, Rutledge found unacceptable Stone's argument that neither the articles of war nor the Geneva Convention of 1929 applied to Yamashita. The cases of both Stone and Rutledge rested largely on their interpretation of the intent of Congress, on the one hand, and of the signatory powers of Geneva, on the other. Examining and citing many of the same documents and records of testimony, they reached totally opposite conclusions. While Stone argued that Congress had identified two separate categories of prisoners subject to trial by military commission, Rutledge believed there was only one. If Stone were right, Yamashita could be tried in a court unfettered by the restrictions imposed by Articles of War 25 and 38. If Rutledge were right, the military commission trying Yamashita would have been prevented by those articles from admitting into evidence depositions without first securing the approval of the defense counsel; from admitting into evidence hearsay, affidavits, and opinion; and from exercising that power granted by MacArthur that made it the sole judge of evidence utilizing the probative value concept.

While Rutledge's method may have been more traditional in its refutation of Stone's articles of war contentions, his own anger surfaced occasionally. To adopt Stone's reasoning would indicate judicial acceptance of the types of evidence admitted during the Yamashita trial. For Rutledge that was intolerable. He revealed his dissatisfaction on this point at the conclusion of his discussion of MacArthur's rules of evidence:

> A more complete abrogation of customary safeguards relating to the proof, whether in the usual rules of evidence or any reasonable substitute and whether for use in the trial of crime in the civil courts or military tribunals, hardly could have been made. So far as the admissibility and probative value of evidence was concerned, the directive made the commission a law unto itself.

The court's arbitrariness in admitting evidence, even though based on MacArthur's procedures, and its prejudicial and unfair limitation of cross-examination, Rutledge concluded, convinced him "that this was no trial in the traditions of the common law and the Constitution."

---

[48]Thomas, *Frankfurter*, p. 348. For the views of Stone and Black, see Mason, *Stone*, pp. 776, 786; and Black, *Constitutional Faith*, pp. 10, 14.
[49]90 L. Ed. 499.

The aberrant decisions relating to evidence and cross-examination alone warranted the voiding of Yamashita's sentence even if one accepted Stone's interpretation of congressional intent in formulating the articles of war, at least so Rutledge reasoned. After all, he continued, Article 63 of the Geneva Convention of 1929 required that "sentence . . . be pronounced against a prisoner of war only by the same courts and according to the same procedure as in the case of persons belonging to the armed forces of the detaining Power." By that rule the articles of war would apply to Yamashita's trial just as they applied to the trial of American soldiers.

Stone disagreed. Rutledge had misinterpreted that particular article, or, more to the point, had failed to place it in the context of the overall document. When reviewing the entire agreement, Stone added, it is clear that the signatory powers meant Article 63 to apply to trials of prisoners of war for offenses committed while prisoners of war. Since Yamashita had been charged with crimes preceding his detention as an American prisoner, the Geneva Convention was inapplicable. On that point Stone, Frankfurter, Reed, Burton, Black, and Douglas agreed.[50]

The issue that had almost cost Stone his majority lay not in questions one through four but in question five. Did the Fifth Amendment of the U.S. Constitution, with its guarantee of due process of law, apply to a defeated Japanese general? Originally Stone had not intended to introduce a discussion of the Fifth Amendment. On 26 January, however, Rutledge, who had been working feverishly on the case, circulated his dissent, based in part on a Fifth Amendment argument.[51]

In its final form, Rutledge's dissent argued that justice for all men, whether friend or foe, must be administered according to law, especially according to the Fifth Amendment guarantee of due process.[52] Each decision to circumvent the nation's constitutional guarantees, Rutledge observed, weakened the entire American tradition of fairness and due process. If upheld, the Yamashita case alone would shake the foundations of America's legal traditions. Contrary to American law, the Japanese general had been charged with a crime—command responsibility— formulated after his capture. Despite its failure to prove that Yamashita had known of war violations, the government, again in violation of traditional American legal custom, merely assumed he must have known. The commission's rulings to limit cross-examination so as to conclude the trial more quickly, together with its power to be "the sole and exclusive

---

[50]For Stone's original comments on Article 63 and Rutledge's reaction, see box 137, Rutledge Papers.

[51]Rutledge discusses his hectic schedule in Rutledge to Frank, 13 and 22 February 1946, box 137, Rutledge Papers; and Rutledge to Stone, 1 February 1946, box 76, Stone Papers.

[52]90 L. Ed. 499.

judge of the credibility, probative value and admissibility of whatever may be tendered as evidence," also ran contrary to the basic concepts of American law. By ignoring these basic guarantees of a fair trial, the Court, Rutledge continued, had received into evidence "every conceivable kind of statement, rumor, report, as first, second, third or further hand, written, printed, or oral, and one 'propaganda' film." Receipt of such evidence, Rutledge charged, constituted perhaps the most flagrant departure from "the whole British-American tradition of common law and the Constitution."

As if the commission, by its procedures and rulings, had not deviated sufficiently from the due process guarantees of the Fifth Amendment, it went even further, Rutledge noted. It denied the defense counsel adequate time to prepare its case, especially time to prepare its response to that supplemental bill of particulars of fifty-nine charges submitted three days before the trial began. The acceptance of charges at such a late date, coupled with the Court's refusal to grant a continuance, "was wholly arbitrary, cutting off the last vestige of adequate chance to prepare defense and imposing a burden the most able counsel could not bear. This sort of thing has no place in our system of justice, civil or military," Rutledge concluded. "This wide departure from the most elementary principles of fairness alone vitiated the proceeding."[53] The violation of due process of law, coupled with other wrongful actions of the Court, "deprived the proceeding of any semblance of trial as we know that institution."

Such activities by the commission, Rutledge firmly believed, gutted the Fifth Amendment guarantee of a fair trial for all persons. No "human being heretofore [has] been held to be wholly beyond elementary procedural protection by the fifth amendment. I cannot consent to even implied departure from that great absolute." If the nation dropped its constitutional safeguards for a defeated enemy, it established a dangerous precedent that could enable those same safeguards to be removed from others, "perhaps ultimately for all."

To ignore such a vigorous charge, Stone believed, would be folly. Therefore, working on Saturday and Sunday, he altered his draft so as to address Rutledge's criticisms.[54] On Monday, 28 January, the day he had hoped to announce the formal ruling, he circulated his revised draft. A military commission corresponds more closely to an expert administrative body than to a regular court, Stone countered. Since the Supreme Court had ruled in other cases that administrative bodies could accept such evidence "as a reasonable mind might accept as adequate to support a

---

[53]In an earlier draft Rutledge had stated "this gross departure." See Rutledge draft, 28 January 1946, box 71, Murphy Papers.

[54]For Stone's third draft with the Fifth Amendment arguments, see box 73, Stone Papers. The following paragraphs are based on that draft.

conclusion," Rutledge's objections lacked validity.[55] Recalling his discussion of the articles of war, Stone reminded his dissenting colleague that Congress had not specifically limited the production of that evidence to which Rutledge objected, in trials before military commissions. As a result, "the constitutional requirement of a jury trial does not apply."

Rutledge's argument that the Court had deprived the defense of ample preparation time likewise lacked substance. Stone recalled that the defense on 8 October had requested two weeks for preparation, while the commission granted three. He also noted that even though the commission denied a continuance, it offered several occasions to appoint additional personnel to the defense team, a suggestion not immediately accepted by Clarke, Reel, or Sandberg. Furthermore, the defense's request for a continuance on 20 November in order to prepare for the supplemental bill of particulars occurred only after it had cross-examined the prosecution's witnesses on that same bill.[56] Surely, Stone remarked, if the defense felt adequately prepared to cross-examine the prosecution's witnesses prior to 20 November, it needed no additional time for preparation after that date. "In all this," Stone concluded, "we are unable to find any denial of a fair trial or of due process."

On 27 January, before he considered adding his Fifth Amendment response, Stone already had secured the approval of Frankfurter, Black, Douglas, and Reed concerning his first draft. Since he had received Rutledge's dissent only on Saturday and did not complete his Fifth Amendment comments until late Sunday, he did not consult those four men regarding his revision. He assumed—hoped—they would continue to support his majority opinion with his Fifth Amendment additions. He was wrong.

When Stone circulated his new opinion on the twenty-eighth, he discovered that Frankfurter, Douglas, and Reed remained supportive. His new argument even convinced Burton to join the majority.[57] But Black found the new additions unacceptable. Stone's opinion, he argued, was dangerous on several grounds.[58] First, the chief justice implied that

---

[55]See, for example, Chief Justice Charles Evans Hughes's ruling in December 1938 in Consolidated Edison Co., et al. vs. N.L.R.B., et al., 305 U.S. 197; Stone's opinion in N.L.R.B. vs. Columbian Enameling and Stamping Company, 306 U.S. 300 (February 1939); and the ruling of the Second Circuit Court of Appeals in May 1924 in John Bene & Sons vs. F.T.C., 299 Fed. 468.

[56]On 2 November, in the midst of the Yamashita trial, General Reynolds observed that unless defense objected the Court would assume it was prepared for the supplemental bill of particulars. Defense did not object. See Transcript, p. 713.

[57]See the notations of Douglas and Burton attached to the draft. See Frankfurter to Stone, 30 January 1946, box 73, Stone Papers; Reed to Stone, 30 January 1946; and Stone to Reed, 31 January 1946, ibid.

[58]Black to Stone, 28 January 1946, box 283, Black Papers. Three days later Black circulated a proposed concurring opinion to Justice Reed. Clearly, Stone already had

judicial trials may use the same kind of evidence, based on probative value, as used in administrative hearings. Second, the chief justice implied that had the Court found the commission guilty of failing to give defense adequate time to prepare its case it could have used the Fifth Amendment to invalidate the sentence. Both implications were unacceptable. With relation to the first point, Black did not share Stone's belief that abbreviated evidence used in administrative hearings could be used in judicial trials without violating the Constitution. Concerning the second, he disagreed with Stone's implication that the Court not only had applied the Fifth Amendment, but also that it discovered no violations. "If we are to apply the judicial concept of a 'fair trial,' " Black argued, "I should be inclined to agree with the dissents." Stone's conclusion that the Court had discovered no violation of the due process clause of the Fifth Amendment placed the justices "in the attitude of defending the Commission's action, rather than saying that it is beyond our powers of review."[59] Black found that position highly objectionable.

As Stone's opinion now stood, Black added, it robbed the due process clause "of a large part of its vital strength." Furthermore, Stone's lame arguments that members of military commissions, acting as administrative experts, could evaluate such normally unacceptable evidence as hearsay, rumor, opinion, affidavits, and depositions better than jurors was simply unconvincing. To avoid weakening the Fifth Amendment and to avoid weak, simple-minded justifications, Black appealed to Stone to eliminate his newest additions.[60]

Fearful of the biting criticisms contained in Black's anticipated concurring opinion, Stone dropped his Fifth Amendment arguments on 31 January.[61] In his final opinion he would deal with Rutledge's arguments in one paragraph, a paragraph much to Black's liking and more in line with the earlier decision to decide the case on narrow lines. Stone wrote:

> We hold that the commission's ruling on evidence and on the mode of conducting these proceedings against [Yamashita] are not reviewable by the courts, but only by the reviewing military authorities. From this viewpoint it is unnecessary to consider what, in other situations, the Fifth Amendment might require, and as to that no intimation one way or the other is to be implied. Nothing we have said is to be taken as indicating any opinion on the question of the wisdom of considering such evidence, or whether the action of a military tribunal in admitting evidence, ... may be drawn in question by petition for habeas corpus. . . .[62]

---

received that document. See Black to Reed, 31 January 1946, ibid. For Reed's reply, see ibid. [n.d.].

[59]Black to Stone, 28 January 1946, box 283, Black Papers.

[60]Ibid. Also see Black's proposed concurring opinion, box 283, Black Papers.

[61]Stone's memorandum to Court, 31 January 1946, box 73, Stone Papers.

[62]90 L. Ed. 499.

Four days later on 4 February, Stone formally announced the Court's findings in the Yamashita case. While Murphy and Rutledge lodged vigorous dissents, the remaining justices, including Black, supported Stone's reasoning. By a vote of six to two, the U.S. Supreme Court declined to overturn the sentence of death imposed on Yamashita.

The War Department cabled the news to MacArthur immediately, realizing that, according to the 24 September instructions, he would now personally have to review the trial. The War Department also cabled that, since the defense counsel planned to appeal to President Truman for executive clemency, MacArthur must not execute the defeated foe until the president disposed of the appeal.[63]

Within days of the Court's announcement, MacArthur released his decision. He found no reason why Yamashita should not die. Yamashita's actions reflected badly upon the entire military profession:

> Rarely has so cruel and wanton a record been spread to public gaze. Revolting as this may be in itself, it pales before the sinister and far reaching implication thereby attached to the profession of arms. The soldier, be he friend or foe, is charged with the protection of the weak and unarmed. It is the very essence and reason for his being. When he violates this sacred trust he not only profanes his entire cult but threatens the very fabric of international society. The traditions of fighting men are long and honorable. They are based upon the noblest of human traits—sacrifice. This officer, of proven field merit, entrusted with high command involving authority adequate to responsibility, has failed this irrevocable standard; has failed his duty to his troops, to his country, to his enemy, to mankind; has failed utterly his soldier faith. The transgressions resulting therefrom as revealed by the trial are a blot upon the military profession, a stain upon civilization and constitute a memory of shame and dishonor that can never be forgotten.[64]

The judgment of the commission, therefore, would be enforced.

Whatever slim hope existed that Yamashita might escape the gallows vanished on 8 February. On that date President Truman declined to grant executive clemency.[65] Major General Harry Vaughan, who had consulted with Truman on the matter, later recalled that Truman's traditional policy was "not to interfere with the authority of a commander in a matter which was clearly his responsibility such as military justice within his command."[66] Since MacArthur had launched the trial at the presi-

---

[63]Brigadier General Green to CinCAFPAC, 4 February 1946, 000.5 Yamashita, box 763, RG 331.

[64]MacArthur review, ibid.

[65]Major General Edward F. Witsell to CinCAFPAC, 8 February 1946, ibid.

[66]Major General Harry Vaughan to Richard Lael, 25 August 1980. Also see "Oral Interview with General Harry Vaughan," Truman Library.

dent's urging, since he had adopted procedures prepared by the War Department's U.S. War Crimes Office, and since the articles of war passed by Congress had clearly given him authority to handle military justice, Truman refused to intervene.

Bureaucratic delays in Tokyo, coupled with inclement weather between Tokyo and Manila, forced Styer to postpone Yamashita's execution until he had received the necessary military paperwork from MacArthur's headquarters.[67] Not until late February did Styer execute the sentence imposed by the U.S. military commission two and one-half months earlier. The false floor under Yamashita's feet dropped open shortly after 3:00 A.M. on 23 February 1946.[68] An officer's personal responsibility for the activities of his soldiers had been dramatically affirmed. Only time would reveal whether Justice Murphy had been right when he stated that no one in command of military forces, from sergeants to generals, could escape the Yamashita precedent. He had prophesied that "indeed the fate of some future President of the United States and his chiefs of staff and military advisers may well have been sealed by this decision."[69]

---

[67]See CG, AFWESPAC to CinCAFPAC, 20 February 1946; and CinCAFPAC to CG, AFWESPAC, 20 February 1946, 000.5 Yamashita, box 763, RG 331.

[68]A military physician pronounced Yamashita dead at 0327 hours.

[69]90 L. Ed. 516.

CHAPTER SIX
COMMAND RESPONSIBILITY SINCE
IN RE YAMASHITA

Neither Frank Murphy nor Wiley Rutledge lived to see the major reforms in the war-crimes process they believed so necessary in 1946. Ironically, however, their deaths in July and September 1949, respectively, bracketed the completion of a new Geneva accord in August which, when ratified by the U.S. Senate, corrected some of the abuses evident to both jurists in the Yamashita proceedings.[1] While the section of the 1949 Geneva Convention relating to the treatment of prisoners of war clearly authorized their trial by military courts, it simultaneously extended to defendants in those trials certain crucial procedural safeguards lacking at the 1929 convention. Article 85, for example, ruled that the protection and benefits of the new international accord applied to prisoners who faced charges for acts committed prior to, as well as after, capture. It had been the ambiguity of the old convention on this point that had prompted Chief Justice Stone in 1946 to find that the protections of the 1929 convention did not apply to Yamashita, a decision that helped spark the Rutledge and Murphy dissents. The adoption of Article 85, when coupled with the convention's reaffirmation that sentences could be validly imposed only by the same courts and according to the same procedures governing trials of the armed forces of the detaining power, ensured that in future trials war criminals held by the United States would be granted the same procedural safeguards covering members of the U.S. military. Future courts, at least, could no longer admit the same type of hearsay evidence, depositions, and affidavits accepted by the Reynolds commission in Manila. To further ensure the defendant's basic rights, the conferees at Geneva also readopted those 1929 provisions that specifically guaranteed suspected war criminals the right to legal counsel, to an interpreter, and to the same appellate procedures granted members of the detaining power's armed forces. Furthermore, they agreed for the first time that a prisoner of war must also be informed of the charges against him "in good time before the opening of the trial," and that he must be

---

[1]See Geneva convention (III) in Leon Friedman, ed., *The Law of War: A Documentary History* (New York: Random House, 1972), 1: 589–60.

granted ample time, no less than two weeks, to consult his counsel and prepare a defense.[2]

Despite its support of those guarantees, the Truman administration postponed consideration of the 1949 Geneva document until it had concluded the Korean War. As a result, the U.S. Senate did not actually discuss ratification until July 1955. In that month, following a short debate, the senators unanimously approved the agreement, expressing in the process their hearty endorsement of Article 85 in particular. Rutledge and Murphy would have been pleased.[3]

On the second major issue, which had sparked the Murphy and Rutledge dissents, the 1949 convention remained ambiguous. The conferees at Geneva simply failed to address the broad issue of command responsibility any more fully than their 1929 counterparts. By so doing, they left to the judgment of future courts the issue of whether command responsibility, as defined at Manila, correctly reflected international legal reasoning. In avoiding this question, they also failed to uphold either Stone's argument that Yamashita had been charged with a normally recognized violation of the law of war, or Rutledge and Murphy's argument that he had faced trial for a crime created only after the fact. Despite their failure to address the wider implications of command responsibility, the conferees, however, considered one aspect of that issue. They adopted a new provision that held that "no prisoner of war may be tried or sentenced for an act which is not forbidden by the law of the Detaining Power or by international law in force at the time said act was committed."[4] Adopting that stipulation, a state, once it ratified the new convention, could no longer try prisoners of war for acts that were not clearly criminal at the time of their commission.

Even if that provision had been in effect in 1945, Yamashita probably still would have faced trial for failure to exercise his command responsibility. Stone, Black, Frankfurter, Reed, Douglas, and Burton all firmly believed that the Hague and Geneva conventions had imposed on commanders during the Second World War an affirmative responsibility to control their forces. Indeed, their arguments had persuasively refuted the counterarguments of Rutledge and Murphy that those same international accords sanctioned no such interpretation. Since they believed two international accords imposed certain duties upon military officers, trial of any officer suspected of a dereliction of duty would still have been valid even if the 1949 provisions had been in effect four years earlier.

For the United States after 1955, therefore, the prevailing legal precedent for assessing the degree of a commander's responsibility still

---

[2]Ibid.

[3]For the Senate discussion and vote, see U.S., Congress, Senate, *Congressional Record*, 84th Cong., 1st sess., 6 July 1955, 101:9958–73.

[4]Friedman, *Law of War*, 1:624.

remained the Yamashita proceedings. More specifically, that precedent lay in the decision of the Reynolds commission rather than in Stone's ruling of early 1946. The chief justice and his brethren, in fact, had pointedly avoided an evaluation of whether the verdict rendered in Manila accurately reflected the degree of Yamashita's guilt. Associate Justice Black particularly had wanted to avoid any semblance of approving the commission's verdict. Not surprisingly, therefore, Stone's final draft had noted on three separate occasions (twice in the text and once in a footnote) that the Court only considered whether the military commission could legally try and sentence Yamashita, not whether that body had accurately interpreted the evidence and had delivered a just verdict.[5] The Court, as Stone's opinion revealed, simply refused to evaluate the impact of a divided command, active guerrilla resistance, the loss of reliable communications, and the intense American military pressure on Yamashita's ability to discharge adequately his command responsibilities. That evaluation, Stone had concluded, was "within the peculiar competence of the military officers composing the commission and were for it to decide."[6]

In exercising their powers, the five military officers in Manila imposed an awesome standard on commanding officers. By accepting the prosecution's argument that Yamashita either must have known or should have known of the widespread violations of the law of war, the court firmly rejected the defense argument that extenuating circumstances should mitigate, at the very least, any sentence imposed on a commanding officer who faced adverse battle conditions. Yamashita, the court reasoned, had an affirmative duty to control his men, a duty not offset by the unique battle conditions existing in the Philippines in 1944 and 1945.

While the U.S. Supreme Court's opinion implied no approval or disapproval of the military commission's findings, it upheld that body's verdict. That action led many who had not reviewed the findings carefully and who were unaware of the justices' interoffice correspondence to assume that the Court not only sustained the verdict but also approved the commission's reasoning. That misinterpretation of Stone's opinion made the Yamashita decision a much more potentially dangerous one to high-ranking military and civilian leaders than would otherwise have been the case. Indeed, the mistaken assumption that the Supreme Court had approved the military court's reasoning relegated two cases tried at Nuremberg in 1948 into a legal backwater. Had those two cases been more carefully considered, the debate over "should have known" logic and the concept of command responsibility perhaps would not have favored the Reynolds commission's reasoning so completely.[7]

---

[5] See Stone's opinion in 327 U.S. 1.

[6] Ibid.

[7] For information on the two Nuremberg courts, see the Hostage and the High Command cases in *Trials of War Criminals Before the Nuernberg Military Tribunals* (Washington: Government Printing Office, 1950), 11: 1–1332.

Two years following the U.S. Supreme Court's ruling in the Yamashita case, American prosecutors at Nuremberg, in the Hostage case, charged twelve German officers with the deaths of hundreds of thousands of civilians in southeastern Europe. Evaluating the evidence presented during that trial, three American judges abandoned the "must have known" reasoning espoused by Major Kerr and General Reynolds in Manila. "In determining the guilt or innocence of these defendants," they ruled, "we shall require proof of a causative, overt act or omission from which a guilty intent can be inferred before a verdict of guilty will be pronounced."[8] Even though an officer might be aware of the commission of criminal acts, that alone, the judges held, provided insufficient grounds for conviction. In order to convict, that officer "must be one who orders, abets, or takes a consenting part in the crime." Commanding officers, even if they did not order the commission of acts in violation of the law of war, could be convicted, however, if they ignored reports of such violations and, if having the power to stop them, permitted them to continue. Normally, the court added, an officer could not claim ignorance of violations within his own area of command or ignorance of reports of such violations that reached his headquarters. Only in cases where he faced exceptional circumstances that denied him knowledge of crimes, or prevented his intervention to stop them, should a court refrain from punishing him for violations committed by his subordinates. If an officer had power to stop war crimes, the court noted, and he also had knowledge or should legitimately have had knowledge of their commission but refused to act, he violated his duties and responsibilities as a commander and therefore assumed legal culpability. If, on the other hand, he had or should have had knowledge of the acts but no power to prevent them, or did not know and had legitimate reasons for not knowing, then he should not be held responsible for the actions of his subordinates.

The crucial question facing military tribunals, the judges reasoned, involved the issue of whether a defendant should have known. In the case against Generalfeldmarschall Wilhelm List, for example, German communications among his units were fully operational and reports of violations had in fact reached his headquarters. In the judges' opinion, then, he clearly should have known of those war crimes. The absence of exceptional circumstances, coupled with a commanding officer's failure to stop these violations and to prevent their recurrence, reflected a dereliction of duty for which he could be legitimately punished. "Want of knowledge of the contents of reports made to him is not a defense," the court ruled. Nor did an officer's absence from his headquarters relieve him of responsibility "for acts committed in accordance with a policy he instituted or in which he acquiesced." However, neither List nor other commanding officers, the

---

[8]For a full transcript of the findings, see ibid., pp. 1230–1318.

court quickly added, may "be charged with acts committed on the order of someone else which is outside the basic orders which he has issued." Under those circumstances his duty upon learning of their commission is, "if time permits," to rescind such orders, or, failing that, to prevent their repetition. In conclusion, an officer who, because of exceptional circumstances, legitimately failed to learn of war crimes committed by his subordinates and who had neither ordered, aided, or abetted their commission could not be held personally responsible.[9]

Eight months later three different American justices in the High Command case, involving thirteen high-ranking German officers, further severely undermined the liberal should have known policy adopted in Manila. Not only did their interpretation of when a commander could legitimately be held accountable for the actions of his subordinates differ from that of the Reynolds commission, it also differed from the judgment handed down by their three colleagues in the Hostage case eight months earlier:

> Modern war such as the last war entails a large measure of decentralization. A high commander cannot keep completely informed of the details of military operations of subordinates and most assuredly not of every administrative measure. He has the right to assume that details entrusted to responsible subordinates will be legally executed. The President of the United States is Commander in Chief of its military forces. Criminal acts committed by those forces cannot in themselves be charged to him on the theory of subordination. The same is true of other high commanders in the chain of command. Criminality does not attach to every individual in this chain of command from that fact alone. There must be a personal dereliction. That can occur only where the act is directly traceable to him or where his failure to properly supervise his subordinates constitutes criminal negligence on his part. In the latter case it must be a personal neglect amounting to a wanton, immoral disregard of the action of his subordinates amounting to acquiescence. Any other interpretation of international law would go far beyond the basic principles of criminal law as known to civilized nations.[10]

That reasoning ripped apart the assumptions and conclusions underlying the execution of Yamashita for failure to exercise adequate command responsibility. It found invalid the assumption that a commanding officer must have known of widespread atrocities committed by his subordinates. And it found that in applying that should have known logic the courts, before judging a commanding officer for failure to control

---

[9]Ibid.

[10]This quotation and the following three paragraphs are based on the Court's findings. See ibid., pp. 462–695.

his subordinates, must be very careful to consider the circumstances facing him. Judges should remember, for example, that commanding officers were often far removed from the sites of their subordinates' crimes, and that those subordinates who should perhaps have suppressed such acts often failed to report them to higher authority for fear of being reprimanded or criticized themselves. "We are of the opinion, . . ." Judge Justin Harding argued for the court, "that the occupying commander must have knowledge of [war-crimes] offenses and acquiesce or participate or criminally neglect to interfere in their commission and that offenses committed must be patently criminal." The commission by one's subordinates of violations of the law of war did not, in and of itself, justify prosecution of the commander.

The prosecution must first prove knowledge and then demonstrate a commanding officer's acquiescence, participation, or criminal neglect in refusing to interfere. Unlike the Hostage court, the High Command judges did not assume that under normal circumstances a commanding officer should know of violations within his own area of command. Only in two instances did they appear to flirt with should have known reasoning. In the case against General der Infanterie Hermann Reinecke, the court ruled that, as the officer responsible for prisoner of war camps in his sector, "he had the sources of knowledge and the duty was placed upon him to know and supervise what took place in those camps." But the court then rendered its verdict not on the basis that he should have known but on the grounds that, based on testimony, they believed he had indeed known of atrocities committed against prisoners of war. Earlier in their general commentary, they also had briefly acknowledged a should have known assumption. Numerous reports to an officer's headquarters, which covered a wide period of time, they conceded, "must be presumed in substance to have been brought to his attention." Beyond that, however, they refused to adopt the more liberal should have known policy used in Manila or that endorsed by the earlier Nuremberg tribunal.

Even if a commander learned of abusive actions or killings by subordinates, the High Command court further ruled, he may be held accountable only if he realized they were clearly in violation of the law and then acquiesced in their commission. Criminal acquiescence could entail, for example, transmittal of a clearly illegal order from one's superior to one's subordinates without protest, or the transferral of prisoners to a unit or units that the officer realized killed or tortured those under its control.[11]

The judgment of the High Command justices gave a commanding officer more benefit of doubt than either the Yamashita or the Hostage courts. While it joined the Hostage court in scrapping the must have

----

[11]Ibid.

known assumption, it refused to accept its colleagues' reasoning that under normal circumstances a commanding officer should have known of violations committed by his subordinates in his own area of command. They firmly indicated that in the future the burden of proof should rest on the prosecution to demonstrate the two essential determinants of culpability: a commanding officer's knowledge of, and his criminal acquiescence in, a violation of a law of war.

The rulings from the Yamashita case to the Hostage case to the High Command case progressed naturally. In December 1945 the Reynolds commission had held a commanding officer to strict accountability with its must have known and liberal should have known logic. In February 1948 the Hostage court expressed some doubts over that strictness. Dissatisfied with the Reynolds commission's reasoning, it abolished the must have known assumption and severely curtailed the should have known logic. Rather, it held that courts should assume that an officer had knowledge only if the violations occurred within his sector and no exceptional circumstances prevailed at the time, or if reports had reached his headquarters concerning violations. While the High Command court in October 1948 no doubt considered that a significant improvement, it went one step further. Proof of knowledge and of criminal acquiescence on the part of the commanding officer should be, with possibly only two exceptions, the sole basis for holding such an officer responsible for the illegal activities of his subordinates.

On one point, however, the Manila commission, the U.S. Supreme Court, the Hostage court, and to a much lesser degree even the High Command court agreed. War-crimes courts could legitimately ask the question of whether a commanding officer should have known of violations. How one determined that fact constituted the essential disagreement between the courts in Nuremberg and in Manila.

Even the U.S. Army acknowledged in 1956 that the should have known issue could legitimately be considered in future trials of commanding officers. In its 1956 edition of *The Law of Land Warfare*, the army added a completely new section dealing with an officer's responsibility for the actions of his subordinates:

> In some cases, military commanders may be responsible for war crimes committed by subordinate members of the armed forces, or other persons subject to their control. Thus, for instance, when troops commit massacres and atrocities against the civilian population of occupied territory or against prisoners of war, the responsibility may rest not only with the actual perpetrators but also with the commander. Such a responsibility arises directly when the acts in question have been committed in pursuance of an order of the commander concerned. The commander is also responsible if he has actual knowledge, or should have knowledge, through reports received by

him or through other means, that troops or other persons subject to his
control are about to commit or have committed a war crime and he
fails to take the necessary and reasonable steps to insure compliance
with the law of war or to punish violators thereof.[12]

As army legal experts may well have realized in 1956, if future commissions adopted the liberal interpretation of the Manila commission over
the narrower ones of the Hostage and High Command courts, U.S.
military personnel throughout the chain of command, up to and including
the president of the United States, might be subject to trial for war crimes
committed by subordinates. Not until an army colonel addressed a jury of
combat officers at Ft. McPhearson, Georgia, in September 1971 would
they or their fellow officers learn which of those earlier precedents would
be the most influential.

Revelation in November 1969 of the massacre by U.S. Army
personnel of at least one hundred Vietnamese women, children, and old
men at My Lai (Song My) set the stage for a reexamination of the concept
of command responsibility.[13] The trial of Lieutenant William L. Calley, Jr.,

---

[12]U.S. Department of the Army, *The Law of Land Warfare* (FM 27-10)
(Washington: Government Printing Office, 1956), pp. 178–79. This issue of the *Law of
Land Warfare* has not been superseded by a revised edition.

[13]For an examination of the My Lai massacre and the debate it generated, see
Joseph Goldstein, Burke Marshall, and Jack Schwartz, eds., *The My Lai Massacre and Its
Cover-up* (New York: Free Press, 1976); Richard Falk, "Songmy: War Crimes and
Individual Responsibility," *Trans-Action* 7 (January 1970): 33–40; Neil Sheehan, "Should
We Have War Crime Trials?," *New York Times*, 28 March 1971, pp. 1–3, 30–34; "My Lai:
An American Tragedy," *Time* 94 (5 December 1969): 23–24, 26, 28–32; "Official U.S.
Report on My Lai Investigation," *U.S. News and World Report* 67 (8 December 1969): 78–
79; Kenneth Clark, "Song My's Shock Wave," *Newsweek* 38 (15 December 1969): 38;
John Sheerin, "War Crimes in High Places," *Catholic World* 212 (July 1971): 163–64;
"The Clamor Over Calley: Who Shares the Guilt?," *Time* 97 (12 April 1971): 14–16, 18–
21; Vietnam Veterans Against the War, *The Winter Soldier Investigation: An Investigation
into American War Crimes* (Boston: Beacon Press, 1972); Seymour Hersh, "A Reporter at
Large: Coverup I and II," *New Yorker* 47 (22 and 29 January 1972): 34–69 and 40–71,
respectively; Richard Hammar, "Medina: Another of the Mylai Guiltless," *New York
Times*, 26 September 1971, p. 6E; Robert Johansen, "U.S. War Crimes: The Guilt at the
Top," *The Progressive* 35 (June 1971): 19–23; A. Frank Reel, "Must We Hang Nixon
Too?," *The Progressive* 34 (March 1970): 26–29; "Assessing Songmy," *The Wall Street
Journal*, 1 December 1969, p. 1; "Minnesota Poll: Many Disbelieve My Lai Reports,"
Minnesota Tribune, 21 December 1969, p. 4B; Stanley Hoffman, "War Crimes: Political
and Legal Issues," *Dissent* 18 (December 1971): 530–34; William Parks, "Command
Responsibility for War Crimes," *Military Law Review* 62 (Fall 1973): 1–104; Richard
Falk, ed., *The Vietnam War and International Law* (Princeton: Princeton University Press,
1969), vols. 1–4; Jordan Paust, "My Lai and Vietnam: Norms, Myths and Leader Responsi-
bility," *Military Law Review* 57 (Summer 1972): 99–187; Peter Trooboff, ed., *Law and
Responsibility in Warfare: The Vietnam Experience* (Chapel Hill: University of North
Carolina Press, 1975); Henry King, Jr., ed., Transcript of Proceedings of Program of
International and Comparative Law Section of the American Bar Association entitled
"Nuremberg Revisited," 12 August 1970; "Command Responsibility for War Crimes,"

charged both with ordering his men to kill civilians and with having participated in those killings, involved a traditional violation of the law of war and did not involve either of the three previously discussed precedents. The trial of Captain Ernest Medina, Calley's immediate superior, on the other hand, did resurrect the question of whether commanding officers should be held responsible for the actions of their subordinates. Furthermore, articles appearing in such divergent publications as *Time, Trans-Action, Dissent, The Progressive,* and the *New York Times* inquired whether responsibility for My Lai should not go beyond Calley and Medina and perhaps be shared by civilians and military leaders throughout the military chain of command.[14] Richard Falk, for example, argued in a January 1970 article that "the imposition of responsibility [on Yamashita] sets a precedent for holding principal military and political officials responsible for acts committed under their command, especially when no diligent effort was made to inquire, punish, and prevent repetition." A few pages later he further noted that "the effectiveness of the law of war depends, above all else, on holding those in command and in policymaking positions responsible for the behavior of the rank-and-file soldiers on the field of battle." Falk's train of reasoning led to the conclusion that "responsibility [for atrocities] should be imposed upon those who inflicted the harm, upon those who gave direct orders, and upon those who were in a position of command entrusted with overall battlefield decorum and with the prompt detention and punishment of war crimes committed within the scope of their authority."[15] In Falk's view, the Yamashita precedent held sway over the two judgments at Nuremberg. Similarly, Telford Taylor, professor of law at Columbia University and former chief counsel at Nuremberg, believed the standards imposed on Yamashita in 1945 should be used to scrutinize the behavior of U.S. Army officers in 1970.[16]

When Secretary of the Army Stanley Resor in November 1969 ordered Lieutenant General William R. Peers to conduct a thorough investigation of the My Lai affair, many were skeptical that a fair evaluation

---

Yale Law Journal 82 (May 1973): 1272–1304; Franklin A. Hart, "Yamashita, Nuremberg and Vietnam: Command Responsibility Reappraised," *Naval War College Review* 25 (September–October 1972): 19–36; William O'Brien, "The Law of War, Command Responsibility and Vietnam," *Georgetown Law Journal* 60 (1971–72): 605–64; Herbert Kelman and Lee Lawrence, "American Response to the Trial of Lt. William L. Calley," *Psychology Today* 6 (June 1972): 41–45, 78–81; and Richard Falk, Gabriel Kolko, and Robert Jay Lifton, eds., *Crimes of War* (New York: Vintage Books, 1971).

[14]See appropriate journals in note 13 above.

[15]Falk, "Songmy," pp. 33–40.

[16]*Nuremberg and Vietnam: An American Tragedy* (Chicago: Quadrangle Books, 1970), p. 182. For a critique of Taylor's book, see Leonard Boudin, "War Crimes in Vietnam: The Mote in Whose Eye?," *Harvard Law Review* 84 (March–June 1971): 1940–59.

of the incident could be made by an army commission.[17] No one was certain how high up the chain of command the Peers commission might investigate or what precedents it might accept for guidance. The Peers commission report of March 1970, released to the public four and one-half years later, surprised some of those skeptics when critics learned that the investigative body had compiled a long list of army officers who, in its opinion, might be subject to disciplinary or administrative action for their activities during operations at My Lai or in the subsequent cover-up. Among the list of names they cited were a major general, a brigadier general, four colonels, five lieutenant colonels, three majors, eight captains, a first lieutenant, and five second lieutenants. The list of their omissions and commissions, the report explained to Resor, denoted "instances in which an individual may have failed to perform his duty or may have performed his duty improperly, measured in terms of those responsibilities which were reasonably his under the attendant circumstances." While that careful phrasing more closely coincided with the general caution of the two Nuremberg tribunals rather than with the Reynolds commission in Manila, only the actual trials would reveal the impact of those three cases.

The trial of Calley's immediate superior, Medina, most fully answered the question of whether the Reynolds commission's logic would be extended to U.S. commanding officers: whether they would be held equally responsible for the acts of their subordinates and whether a liberal or narrow should have known reasoning would apply. In late September 1971, Medina's trial, which had lasted three months, went to a jury composed of two colonels, two lieutenant colonels, and a major. But it was the charge to the jury by military judge Colonel Kenneth Howard, rather than the verdict itself, that revealed the impact of those earlier trials. In his comments to the jury, Howard explained the responsibilities of a commander:

> After taking action or issuing an order, a commander must remain alert and make timely adjustments as required by a changing situation. Furthermore, a commander is also responsible if he has actual knowledge that troops or other persons subject to his control are in the process of committing or are about to commit a war crime and he wrongfully fails to take the necessary and reasonable steps to insure compliance with the law of war. You will observe that these legal requirements placed upon a commander require actual knowledge plus a wrongful failure to act. Thus mere presence at the scene without knowledge will not suffice. That is, the commander-subordinate relationship alone will not allow an inference of knowledge. While it is not necessary that a commander actually see an atrocity being committed,

---

[17]For a copy of the Peers report, see Goldstein et al., *My Lai Massacre*.

it is essential that he know that his subordinates are in the process of committing atrocities or are about to commit atrocities.[18]

Furthermore, he informed the jury, in order to find the captain guilty, it needed to be satisfied beyond a reasonable doubt that Vietnamese non-combatants had been killed, that their killing had been unlawful, "that their deaths resulted from omission of the accused in failing to exercise control over subordinates subject to his command after having gained knowledge that his subordinates were killing noncombatants," and that Medina's omission constituted culpable negligence.

For Howard, culpable negligence was as important as actual knowledge:

Culpable negligence is a degree of carelessness greater than simple negligence. . . . Simple negligence is the absence of due care, that is, an omission by a person who is under a duty to exercise due care, which exhibits a lack of that degree of care for the safety of others which a reasonable, prudent commander could have exercised under the same or similar circumstances. Culpable negligence, on the other hand, is a higher degree of negligent omission, one that is accompanied by a gross, reckless, deliberate, or wanton disregard for the foreseeable consequences to others of that omission. . . . It is higher in magnitude than simple inadvertence, but falls short of intentional wrong. The essence of wanton or reckless conduct is intentional conduct by way of omission where there is a duty to act, which conduct involved a high degree of likelihood that substantial harm will result to others.

The jury could not find Medina guilty, Howard noted, unless it believed killing had occurred after he had obtained knowledge of atrocities and that he had then failed to prevent subsequent violations. The jury neither could assume he must have known nor, contrary to the earlier reasoning of the U.S. Supreme Court, the Reynolds commission, and even the two Nuremberg tribunals, could they assume he should have known. They could not assume that Medina's physical presence at My Lai during the atrocities, his observation of dead bodies, or his nearness to the gunfire implied knowledge. Only if they found that he actually knew his men were illegally killing civilians and did nothing could he be convicted.[19]

Howard's interpretation of the law closely followed the decision issued in October 1948 by the High Command court. His culpable negligence paralleled the court's definition of criminal acquiescence and

---

[18]For a copy of Howard's charge to the jury, see Friedman, *Law of War*, 2:1729–37; and Kenneth A. Howard, "Command Responsibility for War Crimes," *Journal of Public Law* 21 (1972): 7–22. For comments on the trial, see Mary McCarthy, *Medina* (New York: Harcourt Brace Jovanovich, 1972).

[19]Ibid.

negligence. His refusal to accept must have known logic and should have known reasoning also reflected the general tenor of that earlier decision. Indeed, his interpretation represented a logical progression from the Yamashita to the Hostage to the High Command cases. While the High Command justices had retained a fragment of should have known logic, Howard simply scrapped it altogether. He carefully emphasized the importance of demonstrating that Medina had actual knowledge. Howard, at least, had totally rejected the reasoning underlying the Reynolds commission's findings in 1945.

Despite Howard's rejection of the Yamashita precedent, that precedent survived. As a mere colonel, Howard's opinion did not carry the same weight as that of five generals, nor did his opinion convert a large number of critics and skeptics in the country. Those critics could argue that Howard's charge violated the army's own *Law of Land Warfare*, which authorized consideration of should have known logic. They could argue that his charge made future enforcement of the law of war a farce, and that it may well have been concerned more with preventing further prosecutions higher in the American chain of command in 1970, rather than a wise interpretation of the applicability and definition of command responsibility. Finally, they could argue, with some legitimacy, that his charge established a reprehensible double standard, one for a defeated Oriental foe and another for a U.S. Army officer.

Supporters of Howard could counter, on the other hand, that his decision more accurately reflected what should reasonably be expected of a commanding officer given battlefield conditions and the psychological impact of war on individual soldiers. They could rightly note that understanding of atrocity-producing stress was far more advanced in the early 1970s than in 1945, and that with that knowledge it was easier to realize just how fragile a commanding officer's control of his men really was.[20]

---

[20]For a discussion of stress and the individual, see William S. Mullins, ed., *Neuropsychiatry in World War II: Overseas Theatres* (Washington: Government Printing Office, 1973); and Samuel Stouffer, et al., *The American Soldier: Combat and Its Aftermath*, vol. 2 (Princeton: Princeton University Press, 1949). Also see Roy Grinker and John Spiegel, *Men Under Stress* (Philadelphia: Blakiston Company, 1945); William C. Menninger, *Psychiatry in a Troubled World* (New York: Macmillan Co., 1948); Erik Erikson, "Stress: On the Battlefield," *Psychology Today* 3 (September 1969): 32–33, 62–63; Chaim Shatan, "The Grief of Soldiers: Vietnam Combat Veterans' Self-Help Movement," *American Journal of Orthopsychiatry* 43 (July 1973): 640–53; William B. Gault, "Some Remarks on Slaughter," the *American Journal of Psychiatry* 128 (October 1971): 450–54; Peter Bourne, *Men, Stress, and Vietnam* (Boston: Little, Brown & Co., 1970); Richard Sipes, "War, Sports and Aggression: An Empirical Test of Two Rival Theories," *American Anthropologist* 75 (February 1973): 64–86; Ladd Wheeler and Seward Smith, "Censure of the Model in the Contagion of Aggression," *Journal of Personality and Social Psychology* 6 (May 1967): 93–98; Tom Pear, ed., *Psychological Factors of Peace and War* (1950; reprint ed., Freeport, NY: Books for Libraries Press, 1971); Peter Watson, *War on the Mind: The*

Furthermore, supporters could argue that Howard was more than justified in rejecting the Reynolds commission's logic, since certain crucial assumptions underlying perceptions of war criminals in 1945 were invalid. Turning to psychological studies prepared in the post-1945 era, as well as to revelations of American atrocities in Vietnam, they could refute the old assumption that war crimes were committed only by a racially and morally inferior enemy who was inherently cruel and bestial. Equally invalid, they might add, was the old assumption that all enemy soldiers were automatons who were manipulated by militaristic fiends into committing bestial acts and whose own personal motivations played little part. Such simple catch-all explanations no longer adequately explained the commission of atrocities. As a result, neither Howard nor other judges should feel bound by old judicial decisions that may have been seriously influenced by those earlier, mistaken assumptions.

Howard's supporters could refer to studies based on World War II and Vietnam experiences, which revealed a complex range of factors that could transform soldiers into men who might commit atrocities. The death of friends, fear, physical fatigue, lack of food, constant enemy contact, repeated enemy air and artillery bombardment, and the absence of leadership were but a few of those factors. No longer, Howard's supporters might continue, could the guilt of a commanding officer for failure to control his men be determined within the rather rigid framework imposed by the Reynolds commission on Yamashita almost thirty years earlier. While Howard's repudiation of the Yamashita precedent admittedly changed the standards used to evaluate command responsibility, it was a change long overdue, one that ensured a fairer trial to future commanding officers than Yamashita had received in 1945.

While critics and supporters of Howard's decision might argue over his motivation, one fact was indisputable. His charge to the jury in September enunciated a new standard in evaluating the concept of command responsibility. It was a concept that he, at least, believed to be more appropriate in assessing a commanding officer's actions during the chaos of combat.

In July 1977, almost six years after Howard's ruling and thirty-two years after the Reynolds commission's findings, international delegates initialed a protocol that reaffirmed the right of enemy war criminals to all legal protections granted by the 1949 conventions and their

---

Military Use and Abuses of Psychology (New York: Basic Books, 1978); S. L. A. Marshall, *Men Against Fire: The Problem of Battle Command in Future War* (New York: William Morrow & Co., 1947); J. Glenn Gray, *The Warriors* (1959; reprint ed., New York: Harper & Row, 1970); Alexander H. Leighton, *Human Relations in a Changing World* (New York: E. P. Dutton & Co., 1949); and Robert Jay Lifton, *Home from the War* (New York: Simon & Schuster, 1973).

subsequent protocols.[21] In addition, they also addressed more directly the question of a commanding officer's responsibility. They not only prohibited the use in future wars of means of warfare that could be expected to cause "widespread, long-term and severe damage to the natural environment," but they also warned military commanders that they must "do everything feasible" to ensure that all potential objectives involved military and not civilian targets. Even in attacks on military objectives, they warned, officers must minimize the loss of civilian life, injury to civilians, and damage to civilian property. Furthermore, if they found, either prior to or during an operation, that civilian losses either would be or were "excessive in relation to the concrete and direct military advantage anticipated," it was their responsibility to cancel those operations.

The conferees did not stop there. In new Articles 86 and 87, they further elaborated on the responsibilities of military commanders. Those officers must not only ensure that their men are aware of the law of war as outlined at the Geneva conventions, but they also must prevent and/or suppress all violations of that law. Even if their subordinates violate the law of war without orders, they might still be held responsible. Article 86 warned:

> The fact that a breach of the Conventions or of this protocol was committed by a subordinate does not absolve his superiors from penal or disciplinary responsibility, as the case may be, if they knew, or had information which should have enabled them to conclude in the circumstances at the time, that he was committing or was going to commit such a breach and if they did not take all feasible measures within their power to prevent or repress the breach.

The insistence of the High Command court and of Howard that a military commander, in order to be held responsible for the actions of his subordinates, must be proven to have had knowledge of war violations had finally been vindicated by those international delegates at Geneva in 1977. Those same delegates also had agreed with the findings of the earlier courts that once a commanding officer had knowledge he was bound to "take all feasible measures within [his] power to prevent and repress the breach." But only if he had knowledge of war crimes and then still failed to take action would he, too, share the responsibility of his subordinates.

In adopting that reasoning, the delegations firmly rejected two proposals containing a should have known clause.[22] They not only rejected

---

[21]The following discussion of the Geneva protocol is based on the text of that document. See International Committee of the Red Cross, *Protocols Additional to the Geneva Conventions of 12 August 1949* (Geneva: no publisher, 1978).

[22]For a record of the conference debates, see Howard Levie, *Protection of War Victims: Protocol 1 to the 1949 Geneva Conventions*, 4 vols. (Dobbs Ferry, NY: Oceana

the original phrasing, which warned superiors that they could share the penal responsibility of a subordinate "if they knew or should have known that he was committing or would commit such a breach and if they did not take measures within their power to prevent or repress the breach," but they also rejected a U.S. amendment that substituted a weaker version of the should have known phrasing. The defeated American amendment warned superiors that they could share the responsibility of a subordinate "if they knew or should reasonably have known in the circumstances at the time that he was committing or was going to commit such a breach. . . ."

That amendment proved unacceptable. A second American proposal affecting Article 87 also failed passage. The American delegation had hoped that the assembly would at least accept a clause requiring commanding officers to "exercise reasonable supervision and control under the circumstances over members of the armed forces under their command in order to ensure they are properly implementing the Conventions and this Protocol." By rejecting that amendment as well and by adopting the final text of Articles 86 and 87, the Geneva delegations completed the erosion of the Yamashita precedent begun in 1948 at Nuremberg and continued in 1971 by Colonel Howard. Or, at least, it appeared that their decisions had invalidated the earlier case as an acceptable basis for future war-crimes prosecutions. But as of November 1981 only eighteen nations had formally adhered to Protocol I.[23] And in Washington, the U.S. Department of State had so far declined to submit that protocol to the Senate for consideration.

Publications, 1979–81); and *Official Records of the Diplomatic Conference on the Reaffirmation and Development of International Humanitarian Law Applicable in Armed Conflicts, Geneva, 1974–1977,* 17 vols. (Bern: Government of Switzerland, 1978).

[23]J. J. Surbeck, deputy head, Dissemination and Documentation Division, Comité International de la Croix-Rouge, to Richard L. Lael, 17 November 1981.

CHAPTER SEVEN
REFLECTIONS

Despite Secretary of War Henry Stimson's fervent desire that all war-crimes trials should be conducted in a fair manner capable of meeting the judgment of history, the prosecution of General Tomoyuki Yamashita fell short of that standard. The blame for that failure must be shared collectively by top civilian and military officials in Washington, Tokyo, and Manila. No one individual can legitimately be singled out as the villain, not even General Douglas MacArthur who has heretofore received the harshest criticism.

MacArthur's choice of Yamashita as the first prisoner to face trial, his preparation of the 24 September regulations that governed the military commission, his emphasis on speed, and his efforts to hamper defense appeals to civilian courts can be attributed, in large measure, to his logical interpretation of actions and instructions of Washington policymakers. Ordered by the president in early September to proceed with war-crimes trials "without avoidable delay," MacArthur and his staff chose what appeared to be a rather routine, uncomplicated case involving a major Japanese officer. Since the charges against Yamashita only involved traditional violations of the law of war, or at least so they believed at the time, and since they also addressed only war violations committed on American territory, his prosecution seemed simple indeed. MacArthur not only could try Yamashita without allowing additional time for the preparation of charges involving such new legal concepts as conspiracy but also could avoid the laborious process of selecting judges and preparing rules for a trial before an international court. And even if he had discovered some high-ranking Tokyo official whose trial also involved only traditional war crimes committed solely on American territory, the trial still would have been delayed for weeks or even months. United States investigators would need that time to assemble evidence in a nation only recently occupied. On the other hand, since his army had controlled most of Luzon for months, MacArthur's staff already had accumulated much of the evidence that could be used in proceedings against Yamashita. The selection of the 14th Area Army commander for early trial, therefore, was logical.

Obviously, the choice of Yamashita as the first leader to be prosecuted gave MacArthur personal pleasure as well. He abhorred the needless death and destruction wrought by Japanese forces in the Philippines in late 1944 and early 1945. More than that, the slaying of tens of thousands of civilians, the brutal rape of hundreds of women and girls, and the leveling of the Philippine capital angered him. For MacArthur, Yamashita's failure to control his subordinates violated his duty to his profession, to his country, and to civilization. It was, therefore, appropriate as well as practical that his trial be first.[1]

In formulating the 24 September regulations that governed the trial, MacArthur did not arbitrarily "stack the deck" against his foe. He based those rules not on personal whim but on procedures and policies already adopted by the British, General Eisenhower, President Roosevelt, and the conferees at London in August 1945. Indeed, only a few of the many provisions in that 24 September document originated at MacArthur's headquarters. Had he really been out "to get" Yamashita, he could easily have adopted a much more restrictive and arbitrary set of rules. Nor would he have violated the law in formulating such procedures. His power to do so had been affirmed by the secretary and assistant secretary of war, the Joint Chiefs of Staff, the judge advocate general, Congress, the president, and the U.S. Supreme Court.[2]

While MacArthur may escape severe criticism for selecting Yamashita as the first defendant or for adopting policies that originated in Washington, he does merit severe criticism for his overemphasis on speed once the Yamashita trial began. Clearly he and his staff pressured the commission to avoid all unnecessary delays. That emphasis on speed not only occurred in the absence of further presidential directives but also sparked a series of questionable rulings by that court, including its decision to receive affidavits into evidence without accompanying oral testimony, its instructions to defense counsel to shorten its cross-examinations, and its orders that no criticism could be made in open court of inaccurate translations by the official interpreters. Additionally, Mac-Arthur's refusal to permit either the commission or Lieutenant General

---

[1]Ironically, despite the fact that most of the war crimes occurred in that sector directly controlled by Lieutenant General Yokoyama, MacArthur held Yamashita personally responsible. According to SCAP's case index of war-crimes trials in boxes 1348 and 1349, RG 331, Yokoyama never faced trial as a war criminal. Colonel Fujishige, however, was tried and executed. See box 1678, RG 331.

[2]Assistant Secretary McCloy conferred with MacArthur in Tokyo on 22 and 23 October for over eleven hours. Since Colonel Carpenter, MacArthur's war-crimes adviser, had discussed the upcoming visit with MacArthur on the twentieth, it is a fair assumption that war-crimes policies and the 24 September regulations were discussed during the MacArthur-McCloy conversations. The policies and regulations existing prior to 22 October remained unchanged on 24 October, implying that McCloy had not found them unacceptable. See MacArthur's daily appointments register for 20, 22, and 23 October, box 2, RG 5.

Styer to assist defense efforts in securing civilian review of the military commission's judgment seems rather childish in retrospect, especially in view of the fact that Colonel Abe Goff, acting director of the U.S. War Crimes Office, recommended against such refusal. While MacArthur could validly argue that the 24 September regulations clearly forbade any such appeal and that civilian review could complicate and lengthen the war-crimes process, his decision to order Styer to avoid a bailiff of the Philippine Supreme Court, for example, created an image of an overly sensitive, cantankerous officer who was more interested in upholding his own regulations than in ensuring that Yamashita had every opportunity to appeal his sentence of death.

Despite the emphasis on speed, the 24 September regulations, the questionable rulings by the commission, and even the concept of command responsibility, Yamashita could legitimately have been found innocent had the five generals sitting in judgment not imposed such unreasonably high standards of conduct upon him. By emphasizing his paper control over his subordinates and by refusing to consider in mitigation the exceptional battle conditions in the Philippines, they dramatically downplayed the impact of continuous battle, defeat, and retreat on individual Japanese soldiers; downplayed the impact of encirclement, artillery and air attacks, physical fatigue, hunger, fear, and the smell of death; and downplayed the argument that even the best of troops—and those in Manila and Batangas were not in that category—might "crack" under such circumstances. They also disregarded the fact that house-to-house fighting, coupled with poor communications among units, not only isolated men from high-ranking officers such as Rear Admiral Iwabuchi, Lieutenant General Yokoyama, and General Yamashita but also isolated them from their own company commanders and sergeants. They failed to realize that such isolation, combined with intense combat and the fear that upon capture they might be enslaved, starved, or physically mutilated, might just create circumstances leading individual soldiers and squads to commit atrocities regardless of orders from higher authority.

The Reynolds commission further erred in not considering more carefully the sites of war crimes. Had the officers studied more carefully the map of atrocities available to them, they would have realized that only 135 civilian deaths had occurred in 1945 in that region directly controlled by Yamashita, while over thirty-five thousand had occurred in that sector controlled by Lieutenant General Yokoyama. Such figures clearly should have demonstrated to the court that Yamashita had not embarked on a systematic campaign of murder and torture of civilians. Furthermore, it should have demonstrated that the vast majority of those war crimes occurred during the month of February, a time when Yamashita was over one hundred miles to the north battling for his own unit's survival.

In addition, Generals Reynolds, Lester, Bullene, Handwerk, and

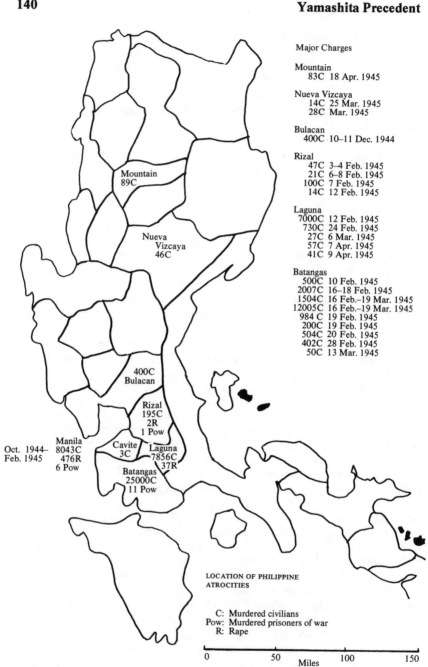

Major Charges

Mountain
  83C 18 Apr. 1945

Nueva Vizcaya
  14C 25 Mar. 1945
  28C Mar. 1945

Bulacan
  400C 10–11 Dec. 1944

Rizal
  47C 3–4 Feb. 1945
  21C 6–8 Feb. 1945
  100C 7 Feb. 1945
  14C 12 Feb. 1945

Laguna
  7000C 12 Feb. 1945
  730C 24 Feb. 1945
  27C 6 Mar. 1945
  57C 7 Apr. 1945
  41C 9 Apr. 1945

Batangas
  500C 10 Feb. 1945
  2007C 16–18 Feb. 1945
  1504C 16 Feb.–19 Mar. 1945
  12005C 16 Feb.–19 Mar. 1945
  984 C 19 Feb. 1945
  200C 19 Feb. 1945
  504C 20 Feb. 1945
  402C 28 Feb. 1945
  50C 13 Mar. 1945

Mountain
89C

Nueva
Vizcaya
46C

400C
Bulacan

Rizal
195C
2R
1 Pow

Manila
8043C
476R
6 Pow

Oct. 1944–
Feb. 1945

Cavite
3C

Laguna
7856C
37R

Batangas
25000C
11 Pow

LOCATION OF PHILIPPINE
ATROCITIES

C: Murdered civilians
Pow: Murdered prisoners of war
R: Rape

0   50   100   150
                    Miles

Donovan too quickly discounted Yamashita's assertions that he had no knowledge of those atrocities. Rather than seriously consider the reality of battle conditions, the independence and self-sufficiency of the three army groups, the air superiority of the U.S. forces, the guerrilla harassment, the collapse of the Japanese transportation system, and the severely impaired intergroup communications, the court cavalierly assumed that Yamashita either must have known, or at least should have known, of criminal violations. By forcing Yamashita to shoulder the burden of guilt, the five generals failed to consider sufficiently the erratic actions of men and officers facing death, the army's ambiguous control over Okochi's forces in Manila, the independent decisions taken by subordinate officers to achieve their own goals, and the misinterpretation of military directives by subordinates such as Fujishige.[3] Ultimately, then, the Manila commission erred, not in asking whether Yamashita should have known of atrocities but in failing to consider adequately in mitigation those exceptional circumstances existing in the Philippines in 1944 and 1945.

While the Reynolds tribunal was too strict in its evaluation of an officer's obligations, the High Command and the Medina courts were too lenient. By adopting the actual knowledge and the culpable negligence arguments, they lifted too much of the responsibility for controlling wartime violations from the shoulders of high-ranking officers. Realizing that a prosecutor could find proof of knowledge and culpable negligence extremely difficult, future officers might be tempted under such conditions to focus their energies elsewhere, while simultaneously relaxing their enforcement of the law of war.

That need not happen. Nor do future courts need to revert to the strict accountability of the Yamashita precedent. The ruling of those American judges sitting on the Hostage court offers a more reasonable strategy for assessing the degree of an officer's command responsibility than either the Yamashita commission's judgment or that of the High Command and Medina courts. By rejecting the concept of strict accountability while, at the same time, acknowledging an officer's affirmative responsibility to control the actions of his subordinates, those men rectified the major flaw in the logic of Reynolds and his military colleagues without going to the lenient excesses of the High Command and Medina tribunals. By arguing that a commanding officer normally must be shown to have ordered, aided, or abetted the commission of war crimes, they emphasized the pursuit of those officers who knowingly failed to perform their duty rather than those who may merely have held prestigious positions in the army of the defeated foe. However, by also asserting that

---

[3]Kobayashi and the officers of the Southwest Area Fleet contingent remaining in Manila in late January are examples of subordinates who manipulated decisions to fit their own goals.

an officer could be held responsible for crimes committed by his subordinates if no exceptional circumstances existed, which could adequately explain his failure to prevent violations within his area of command or to avert a recurrence, those justices additionally provided leaders incentive to control their men.

That seems a rational modification of the Yamashita precedent. While, even if universally adopted, such logic would not prevent future armies from violating international law, it can serve notice on all personnel in command that they will be judged by a reasonable should have known standard and can remind them that, should they choose not to enforce energetically the law of war, they do so at their own peril.

APPENDIX

ARTICLES OF WAR

25: A duly authenticated deposition taken upon reasonable notice to the opposite party may be read in evidence before any military court or commission in any case not capital, or in any proceeding before a court of inquiry or a military board, if such deposition be taken when the witness resides, is found, or is about to go beyond the State, Territory, or district in which the court, commission, or board is ordered to sit, or beyond the distance of one hundred miles from the place of trial or hearing, or when it appears to the satisfaction of the court, commission, board, or appointing authority that the witness, by reason of age, sickness, bodily infirmity, imprisonment, or other reasonable cause, is unable to appear and testify in person at the place of trial or hearing: Provided, That testimony by deposition may be adduced for the defense in capital cases.

38: The President may, by regulations, which he may modify from time to time, prescribe the procedure, including modes of proof, in cases before courts-martial, courts of inquiry, military commissions, and other military tribunals, which regulations shall, insofar as he shall deem practicable, apply the rules of evidence generally recognized in the trial of criminal cases in the district courts of the United States: Provided, That nothing contrary to or inconsistent with these articles shall be so prescribed: Provided further, That all rules made in pursuance of this article shall be laid before the Congress annually.

ANNEX TO THE FOURTH HAGUE CONVENTION (1907)

1: The laws, rights, and duties of war apply not only to armies, but also to militia and volunteer corps fulfilling the following conditions:

1. To be commanded by a person responsible for his subordinates. . . .

43: The authority of legitimate power having in fact passed into the hands of the occupant, the latter shall take all measures in his power to restore, and ensure, as far as possible, public order and safety, while respecting, unless absolutely prevented, the laws in force in the country.

ADAPTATION TO MARITIME WARFARE OF THE PRINCIPLES OF THE GENEVA CONVENTION (HAGUE, X, 1907)

19: The commanders-in-chief of belligerent fleets shall see to the execution of the details of the preceding articles, as well as to unforeseen cases, according to the instructions of their respective governments and conformably to the general principles of the present convention.

GENEVA RED CROSS CONVENTION (1929)

26: It shall be the duty of the commanders-in-chief of the belligerent armies to provide for the details of execution of the foregoing articles, as well as for unforeseen cases, in accordance with the instructions of their respective Governments, and conformably to the general principles of this Convention.

CONVENTION ON TREATMENT OF PRISONERS OF WAR (1929)

63: Sentence may be pronounced against a prisoner of war only by the same courts and according to the same procedure as in the case of persons belonging to the armed forces of the detaining Power.

UNITED STATES CONSTITUTION, FIFTH AMENDMENT

No person shall be held to answer for a capital, or otherwise infamous crime, unless on a presentment or indictment of a Grand Jury, except in cases arising in the land or naval forces, or in the militia, when in actual service in time of war or public danger; nor shall any person be subject for the same offense to be twice put in jeopardy of life or limb; nor shall be compelled in any criminal case to be a witness against himself, nor be deprived of life, liberty, or property, without due process of law; nor shall private property be taken for public use, without just compensation.

SELECTED BIBLIOGRAPHY

MANUSCRIPT SOURCES

MacArthur Memorial & Archives, Norfolk, Virginia
RG 5 Records of General Headquarters, Supreme Commander for the
  Allied Powers, 1945–51

Center for Military History, Washington, DC
10th Information and Historical Service Studies
Imperial General Headquarters Army Orders
Statements of Japanese Officials on World War II
Historical Manuscript File
Interrogations of Japanese Officials on World War II
Translation of Japanese Documents
Japanese Monograph Series

National Archives, Washington, DC
RG 59 Records of the U.S. Department of State
RG 107 Records of the Secretary of War
RG 218 Records of the U.S. Joint Chiefs of Staff
RG 226 Records of the Office of Strategic Services
RG 238 Records of the U.S. Counsel for the Prosecution of Axis
  Criminality, Nuremberg
RG 243 Records of the U.S. Strategic Bombing Survey
RG 319 Records of the Army Staff

Washington National Records Center, Suitland, Maryland
RG 153 Records of the Judge Advocate General (Army)
RG 165 Records of the War Department General Staff
RG 331 Records of the U.S. Army Forces, Pacific
RG 407 Records of the Adjutant General's Office

Library of Congress Manuscript Division, Washington, DC
Papers of Hugo Black
Papers of Harold Burton

147

Papers of Felix Frankfurter
Papers of Wiley B. Rutledge
Papers of Henry Stimson
Papers of Harlan Fiske Stone

Franklin D. Roosevelt Library, Hyde Park, New York
Papers of Franklin D. Roosevelt
Papers of Oscar Cox
Papers of W. D. Hassett

Harry S Truman Library, Independence, Missouri
Papers of Harry S Truman
Papers of Eleanor Bontecou
Papers of Samuel I. Rosenman
Oral Interview Files

Michigan Historical Collections, Bentley Historical Library, University of Michigan, Ann Arbor
Papers of Frank Murphy

GOVERNMENT PUBLICATIONS

Public Papers of the Presidents of the United States: Harry S Truman, 1945. Washington: Government Printing Office, 1961.

U.S. Congress. *Congressional Record.* 75th Cong., 1st sess. to 84th Cong., 2d sess.

U.S. Congress, Senate. Committee on the Judiciary. *Morgenthau Diary (Germany)* by Henry Morgenthau. Vol. 1. Washington: Government Printing Office, 1967.

U.S. Department of the Army. M. Hamlin Cannon, *U.S. Army in World War II: Leyte, The Return to the Philippines.* 1954; reprint ed. Washington: Government Printing Office, 1978.

————. *The Law of Land Warfare* (FM 27-10). Washington: Government Printing Office, 1956.

————. *A Manual for Courts-Martial.* Washington: Government Printing Office, 1943 and 1951.

————. Louis Morton, *U.S. Army in World War II: The Fall of the Philippines.* Washington: Government Printing Office, 1953.

————. William S. Mullins, ed. *Neuropsychiatry in World War II: Overseas Theatres.* Washington: Government Printing Office, 1973.

———. *Rules of Land Warfare* (FM 27-10). Washington: Government Printing Office, 1947.

———. Robert R. Smith, *U.S. Army in World War II: The Approach to the Philippines.* Washington: Government Printing Office, 1953.

———. Robert R. Smith, *U.S. Army in World War II: Triumph in the Philippines.* Washington: Government Printing Office, 1963.

———. *Trials of War Criminals Before the Nuernberg Military Tribunals.* Vol. 11. Washington: Government Printing Office, 1950.

———. *U.S. Army and Navy Field Manual of Military Government and Civil Affairs* (FM 27-5). Washington: Government Printing Office, 1945.

U.S. Department of State. *International Conference on Military Trials.* Washington: Government Printing Office, 1945.

———. *Foreign Relations of the United States.* Washington: Government Printing Office.

———. *Trial of Japanese War Criminals.* Washington: Government Printing Office, 1946.

———. *Trial of War Criminals.* Washington: Government Printing Office, 1945.

U.S. Supreme Court. *United States Reports.* Washington: Government Printing Office.

BOOKS

Anesaki, Masaharu. *History of Japanese Religion.* 1930; reprint ed. Tokyo: Charles Tuttle Co., 1963.

Appleman, John A. *Military Tribunals and International Crimes.* Westport, CT: Greenwood Press, 1971.

Baird, Jay, ed. *From Nuremberg to My Lai.* Lexington, MA: D. C. Heath & Co., 1972.

Barker, A. J. *Yamashita.* New York: Ballantine Books, 1973.

Beck, John J. *MacArthur and Wainwright.* Albuquerque: University of New Mexico Press, 1974.

Berry, Mary F. *Stability, Security and Continuity: Mr. Justice Burton and Decision-Making in the Supreme Court, 1945–1958.* Westport, CT: Greenwood Press, 1978.

Black, Hugo. *A Constitutional Faith.* New York: Alfred A. Knopf, 1969.

Blum, John M., ed. *From the Morgenthau Diaries: Years of War, 1941–1945.* Boston: Houghton Mifflin Co., 1967.

Bosch, William J. *Judgment on Nuremberg: American Attitudes Toward the Major German War-Crimes Trials.* Chapel Hill: University of North Carolina Press, 1970.

Bourne, Peter. *Men, Stress, and Vietnam.* Boston: Little, Brown & Co., 1970.

———, ed. *The Psychology and Physiology of Stress: With Reference to Special Studies of the Viet Nam War.* New York: Academic Press, 1969.

Brown, Delmer M. *Nationalism in Japan.* Los Angeles: University of California Press, 1955.

Calvocoressi, Peter. *Nuremberg: The Facts, the Law, and the Consequences.* New York: Macmillan Co., 1948.

Churchill, Winston S. *The Second World War: Closing the Ring.* Boston: Houghton Mifflin, 1951.

Davidson, Eugene. *The Nuremberg Fallacy: Wars and War Crimes Since World War II.* New York: Macmillan Co., 1973.

Dilks, David, ed. *The Diaries of Sir Alexander Cadogan.* New York: G. P. Putnam's Sons, 1972.

Earhart, H. Byron. *Japanese Religion: Unity and Diversity.* Encino, CA: Dickenson Publishing Co., 1974.

Fairman, Charles. *The Law of Martial Rule.* 2d ed. Chicago: Callaghan & Co., 1943.

Falk, Richard; Kolko, Gabriel; and Lifton, Robert Jay, eds. *Crimes of War.* New York: Vintage Books, 1971.

Falk, Richard, ed. *The Vietnam War and International Law.* Vols. 1–4. Princeton: Princeton University Press, 1969.

Frank, John P. *Mr. Justice Black: The Man and His Opinions.* New York: Alfred A. Knopf, 1949.

———. *Marble Palace: The Supreme Court in American Life.* New York: Alfred A. Knopf, 1961.

Friedman, Leon, ed. *The Law of War: A Documentary History.* Vols. 1 & 2. New York: Random House, 1972.

Friend, Theodore. *Between Two Empires: The Ordeal of the Philippines, 1929–1946.* New Haven: Yale University Press, 1965.

Fujisawa, Chikao. *Concrete Universality of the Japanese Way of Thinking.* Japan: Hokuseido Press, 1958.

Gerhart, Eugene. *America's Advocate: Robert H. Jackson.* New York: Bobbs-Merrill, 1958.

Goldstein, Joseph; Marshall, Burke; and Schwartz, Jack, eds. *The My Lai Massacre and Its Cover-up.* New York: Free Press, 1976.

Gray, J. Glenn. *The Warriors.* 1959; reprint ed. New York: Harper & Row, 1970.

Grinker, Roy, and Spiegel, John. *Men Under Stress.* Philadelphia: Blakiston Company, 1945.

Grunder, Garel A., and Livezey, William E. *The Philippines and the United States.* Norman: University of Oklahoma Press, 1951.

Hall, Robert, ed. *KOKUTAI NO HONGI*. Translated by John Gauntlett. Newton, MA: Crofton Publishing Co., 1974.

Harper, Fowler. *Justice Rutledge and the Bright Constellation.* New York: Bobbs-Merrill, 1965.

Harris, Whitney. *Tyranny on Trial: The Evidence at Nuremberg.* Dallas: Southern Methodist University Press, 1954.

Herbert, Jean. *Shinto: At the Fountain-head of Japan.* New York: Stein and Day, 1967.

Holtom, D. C. *Modern Japan and Shinto Nationalism.* Chicago: University of Chicago Press, 1947.

Howard, J. Woodford, Jr. *Mr. Justice Murphy: A Political Biography.* Princeton: Princeton University Press, 1968.

Hull, Cordell. *The Memoirs of Cordell Hull.* Vol. 2. New York: Macmillan Co., 1948.

Hunt, Frazier. *The Untold Story of Douglas MacArthur.* New York: Devin-Adair Co., 1954.

International Committee of the Red Cross. *Protocols Additional to the Geneva Conventions of 12 August 1949.* Geneva: no publisher, 1978.

Jackson, Robert H. *The Case Against the Nazi War Criminals.* New York: Alfred A. Knopf, 1946.

———. *The Nuremberg Case.* New York: Alfred A. Knopf, 1947.

James, D. Clayton. *The Years of MacArthur.* Vols. 1 & 2. Boston: Houghton Mifflin Co., 1970, 1975.

James, Robert Rhodes, ed. *Winston S. Churchill: His Complete Speeches, 1897–1963.* Vol. 6. London: Chelsea House Publishers, 1974.

Karsten, Peter. *Law, Soldiers, and Combat.* Westport, CT: Greenwood Press, 1978.

Keenan, Joseph, and Brown, Brendan. *Crimes Against International Law.* Washington: Public Affairs Press, 1950.

Kenney, George C. *General Kenney Reports.* New York: Duell, Sloan & Pearce, 1949.

Kenworthy, Aubrey. *The Tiger of Malaya.* New York: Exposition Press, 1953.

Kirby, S. Woodburn. *The War Against Japan: The Loss of Singapore.* London: Her Majesty's Stationery Office, 1957.

Kitagawa, Joseph. *Religion in Japanese History.* New York: Columbia University Press, 1966.

Knoll, Edwin, and McFadden, Judith, eds. *War Crimes and the American Conscience.* New York: Holt, Rinehart & Winston, 1970.

Krueger, Walter. *From Down Under to Nippon: The Story of the Sixth Army in World War II.* 1953; reprint ed. Washington: Zenger Publishing Co., 1979.

Kurland, Philip B. *Mr. Justice Frankfurter and the Constitution.* Chicago: University of Chicago Press, 1971.

Leasor, James. *Singapore: The Battle That Changed the World.* Garden City, NY: Doubleday & Co., 1968.

Leighton, Alexander H. *Human Relations in a Changing World.* New York: E. P. Dutton & Co., 1949.

Levie, Howard. *Protection of War Victims: Protocol 1 to the 1949 Geneva Conventions.* Vols. 1–4. Dobbs Ferry, NY: Oceana Publications, 1979–81.

Lifton, Robert Jay. *Home from the War.* New York: Simon & Schuster, 1973.

Loewenheim, Francis; Langley, Harold; and Jonas, Manfred, eds. *Roosevelt and Churchill: Their Secret Wartime Correspondence.* New York: E. P. Dutton, 1975.

Luvaas, Jay, ed. *Dear Miss Em: General Eichelberger's War in the Pacific, 1942–1945.* Westport, CT: Greenwood Press, 1972.

MacArthur, Douglas. *Reminiscences.* Greenwich, CT: Fawcett Publications, 1965.

Manchester, William. *American Caesar: Douglas MacArthur, 1880–1964.* New York: Dell Publishing Co., 1979.

Marshall, S. L. A. *Men Against Fire: The Problem of Battle Command in Future War.* New York: William Morrow & Co., 1947.

Maruyama, Masao. *Thought and Behavior in Modern Japanese Politics.* London: Oxford University Press, 1969.

Mason, Alpheus T. *Harlan Fiske Stone: Pillar of the Law.* New York: Viking Press, 1956.

McCarthy, Mary. *Medina.* New York: Harcourt Brace Jovanovich, 1972.

Melman, Seymour. *In the Name of America: The Conduct of the War in Vietnam by the Armed Forces of the United States as Shown by Published Reports.* Annandale, VA: Turnpike Press, 1968.

Mendelson, Wallace, ed. *Felix Frankfurter: The Judge.* New York: Reynal & Co., 1964.

Menninger, William C. *Psychiatry in a Troubled World.* New York: Macmillan Co., 1948.

Miller, Richard, ed. *The Law of War.* Lexington, MA: D.C. Heath & Co., 1975.

Moran, Lord. *Winston Churchill.* London: Constable & Co., 1966.

Morgenthau, Henry, Jr. *Germany Is Our Problem.* New York: Harper & Brothers, 1945.

Morison, Samuel E. *History of United States Naval Operations in World War II: Leyte, June 1944–January 1945.* Vol. 12. Boston: Little, Brown & Co., 1966.

———. *History of United States Naval Operations in World War II: The Liberation of the Philippines: Luzon, Mindanao, the Visayas, 1944–1945.* Vol. 13. Boston: Little, Brown & Co., 1965.

Mullins, Claud. *The Leipzig Trials.* London: H. F. & G. Witherby, 1921.

Official Records of the Diplomatic Conference on the Reaffirmation and Development of International Humanitarian Law Applicable in Armed Conflicts, Geneva, 1974–1977. Vols. 1–17. Bern: Government of Switzerland, 1978.

Pear, Tom, ed. *Psychological Factors of Peace and War.* 1950; reprint ed. Freeport, NY: Books for Libraries Press, 1971.

Percival, Sir Arthur. *The War in Malaya.* London: Eyre & Spottiswoode, 1949.

Piccigallo, Philip. *The Japanese on Trial: Allied War-Crimes Operations in the East, 1945–1951.* Austin: University of Texas Press, 1979.

Potter, John Dean. *The Life and Death of a Japanese General.* New York: New American Library, 1962.

Pritchett, C. Herman. *The Roosevelt Court: A Study in Judicial Politics and Values, 1937–1947.* New York: Macmillan Co., 1948.

Quirino, Carlos. *Quezon: Paladin of Philippine Freedom.* Manila: Filipiniana Book Guild, 1971.

Reel, A. Frank. *The Case of General Yamashita.* 1949; reprint ed. New York: Octagon Books, 1971.

Roosevelt, Elliott. *As He Saw It.* New York: Duell, Sloan & Pearce, 1946.

Rosenman, Samuel I. *The Public Papers and Addresses of Franklin D. Roosevelt.* New York: Harper & Brothers, 1950.

Schindler, Dietrich, and Toman, Jiri, eds. *The Laws of Armed Conflict.* Leiden: A. W. Sijthoff, 1973.

Simson, Ivan. *Singapore: Too Little, Too Late.* London: Leo Cooper, 1970.

Smith, Bradley F. *Reaching Judgment at Nuremberg.* New York: Basic Books, 1977.

———. *The Road to Nuremberg.* New York: Basic Books, 1981.

Stouffer, Samuel, et al. *The American Soldier: Combat and Its Aftermath.* Vol. 2. Princeton: Princeton University Press, 1949.

Swinson, Arthur. *Four Samurai.* London: Hutchinson & Co., 1968.

Taylor, Telford. *Nuremberg and Vietnam: An American Tragedy.* Chicago: Quadrangle Books, 1970.

Thomas, Helen. *Felix Frankfurter: Scholar on the Bench.* Baltimore: Johns Hopkins Press, 1960.

Toland, John. *The Rising Sun.* New York: Random House, 1971.

Trooboff, Peter, ed. *Law and Responsibility in Warfare: The Vietnam*

Experience. Chapel Hill: University of North Carolina Press, 1975.
Tsuji, Masanobu. *Singapore: The Japanese Version.* Translated by Margaret Lake. New York: St. Martin's Press, 1960.
Tsunoda, Ryusaku, et al. *Sources of Japanese Tradition.* New York: Columbia University Press, 1958.
Vietnam Veterans Against the War. *The Winter Soldier Investigation: An Investigation into American War Crimes.* Boston: Beacon Press, 1972.
Wainwright, Jonathan. *General Wainwright's Story.* Garden City, NY: Doubleday & Co., 1946.
Watson, Peter. *War on the Mind: The Military Uses and Abuses of Psychology.* New York: Basic Books, 1978.
Whan, Vorin E., Jr., ed. *A Soldier Speaks: Public Papers and Speeches of General of the Army Douglas MacArthur.* New York: Praeger, 1965.
Whitney, Courtney. *MacArthur: His Rendezvous with History.* New York: Alfred A. Knopf, 1956.
Willoughby, Charles, and Chamberlain, John. *MacArthur, 1941–1951.* New York: McGraw-Hill, 1954.
Woetzel, Robert K. *The Nuremberg Trials in International Law.* New York: Praeger, 1962.
Woodward, Sir Llewellyn. *British Foreign Policy in the Second World War.* London: Her Majesty's Stationery Office, 1962.
Zaide, Gregorio F. *Philippine Constitutional History and Constitutions of Modern Nations.* Manila: Modern Book Co., 1970.

ARTICLES

"Assessing Songmy." *The Wall Street Journal,* 1 December 1969, p. 1.
Bevans, Charles, comp. "Contemporary Practice of the United States Relating to International Law." *American Journal of International Law,* 1968, pp. 754–75.
Boudin, Leonard. "War Crimes in Vietnam: The Mote in Whose Eye?" *Harvard Law Review* 84 (March–June 1971): pp. 1940–59.
Bourne, Peter. "Military Psychiatry and the Viet Nam Experience." *American Journal of Psychiatry,* October 1970, pp. 481–88.
"The Clamor Over Calley: Who Shares the Guilt?" *Time* 97 (12 April 1971): 14–16, 18–21.
Clark, Kenneth. "Song My's Shock Wave." *Newsweek* 38 (15 December 1969): 38.
"Command Responsibility for War Crimes." *Yale Law Journal* 82 (May 1973): 1272–1304.

Cowles, Willard B. "Trial of War Criminals by Military Tribunals." *American Bar Association Journal*, June 1944, pp. 330–33.

Cramer, Myron C. "Military Commission: Trial of the Eight Saboteurs." *Washington Law Review*, November 1942, pp. 247–55.

Erikson, Erik. "Stress: On the Battlefield." *Psychology Today* 3 (September 1969): 32–33, 62–63.

Falk, Richard. "Songmy: War Crimes and Individual Responsibility." *Trans-Action* 7 (January 1970): 33–40.

Feldhaus, J. Gordon. "The Trial of Yamashita." *South Dakota Bar Journal* 15 (October 1946): 181–93.

———. "The Trial of Yamashita." *Current Legal Thought*, 1946–47, pp. 251–62.

Ganoe, John. "The Yamashita Case and the Constitution." *Oregon Law Review*, April 1946, pp. 143–58.

Gault, William B. "Some Remarks on Slaughter." *American Journal of Psychiatry* 128 (October 1971): 450–54.

"G.I.'s Near Songmy Doubt Any Massacre." *New York Times*, 1 December 1969, p. 12

Guy, George. "The Defense of Yamashita." *Wyoming Law Journal* 4 (Spring 1950): 153–80.

Hammar, Richard. "Medina: Another of the Mylai Guiltless." *New York Times*, 26 September 1971, p. 6E.

Hart, Franklin A. "Yamashita, Nuremberg and Vietnam: Command Responsibility Reappraised." *Naval War College Review* 25 (September–October 1972): 19–36.

Hersh, Seymour. "A Reporter at Large: Coverup I & II." *New Yorker* 47 (22 and 29 January 1972): 34–69 and 40–71, respectively.

Hoffman, Stanley. "War Crimes: Political and Legal Issues." *Dissent* 18 (December 1971): 530–34.

Holtom, Daniel C. "The Political Philosophy of Modern Shinto: A Study of the State Religion of Japan." Ph.D. dissertation, University of Chicago, 1922.

Howard, Kenneth A. "Command Responsibility for War Crimes." *Journal of Public Law* 21 (1972): 7–22.

Jackson, Robert H. "War Criminals and International Law." *Saturday Review of Literature*, 2 June 1945, pp. 7–8, 29.

Johansen, Robert. "U.S. War Crimes: The Guilt at the Top." *The Progressive* 35 (June 1971): 19–23.

Kelman, Herbert, and Lawrence, Lee. "American Response to the Trial of Lt. William L. Calley." *Psychology Today* 6 (June 1972): 41–45, 78–81.

Kuhn, Arthur. "International Law and National Legislation in the Trial of War Criminals—The Yamashita Case." *American Journal of International Law*, July 1950, pp. 559–62.

"Landing of American Forces in the Philippines." U.S. Department of
State *Bulletin* 11 (July–December 1944): 454–55.

"Minnesota Poll: Many Disbelieve My Lai Reports." *Minnesota Tribune*, 21 December 1969, p. 4B.

Murphy, Frank. "Frank Murphy: Civil Liberties and the Cities." *Vital Speeches* 5 (15 June 1939): 542–44.

"My Lai: An American Tragedy." *Time* 94 (5 December 1969): 23–24, 26, 28–32.

Novak, Michael. "The Battle Hymn of Lt. Calley . . . and the Republic." *Commonweal*, 20 April 1970, pp. 183–87.

O'Brien, William. "The Law of War, Command Responsibility and Vietnam." *Georgetown Law Journal* 60 (1971–72): 605–64.

"Official U.S. Report on My Lai Investigation." *U.S. News and World Report* 67 (8 December 1969): 78–79.

Parks, William. "Command Responsibility for War Crimes." *Military Law Review* 62 (Fall 1973): 1–104.

Paust, Jordan. "My Lai and Vietnam: Norms, Myths and Leader Responsibility." *Military Law Review* 57 (Summer 1972): 99–187.

Poirier, Norman. "An American Atrocity." *Esquire*, August 1969, pp. 59–63, 132–41.

"Poll Finds Doubters on Mylai." *Washington Post*, 22 December 1969, p. A9.

"President Nixon's News Conference on 8 December." U.S. Department of State *Bulletin*, 29 December 1969, pp. 618–21.

Redford, L. H. "The Trial of General Tomoyuki Yamashita: A Case in Command Responsibility." Master's thesis, Old Dominion University, 1975.

Reel, A. Frank. "Must We Hang Nixon Too?" *The Progressive* 34 (March 1970): 26–29.

Resor, Stanley. "Official U.S. Report on My Lai Investigation." *U.S. News and World Report*, 26 November 1969, pp. 78–79.

Reston, James B., Jr. "Is Nuremberg Coming Back to Haunt Us?" *Saturday Review*, 18 July 1970, pp. 14–17, 61.

"Russia's Declaration for War Crimes Trials." *New York Times*, 16 October 1942, p. 8.

Shatan, Chaim. "The Grief of Soldiers: Vietnam Combat Veterans' Self-Help Movement." *American Journal of Orthopsychiatry* 43 (July 1973): 640–53.

Sheehan, Neil. "Should We Have War Crimes Trials?" *New York Times*, 28 March 1971, pp. 1–3, 30–34.

Sheerin, John. "War Crimes in High Places." *Catholic World* 212 (July 1971): 163–64.

Shepard, Jack. "Incident at Van Duong." *Look*, 12 August 1969, pp. 26–31.

Sipes, Richard. "War, Sports and Aggression: An Empirical Test of Two

Rival Theories." *American Anthropologist* 75 (February 1973): 64–86.

Stone, Harlan F. "The Common Law in the United States." *Harvard Law Review*, November 1936, pp. 4–26.

Stratton, Samuel S. "Tiger of Malaya." *U.S. Naval Institute Proceedings* 80 (February 1954): 136–43.

"Training for Song My." *The Nation*, 26 December 1969, p. 716.

Wheeler, Ladd, and Smith, Seward. "Censure of the Model in the Contagion of Aggression." *Journal of Personality and Social Psychology* 6 (May 1967): 93–98.

Whitney, Courtney. "The Case of General Yamashita: A Memorandum." 27 January 1950. A copy is located at the University of North Carolina Law Library, Chapel Hill.

"Yamashita: Too Busy." *Newsweek*, 10 December 1945, p. 44.

NEWSPAPERS

Chicago Daily Tribune, October–December 1945.
Dallas Morning News, October–December 1945.
Los Angeles Times, October–December 1945.
New York Herald Tribune, October–December 1945.
New York Times, September 1945–October 1946.
Philadephia Inquirer, October–December 1945.
The Sun (Baltimore), October–December 1945.
Washington Post, October–December 1945.

INDEX

159

Y